REVISED SECOND EDITION

WOMEN AND COMMUNITY ACTION

Lena Dominelli

Consultant Editor: Jo Campling

BASW
BRITISH ASSOCIATION
OF SOCIAL WORKERS

First edition published in paperback 1990 by Venture Press Ltd,
16 Kent Street, Birmingham B5 6RD, UK

This revised second edition published in Great Britain in May 2006 by

The Policy Press
University of Bristol
Fourth Floor
Beacon House
Queen's Road
Bristol BS8 1QU
UK

Tel +44 (0)117 331 4054
Fax +44 (0)117 331 4093
e-mail tpp-info@bristol.ac.uk
www.policypress.org.uk

British Library Cataloguing in Publication Data
A catalogue record for this book is available from the British Library.

Library of Congress Cataloging-in-Publication Data
A catalog record for this book has been requested.

ISBN-10 1 86134 708 1 paperback
ISBN-13 978 1 86134 708 4 paperback
ISBN-10 1 86134 709 X hardcover
ISBN-13 978 1 86134 709 1 hardcover

Cover design by Qube Design Associates, Bristol.
Printed and bound in Great Britain by Hobbs the Printers, Southampton.

For women struggling to make the world a better place for all

Contents

Acknowledgments

The world has changed substantially since I wrote the first edition of *Women and Community Action* in the late 1980s. Much of the optimism around at the time has fallen as natural disasters, armed conflicts, terrorist attacks, environmental degradation and pollution have increased. Women and children have been disproportionately affected by many of these events; the lives of women and children throughout the world have become more precarious as poverty has intensified and many of the amenities that had been promised – safe water, sanitation, health services and education – seem as distant as ever for large numbers of them (Hocking, 2003).

Despite this gloomy picture, women have remained undaunted by the obstacles they face in reaching equality and providing their families with a better quality of life. They remain the unsung heroes of our age as they stitch together the fabric of social solidarity among the weakest segments of society. I am humbled by their courage in taking action to safeguard the future of us all. These women are many and their visions for healthy, happy communities underpin this book. But they are too numerous to mention, and they live in countries across the globe – Argentina, Australia, Canada, Chile, China, Ethiopia, Iceland, India, Italy, Jamaica, Japan, Northern Ireland, New Zealand/Aotearoa, South Africa, Zimbabwe, to mention a few places where women have unstintingly shared their experiences with me.

Age has caught up with some people, and others are no longer alive to share their dreams with us. But I remember them and their words of wisdom as those of us left behind sustain their hopes amidst losses that continue to be keenly felt – my father, my sister-in-law, mother-in-law, aunts, uncles, other relatives and close friends lost to cancer and other diseases.

People continue the struggle to create a better world. Among these are poor women whose strengths inspire us through their dreams of change despite conditions of being disenfranchised and dispossessed. To them, I also express my heartfelt thanks.

Finally, I thank: Jo Campling for insisting that I write a new edition of this book; Connie, Maria, Rita, Nic, Sam, David and Nicholas for supporting me with their love and understanding while I lose myself in writing instead of enjoying their company during precious life moments; and my mother for being there with words of encouragement.

Lena Dominelli

Notes on the author

Lena Dominelli is Chair of Applied Social Sciences, University of Durham, UK. Her extensive knowledge as a practitioner, researcher and educator is reflective in the extensive and impressive list of publications in the fields of social work, social policy and sociology, including *Social Work*; *Broadening Horizons*; *Anti-Oppressive Social Work Theory and Practice*; *Feminist Social Work Theory and Practice*; *Anti-Racist Social Work*; *Sociology for Social Work*; and *Women Across Continents*. Lena was President of the International Association of Schools of Social Work (IASSW), 1996 to 2004, and currently Past President and IASSW United Nations Liaison Officer.

Introduction

Communities are constantly changing entities with shifting and contested boundaries. Politicians, policy makers and practitioners like the term 'community' because they envisage this as a unitary fixed site where things happen and people enjoy warm feelings of solidarity and belonging. When a community 'breaks down', they see this as cause for concern. This is a very partial view of communities – who constitutes them, how they operate and what activities are included within them. Although touching on important elements of what holds people together in specific groupings, this conceptualisation of communities can be considered as out of touch with lived realities and discounted as essentialist. Different kinds of communities exist; people's allegiances to these alter over time; many communities are transient; and people can belong to more than one community simultaneously.

Communities have been thought about as being formed according to geographical affinities, identity traits or interests. They are constituted to provide a sense of unity or belonging that leaves a warm glow. Celebrated as inclusive, communities are simultaneously exclusive because the criteria for inclusion spurn those in a given locality who do not meet these requirements, and barriers are often erected around their borders to prevent those outside from entering. Communities are divided entities even if strategic decisions are taken to focus on one particular constituent element that binds diverse groups together for a specific purpose. People's experiences of the 'community' formed by the nation-state as either a geographical or citizenship-based (identity trait) entity, are varied. Women, minority ethnic groups and disabled people have complained about being excluded from being treated as equals within it, even when they are nationals (Williams, 1989; Dominelli, 1991; Lister, 1997). A nation-state can be home to people who are not nationals, but who contribute to its economic and social well-being. Yet, they are often defined as outsiders as current European discourses around migrants, asylum seekers and refugees indicate (Lorenz, 1994; EUMC, 2005). Communities are fraught with contradictions and tensions (Craig et al, 2000) that fracture and contest their alleged unity. They are unable to foreground all the myriad voices encompassed by a particular community, or acknowledge the asymmetrical power relations that rupture well-intentioned strivings for equality within them.

Virtual communities have caused notions of place and space to implode as geographical boundaries are transcended, bringing people together while fragmenting and segmenting locality and transcending its physical constraints (Burrows et al, 2005). Additionally, virtual communities are gendered and women's lesser usage of electronic information technologies has implications for the range of communities created by women and their participation in those dominated by men (CWIT, 2005).

Despite the lack of equality in the inclusion of women in national communities, 'the community' at the neighbourhood level is popularly acknowledged as *women's place and space*. The role of women in developing communities has become an integral part of official social development agendas (UNDP, 1998). Linked to their activities as nurturers and bearers of continuity between the past, present and future, women are targeted to uplift their communities in ways that men are not (Haidari and Wright, 2001). But the work that women undertake in the community on behalf of its members is often invisible. And so, women are excluded from its remit while being included within it.

Community work has drawn on women's struggles to gain a real voice in their communities and foster social change within them, even when these have been downgraded as 'soft' issues of lesser importance than 'hard' ones involving men. Women's heroic efforts to reshape the world in more humane directions by working through the local level inspire both practitioners and educators, and challenge those who seek to write these stories to do so in ways that accurately portray women's voices, concerns and achievements.

The structure of the book

This book celebrates women's involvement in community action, acknowledging the diversity of women who participate in making communities better places in which to live and valuing the vast variety of activities and techniques that women use in realising their ambitions for communities. Elements of community work, especially techniques and skills and some action goals, apply to men and women, and different groups of women. The book is structured around the idea that some community work values, philosophies, skills and techniques apply to all community work models; others are gender specific and have to be articulated separately for a full appreciation of the contributions that women make to community work and within that community action as professional practice. Women's endeavours in making communities more humane places for people are to be recognised and celebrated.

Gender is fractured along and interacts with a number of social divisions that intersect with each other rather than being additive. I refer to 'women' in the community, but this should not be taken as endorsing a homogeneous view of women, nor of the sameness of their experiences of community. Differences based on class, 'race', ethnicity, age, disability, sexual orientation and mental ill health configure women's experiences of gendered relations in diverse ways. These have to be specifically contextualised and addressed when organising any group of women. But there are commonalities in women's experiences of oppression, and in the dynamics of oppression that should not be lost. Similarities are important in forming alliances across difference, provided that the disparate starting point of each constituent member is recognised. Celebrating diversity while working for unity can form the basis for collective action among women. These may be constituted as temporary coalitions created through interaction and dialogue that bridges differences and diversities around common goals.

In revising this book for the second edition, I hung on to those aspects of the first one that have retained their currency including historical examples that carry messages for us today; updated other elements; and made new additions. Basic community work skills and organising techniques remain relevant and can be transferred from one setting to another provided that they are contextualised and adapted to a given situation. Meanwhile, the new information technologies have opened new opportunities for community organisation and women have been taking advantage of these, adding to their repertoire of knowledge (CWIT, 2005).

The book's overall structure remains the same. I focus primarily on community action as a model of community work that has considerable implications for women without losing sight of the broader community work canvas within which it is located. In the pages that follow I consider the difficulties surrounding the (re)defining of communities, processes of engaging people in community action and bases for their coming together in collective action to do something about their living conditions. In doing so, I focus on recent debates about the role and purpose of community work in contemporary British society, updating materials from the first edition, highlighting the themes that are elaborated in the remainder of the book and concluding that community workers have to *work for* inclusivity rather than *taking it for granted*, using notions of citizenship, solidarity, social justice and human rights that acknowledge the differentiated nature of women's experiences of these concepts.

In Chapter One, I concentrate on defining and redefining 'community' and women's place within it. I examine models of community work utilised in mobilising people for both their overall purpose and the positioning of women's activities within them. I acknowledge women's identity as multidimensional, multifaceted and fluid. And I view the category 'woman' as diverse, while anticipating that women share some commonalities across various social divisions that separate them. Finding unity within this diversity is a key challenge for practitioners but underpins a community work that aims to bring women together in collective action around agreed objectives.

I deconstruct gendered communities and endeavour to reveal women's roles within them in Chapter Two. I expose the normalisation of men's activities in community work and show that this devalues women's contribution to the profession. Gendering women's bodies within communities indicates how gender is articulated in practice. I also introduce key concepts such as empowerment, participation, exclusion and social capital because these are central to community work approaches to social problems, especially those intended to eliminate structural inequalities, alongside transforming the roles that individual women play in their communities (Fraser, 2005).

In Chapter Three, I explore the state's relationship with communities and how it has portrayed them as safe havens to promote their use as sites for social cohesion while at other times the state fragments communities to keep people divided in pursuit of policies that exacerbate existing tensions between them. Policies fostered by the state have been central to expropriating women's unpaid labour to improve the quality of life in communities and to provide the caring services that can be offloaded onto them.

I highlight feminist challenges to traditional community work and move on to consider feminist community action and its achievements in Chapter Four. Feminist community action has been crucial in creating facilities for women and ensuring that these are also run by them. They cover a vast array of endeavours ranging from the home to the environment. And they have challenged traditional forms of community involvement and participation, and posited new ones in their stead (Fraser, 2005).

In Chapter Five, I consider feminist campaigns and networks as major vehicles through which women have undertaken social action that promotes their interests. These have concentrated on a number of spheres – the home, workplace and physical environments – and redefined their meaning and relevance to quality of life issues.

In Chapter Six I turn to the concern of feminists to address women's individual needs including emotional ones alongside their preoccupation with structural inequalities. I consider various forms of intervention, including feminist therapy and counselling. I also problematise worker–service user relationships.

The roles of women in the workplace and traditional gendered expectations about their potential to act within it have been challenged by women entering waged work. This has included demanding equal pay, crèche provisions, flexible working and an end to sexual harassment at work. Their treatment as workers and the links between their waged economic activities and domestic responsibilities have been important sites for feminist community action. In Chapter Seven, I consider some of women's activities in the sphere of working relations.

I examine feminist social action in electoral politics in Chapter Eight. Women have played limited roles in party politics, which have traditionally been conceptualised as the prerogative of men. Their engagement in political social action has initiated changes in how traditional parties have related to women and failed to promote their issues or interests. Women have also redefined the meaning of the term 'political'.

I conclude with ways in which women's contributions to their communities can be recognised and celebrated. And I consider how community workers can transform their work in communities to improve the position, status and action of women within them.

ONE

Constructing, deconstructing and reconstructing communities

Introduction

Definitions of community are many, varied and contested. People argue over its meaning; those it includes or excludes; reasons for its existence; and where its locational boundaries are drawn. In this chapter I examine different definitions of community, identify how these are linked to context and purpose, and consider their significance. The impact of social divisions on social constructions of particular communities, their destruction and reconstruction, is integral to these discussions. The dynamics of creating, destroying and rebuilding communities make 'community' a highly politicised term and legitimate discourses that favour one of them over another.

Certain models of community dominate the social landscape and are encapsulated into different models of community work, namely, community care, community organisation, community development and community action. I reflect on flows of change and stability within communities for each model and utility in achieving specific ends. I highlight the racialised and gendered assumptions underpinning each genre alongside those of other social divisions. I also interrogate the transformative potential of community action and its use by women in initiating social change.

(Re)conceptualising communities

Bell and Newby (1971) unearthed 98 definitions for 'community'. These focused on geography or location, identity and interests, and have underpinned these three basic approaches to communities. Despite this variety, popular discourses, as the Collins Dictionary (1979, p 306) indicates, define community 'as the people living in one locality; a group of people having cultural, religious, ethnic or other characteristics in common; similarity or agreement'. These assume a unitary and unchanging view of the notion – a conceptualisation still evident in current texts, for example, Fellin (2001).

Töennies (1957), in writing about rural communities, articulates a homogeneous view of community. He calls it *Gemeinschaft* and argues that it is a self-contained entity united by kinship and a sense of belonging, which stands in counter-distinction to *Gesellschaft*, which involves a loose association of individuals. Töennies' (1957) insights weave a totalising discourse around the notion of *Gemeinschaft* that ignores divisions within a given community and treats it as an undifferentiated entity, regardless of the many different social groupings comprising it. This approach endorses an idealising of *Gemeinschaft* over *Gesellschaft*. It visualises community as an exclusionary phenomenon that creates insiders and outsiders at many levels. Current illustrations include national communities that are defined as unitary, despite the diversity of peoples residing within specified territorial boundaries. These views of community also persist in the works of communitarians such as Etzioni (1993), whose vision of the world underpins New Labour rhetoric (Blair, 2002), and social capital theorists such as Putnam (1993, 2000). Communitarian concepts have had a major impact on community initiatives since *Women and Community Action* was first published (Dinham, 2005). However, like *Gemeinschaft*, communitarian notions of community decry the loss of traditional associational bonds while devaluing new forms of linkage between peoples (Ladd, 1999).

Women were neglected in community work discourses until Marjorie Mayo (1977) highlighted the relevance of gender. Women have always participated in community activities, but their significance has been relegated in favour of men's actions, an enduring feature that was recently uncovered by the survey of community work conducted by the Community Development Foundation (CDF) (Glen et al, 2004). Yet community is the site where women live, work and ensure the survival of the species (Wilson, 1977a). They do so by defending the right of their families to enjoy decent standards of living, to acquire facilities that enhance their lives and to be treated with dignity and respect. Women act as mediators between local communities and the nation-state, which is represented through officials who take an interest in what people do, including when they are unable to fulfil their obligations as citizens.

Elizabeth Wilson (1977a) has called community a 'portmanteau' word, stuffed with diverse meanings that lack clarity, a point later echoed by Abercrombie et al (1994). Politicians have used these features to offload state responsibility for the care of children and older people onto 'communities', namely women (Finch and Groves, 1983; Ungerson, 1990; Orme, 2000). And so, for women, community can be a site of exploitation, especially of their caring capacities. This issue is of particular concern in countries where public provisions have been reduced in favour of 'community care' without the necessary resources accompanying such moves (Orme, 2000), and in those where 'family values' are anticipated as ensuring that welfare needs are met.

In deeming community an 'elusive' term 'without clear meaning', Abercrombie et al (1994, p 75) have destabilised unitary and clear-cut conceptualisations of it. I have argued that although community affiliations are configured on the bases of geography, identity and interests, these are multidimensional, interactive and fluid, with individuals and groups belonging to more than one community simultaneously even when they choose to emphasise one over the other. Thus, what constitutes a 'community' is contested and ambiguous (Dominelli, 2002a, b, 2004a).

Locational communities

How a community is defined depends on its context, the purposes for which it is being formed and who is configuring it. Traditionally, definitions have focused on geographic locality. Geographical notions, often associated with neighbourhoods, are those that community workers regularly draw on in practice (Fellin, 2001). Virtual communities that exist in cyberspace have augmented physical entities and require us to rethink locationality as fluid and ephemeral, although even these treat community, however defined, as unitary and homogeneous, as an examination of activist websites for women reveals (see www-unix.umbc.edu/~korenman/wmst/links.html and www.apc.org). Geographic locationality remains a popular basis for thinking about communities because it has simplicity and enables community borders to be easily identified and readily drawn. Those included in it may share other characteristics such as culture, religion and language that bind them further. The size of a geographic community varies. It can be very small, comprised of a few streets or a neighbourhood; large or national if constituted at the level of the nation-state; or global if encompassing the entire planet. Those falling within these boundaries become part of a 'community' or belong; those without do not. Formulated in this way, the concept becomes inherently exclusionary.

Within a geographical community, a totalising discourse that constructs all people as the same is perpetrated and reinforced. National configurations of community ignore, deny or suppress differences, especially those linked to ethnic, cultural or linguistic attributes, to create a unity that allows the nation-state to come into being and persist. This has occurred, for example, with people of Scottish and Irish origins within the UK, Basque people in Spain, and First Nations peoples and Quebeçois in Canada. Unitary discourses notwithstanding, these divisions do not go away as current demands for decentralisation and autonomy in these countries indicate.

Gendered relations within national discourses are formulated on a binary dyad that normalises men as the dominant gender. This socially constructed image essentialises men and women by casting each gender category as homogeneous for the strategic purpose of nation building. Termed 'strategic essentialism' (Hartsock, 1987; Harding, 1990), this construct genders women's bodies by their socialising, nurturing and caring capacities. Crucial to communal well-being, these activities are performed within private space and not as valued as those undertaken by men in the public arena. Discourses about national communities ignore the specificities of women's position and differences among women. In strategically essentialist nationalist discourses, women occupy subordinate positions while playing specific roles as 'mothers of the nation' (Yuval-Davis, 1997), safeguarding its culture and tradition and passing these on to subsequent generations through work in the home and waged employment. Women can be excluded from national communities by being configured as having the same characteristics and entitlements to services, power and resources as men, even when prevented from doing so by different working careers and expectations about their roles in society. This was exemplified by the 'cohabitation rule' in Britain that denied women living with men access to Income Support in their own right before 1986, and bedevils discourses about women's entitlements to pensions today.

Töennies' (1957) articulation of community fails to take account of the fragmentation and fracturing of communities over time. Nor can it explain how change occurs within communities to lead to their rise, reformulation or demise. A 'community', expressed through social relations, is an elusive entity and the process of seeking a single definition that encompasses more rather than fewer people masks differences between its constituent parts. And, as 'national' communities reveal, there may be more differences between peoples than 'common' bonds.

Locational communities can be segregated by class. Socialists like John Ruskin, William Morris and the Guild Socialists used class-based notions of community to forge unity across geographical, political, sociological and economic terrains. They did so by idealising '*the* working-class community', treating it as homogeneous and drawing nostalgically on close networks of support that people allegedly had in pre-industrial times when lives were closely attuned to the rhythms of nature. It was also gendered, as the working class consisted primarily of men working in factories. Such conceptualisations of community allow for the lament of its loss, as do Wilmot and Young (1957), in describing working-class communities that have lost their kinship base through urban planning in London, and Etzioni (1993) in the US.

Blagg and Derricourt (1982) also identified the workplace as a site for working-class struggles, and emphasised the importance of community work involving employment issues associated with production above those concerned with 'reproductive' matters that were the prerogative of women (Cowley et al, 1977). These have been termed respectively 'hard' issues as the remit of men and 'soft' ones addressed by women. These varied definitions view 'community' as a local space that is small enough for people to interact with each other. They signify traditional definitions of community that ignore the significance of racialised gendered relations and other social divisions like disability, mental ill health, sexual orientation and age that stratify communities and segregate members. Focusing on geographical locations and spatial arrangements based on class and kinship ties neglects the subordinate position and exclusion of men inscribed with subjugated masculinities alongside that of women, for example, disabled men (Shakespeare, 1999).Van Moorst (1998) makes similar points about the segregated nature of community in Australia where the exclusion of aboriginal peoples further complicates the picture.

Identity-based communities

Communities can be formed on the basis of identity traits. These communities involve interpersonal interactions that revolve around whom people are or how they identify themselves and how others define them. Identity-based communities use gender, ethnicity, disability, sexual orientation, religion or other attributes to differentiate between people and to create an 'in'-group that belong and an 'out'-group that does not.

Identity-based communities risk being cast as fixed or essentialised when identity is considered unitary, natural and immutable. Gendered identities, often presented as totalising and unchanging, are particularly interesting. They rely on a man–woman dyad in which men are configured as superior to women. Some aspects of gender, such as becoming pregnant and giving birth, are seen as legitimately gender-specific, in this case, belonging to women. Other traits are inappropriately usurped for one gender to create relations of domination and subordination, for example, reserving assertiveness exclusively for men (Belotti, 1975). Gender is subjugated within other social divisions when endorsing the interests of wider communities, for example, gendered dichotomous constructions of sexuality between men and women favouring heterosexual relationships. These have been challenged by homosexual, bisexual and transsexual persons, a feature articulated in and reflected through 'queer' theory (Butler, 2000).

Women's subjugated identity within the binary dyad of men and women has been used to uphold the interests of men within ethnic or national groupings where the identity of the nation has been inscribed on women's bodies (Yuval-Davis, 1997; Shakib, 2002). In these, differences between men and women have been configured as a timeless feature of a given community and women are expected to represent that broader community rather than their own personal interests. Other identity attributes are present in such communities, but ethnicity is prioritised as women symbolically represent the nation. This often involves the idealisation of their strengths as women rather than as people, thus emphasising differences between them and men. Sanctions can be imposed on women who challenge racialised configurations of their identity, as occurred to women who did not wear the burkha under the Taliban in Afghanistan (Shakib, 2002).

Women are implicated in reproducing and upholding these constructions of their bodies. Their participation in these communities is based on their consent as women or participation in self-directed 'technologies of governance' (Foucault, 1980) or self-discipline. These definitions of community are predicated on the view of the whole being greater than the sum of its parts and underplay women's interests as women in favour of affirming a national identity that transcends local community divisions. And so, women are members of their national or ethnic community while inhabiting that community of women that is accorded lesser significance in defence of the nation.

Racialised representations can both liberate and oppress women, depending on the specific contexts, purposes and mechanisms used to implicate women in them. In some, an entire world view linked to ethnicity is highlighted in creating dichotomised social relations between the 'majority' ethnicity and a 'minority' one to safeguard its survival, for example, reaffirming the uniqueness of First Nations cultures in Canada over the dominant Anglo-Saxon one (Fournier and Crey, 1998); others stress rituals linked to religious observance that uphold homogeneity in a particular culture. Demonstrating national locationality, these characteristics also encompass identity and interest communities and blur the boundaries between the three types of communities.

Unitary notions of identity communities can cross borders, as happens in diasporic ones. Conceptualising communities within a unitary diaspora has been crucial in ensuring survival, for example, Jewish communities and those of people with African origins (Asante, 1987; Brah, 1996; John-Baptiste, 2001). Transmitting cultural traditions and values across generations has been central to a strategy of maintaining a community's continuity across time and space. Exchanges with others provide the contexts that produce discontinuities within an original culture and beyond, while enacting continuities in both (Dominelli, 2000).

While some aspects of culture, particularly its value system, may be retained, adapting to different geographic terrains and contexts in which people are now located introduces change in the culture, language and traditions of diasporic communities. This occurs through negotiated encounters with other peoples who also occupy these territories. Africentric theories (Asante, 1987) exemplify how African Americans have reclaimed their African cultural heritage to affirm their equal status and position within the broader national community currently represented by the United States. Embedded in homogeneous castings of 'community', their challenge illustrates change occurring in the culture and values of a group as members respond to local conditions.

Internet and email can now be used to transcend national boundaries and maintain ties among members of dispersed communities. In collapsing barriers of time, space and place, links can be electronically maintained to affirm and maintain existing relationships and to create new ones, as occurs in transnational communities that bind people in diasporic configurations, for example, people from Jamaica maintaining active connections with relatives in the UK, the US and Canada (Goulbourne, 1999). These virtual communities are supplemented by visits that occur in real time and place and add complexity to the notion of community and contested meaning (Burrows et al, 2005). Similar exclusionary dynamics are evident in communities acquiring visibility through the Internet, for example, DAWN (www.dawn.thot.net) in overcoming disablist framings of disabled women's bodies (Morris, 1991; Begum, 1992, Wendell, 1996).

Interest communities

Interest-oriented communities are those that people create on the basis of shared pursuits. These are more easily understood as temporal. They include sports- or hobby-related activities, time-limited campaigning networks and social action groups that address specific issues. People's interests alter over time as they undergo different experiences or become aware of other possibilities within their environments and change their allegiances. Entry to and exit from various interest communities can be enacted at the individual's or group's desire.

The inherent transience of interest communities suggests that, as organisational forms, these are held together by fewer ties and looser bonds than identity-based ones. Consequently, the departure of one individual in a group is unlikely to be experienced as having a devastating impact on the organisational structures of an interest community. An individual can hold more than one interest and join more than one interest community simultaneously and participate in these while being a member of both locational and identity communities. Communities are, therefore, multilayered and an individual's participation in these can be conceptualised as multidimensional, interactive and fluid, as indicated in Figure 1.1 below.

Figure 1.1: Multidimensional and fluid communities

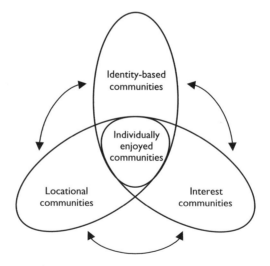

Source: Adapted from *Anti-Oppressive Social Work Theory and Practice* (Dominelli, 2002a)

Models of community work

Whether formed on the basis of geography, identity or interests, community work as collective action undertaken by groupings that share common objectives in reaching specific goals has a long history and is comprised of a variety of models whereby people come together to advance their interests as a community, however defined/Community work can be postulated as having begun in the days when human beings first began to work collaboratively to maximise their capacity in achieving desired outcomes. Its development has been varied, but it is recognised as a professional activity throughout the globe. Community work has been considered one of the three arms of social work, alongside casework and groupwork (Younghusband, 1978). This position pertained in the UK until the mid-1980s when the then Central Council for Education and Training in Social Work (CCETSW) removed it from the social work curriculum. Its radical potential undermined its popularity as a state-funded activity in the West; its capacity to mobilise poor communities popularised it in industrialising countries where direct links to social work were detached (Kaseke, 1994) to make it central to social development initiatives (Sewpaul and Hölscher, 2004).

Nation-states formally acknowledged community work during the heyday of imperialism. As community development, it drew non-industrialised parts of the world into capitalist industrial production (Mayo, 1977; Marsden and Oakley, 1982) and laid foundations for capitalist economic and political infrastructures that integrated colonial territories into a world capitalist system. These introduced industrial forms of production, transportation, communication, Western education, cultures, religions and institutions, including social services, the rule of law, judicial systems and state administration, to pre-capitalist social formations (Kwo, 1984; Sewpaul and Hölscher, 2004).

Community development initiatives incorporated traditional ruling classes into colonial regimes by according them privileged status in the civil service and state bureaucracy in return for support of colonial policies (Halpern, 1963; Dominelli, 1974, 1986a). By collecting taxes and upholding foreign laws, the elites utilised these structures to legitimate private ownership of property and to facilitate the sale or expropriation of common lands. In this way, indigenous elites became integrated into the exploitation of indigenous masses by their colonial masters. And colonial authorities ensured that community development became integrated into the processes of capacity building and social entrepreneurship, concerns that are essential to this model today (LRN,

1999; Kenny, 2002; Williams, C., 2004). After the Second World War, when independence movements secured the liberation of former colonies, community development was used by local elites to prevent the spread of communism (Mayo, 1977; Marsden and Oakley, 1982) and to control troublesome populations.

The lessons learnt in the ex-colonies were subsequently utilised in the imperial heartlands. In Britain and US, community development models were adapted for use in poor working-class communities. In Britain, the Victorian techniques of population control, incorporation of local leaders and reliance on local resources through 'self-help' schemes were revised through philanthropic initiatives such as the 'Model Dwellings' to relieve 'working-class housing problems'. These practices were later refined for controlling social disorder and working-class militancy during 'the troubles' in Northern Ireland (Griffiths, 1974a; Lovett and Percival, 1982). These trends resonate to the present (L. Morris, 1995), while the ongoing struggles over the heart and soul of the social work profession indicate its contested and unresolved nature.

Identifying models of community work is as problematic as defining the term 'community'. Models are arbitrary constructs that depend on which features theorists choose to highlight. There are overlaps between different models, especially in the techniques and skills associated with each. Jack Rothman's (1970) influential work proposed the following models as central to mainstream community work:

- community care;
- community organisation;
- community development; and
- community action (which I [Dominelli, 1990] subdivided on an identity basis into class-based community action, feminist community action and community action from a black perspective).

Community care

Community care draws on social networks and voluntary activities that offer a direct caring service to residents, especially those who are sick, disabled or aged. It is a locational model with a touch of identity trait because women undertake the bulk of its caring work (Finch, 1982; Finch and Groves, 1983; Knijn and Ungerson, 1997) and are central to its realisation, for example, Good Neighbourhood Schemes, Neighbourhood Watch, Meals-on-Wheels and tenants' associations that simply pass on requests for improving certain buildings.

Community workers in these schemes are often unpaid volunteers, estimated to contribute £40 billion to the economy yearly (Hirst, 1999, p 20).

Volunteers in the community care model are motivated by altruism and a desire to do something useful in their spare time. They usually consider themselves 'apolitical' and believe that this stance is reflected in the services provided. They accept the basic soundness of an existing social system while recognising that it produces minor problems that can be alleviated through voluntary work. This goal underpins their involvement in community care. By relying on unpaid volunteers, although nominal payments are occasionally given (Ungerson, 1990), community care provides opportunities for middle-class women not engaged in waged work and retired people using 'free' time to perform duties that meet other people's needs. However, not paying expenses incurred in doing voluntary work assumes the volunteer has the wherewithal to cover these, inhibits low-income people from volunteering and privileges middle-class participants (Hirst, 1999).

Recruiting volunteers on this basis can enforce paternalism towards others and carries the danger of imposing racist, sexist and classist views of the world on those being cared for. White and black working-class women[1] who cannot afford to buy the labour of other women or are refused support from the personal social services have to assume informal community care at home on top of their waged job and normal domestic responsibilities. Lacking other alternatives, they may give up paid work to meet additional caring demands from frail older parents and disabled adult children.

Promoted by a shoal of investigations such as the Barclay (1982), Griffiths (1988) and Wagner (1988) Reports, formal policies of community care that co-opted women's unpaid work were initiated under the 1990 National Health Service and Community Care Act. From the 1990s, community care became the major UK government policy for delivering services to older people (Orme, 2000), and was integrated into the New Deal for Communities (NDC) (Hirst, 1999). Despite state rhetoric on empowering consumers and increasing 'choice', users and volunteers were not involved in (re)defining the nature of the services offered or in determining the type and amount of resources available (Dominelli, 2004a). It formalised and intensified one of the model's key problems – using women's unpaid labour to cover gaps in statutory provisions caused by the state's reduced role as a service provider; calling for increased voluntary participation in helping others; demanding more of the family, that is, women, in caring for their own; and commissioning services from voluntary agencies and commercial providers that pay women workers low wages (CPS, 2002).

Hailed as a positive alternative, community care replaced institutionalised residential care that had been critiqued for dehumanising residents, enforcing powerlessness and fostering neglect in places where people expected quality conditions (Hughes, 1995). Initially articulated by the progressive Left, deinstitutionalisation (Scull, 1977) provided the grounds on which governments strapped for cash constructed cases for closing down residential provisions and placing people in the community to receive the caring attention that institutions had failed to provide (Baldwin, 1985). This position was contested by feminists who argued that good residential care was necessary for some people as it could provide more appropriate care for some and could also reduce the caring burden on women and other family members (Finch, 1984). Moreover, locating homes in the private sector has proved a mixed blessing. Residential homes for older people have not provided residents with the high standards of care expected. Closures of 15,000 places a year are disruptive to older people who can be shunted from one location to another. In the UK, the number of private residential homes for older people was halved as profits dwindled (Batty, 2002). Profits can also be made from selling establishments. Residential homes in affluent areas were closed and land sold to property developers building luxury dwellings for well-paid professionals (Summerskill, 2001). Inadequate government payments per place, chronic staff shortages and poorly paid staff – often on a minimum wage that pays less than stacking supermarket shelves (Summerskill, 2001) – also undermine service provision.

Community care isolates both the receiver and deliverer of care, but improvements in delivery have occurred under its auspices. Care in the community is provided on an individual basis; people have remained in their homes longer; and some receive considerable support even if they pay user fees. For those unable to cook, hot rather than tepid Meals-on-Wheels are being served. However, these have been achieved at the expense of the consumer through industrial methods that mass-produce food of limited nutritional value (Weinstock, 2004) and restrict multicultural and vegetarian options. And those running care home establishments have come together to form organisations such as the National Care Homes Association (NCHA) to organise the sector's voice.

Formal community care models symbolised through case (or care) management systems have shifted the terrain of caring from symbolising solidarity with others to profit making. And, being provided on a commercial basis, profit rather than service dominates their delivery (Kenny, 2002). This subjects community care to the vagaries of the market, turning it into a 'stop-go' provision as profit opportunities rise or fall giving priority to commercial imperatives rather than user needs. The architects of care in the community did not address issues of sexism and racism. Recently, dealing with these has been grafted on to equal opportunities legislation and the willingness of individual case managers to tackle them in the workplace.

Community organisation

Community organisation models of community work promote community interests by improving coordination between various welfare agencies. These aim to avoid wasting resources by ending the duplication of efforts, facilitating interagency pooling of resources and managing services more effectively. It has been used extensively in Britain since the 1960s, once government realised its managerial propensities in curtailing expenditures and diverting the radical potential of community development. Community organisation became popularised as part of a corporate approach to welfare. It formed a useful tool in the hands of managers wanting to make the best use of resources when these had to be rationed. Community groups expected to be strengthened in reaching their objectives through such initiatives. The community worker is a paid 'expert', often a male professional with organisational knowledge who gives direct advice to the people being helped and who does not threaten the status quo. Residents can perceive professional advice as paternalistic. Community organisation models are often conducive to those in power retaining their privileges and control over resources. And it has been used to contain working-class anger by channelling it through approved structures and procedures (Dearlove, 1974; Drummond, 2004).

From the late 1990s, community regeneration projects promoted under New Labour's NDC have drawn heavily on community organisation models that reinforce professional power over residents (see SEU, 1999, 2000; Dinham, 2005). Popularised under 'Third Way' policies (Giddens, 1998), this model entrenches highly regulated public–private partnerships and a technical rationalist management style that excludes those unfamiliar with its jargon while empowering recognised groups at the expense of new ones (Diamond, 2004; Gilchrist, 2004). This enhances participation among established groups, usurps grassroots power and inhibits spontaneous group formation (Jordan, 2000). Opposition to proposals in official town plans and road schemes during community participation exercises flounder against this type of locality-based community intervention for it gives people power that lacks substance (Schuftan, 1996). Community organisation models assume homogeneous, unitary views of community; treat people similarly; ignore the needs of women and black people in allocating resources; and neglect conflict (Dinham, 2005). Totalising location-based views of community dominate the community organisation terrain.

Community development

Community work formulated on the community development model helps people acquire the self-help skills necessary for improving their situation through their own endeavours (Ife, 1998). It relies on educational processes initiated by community workers using either directive or non-directive approaches in mobilising people around specific actions (Batten, 1967; Fellin, 2001). Community problems are presumed to indicate backwardness on the part of inhabitants who are believed to lack the skills necessary for enriching their community. This pathological view of residents legitimises bringing in expert 'outsiders' to provide the leadership necessary for mobilising people around specific issues and teaching them how to improve their circumstances. Action is collective and seeks to improve living conditions (Gilchrist, 2000).

The community worker, usually a man, helps people work on problems that they have identified. He is typically a paid professional interested in reforming the existing system through social engineering. His interventions target specific residential areas or geographic locations that the state foresees as requiring assistance in tackling social problems such as poverty through self-help initiatives (SEU, 1997). Locality-based community development models draw heavily on women to provide grassroots support and resources that projects require during implementation. This model has been used to integrate black communities more thoroughly into the capitalist system in subordinate positions (Ng, 1988), and has become increasingly popular in engaging residents in addressing training initiatives aimed at getting poor people into paid work (Perlmutter, 1997; Hoatson, 2001; Dinham, 2005).

Negotiation and discussion are the main tools used in the organising process as long as action remains within the community development paradigm. It acknowledges the possibility of conflict if opponents to residents' proposals do not respond to their demands for meaningful change. Protracted struggles with government officials or corporate managers that do not progress a community's concerns produce disillusionment with community development processes and indicate a need to change the system in which these are embedded (Mowbray, 2005). At this point, community development may turn into community action and lead to more confrontational forms of direct action (Rothman, 1970). I prefer to retain the distinction between community development and community action, even though the Standing Conference for Community Development (SCCD, 2001) and the Federation for Community Development Learning (FCDL, 2004) have blurred it by defining community development as involved in social change that increases participation and affirms the values of social justice and mutual respect.

The paradigmatic shift to community action occurs when community development models that assume community passivity and pathology are challenged through grassroots mobilisation. This happened during the 1960s and 1970s when initiatives in the American War on Poverty and British Community Development Projects (CDPs) became transformed into what became known as community action. State fear of the radical potential of community development has led to constraints being imposed on the autonomy of community workers to respond in accordance with activist pressures (Dominelli, 2004b).

CDPs began with community organisation and community development models of working but became community action oriented when their interventions failed to reduce disadvantage (CDP, 1977a, b). CDP endeavours challenging the housing of tenants in homes unfit for human habitation turned the state that was funding their activities into an object of their interventions and placed it in an intolerable position. So, the state moved quickly to close the more contentious projects despite earlier agreements to extend their remit, as occurred in Batley CDP which was closed down twice for supporting community groups critical of the local authority. Eventually, the state abandoned the whole CDP enterprise and community development ceased to find favour in state circles (Loney, 1983) for several decades. This caused a precipitous decline in the number of community work posts and had a knock-on effect of eliminating community work training in British social work education (Dominelli, 2004b).

Community action

Community action presupposes a conflict model of social organisation that is often identity based. Community work organised according to this model can be militant, bringing people lacking power together to reduce their powerlessness and increase effectiveness in furthering their interests through direct collective action. Community groups using this model focus on social change, expose the contradictions on which society is based and demand a shift in the allocation of power and resources. Confrontation and negotiation are key means for realising their objectives.

The community worker may be either a paid professional or community activist and is usually a man. The community worker is likely to live in the community that is being mobilised. Group members rapidly become activists as they engage in conflict with those in authority. The distinction between the community worker and the rest of the group is blurred when he (or she) becomes an active member of that community and works with others on an egalitarian basis. Thus, the relationship between the community worker and grassroots participants shifts away from the expertise held by the professional to encompass lay knowledge.

Class-oriented community action concentrates on the interests of working-class people. It divides society between the 'bosses' who own the means of production and 'workers' who sell their labour. This binary division was considered inequitable and amenable to social change through community action linked to class struggles that involved alliances between working-class activists in community groups and trade unionists to achieve agreed goals (Leonard, 1975). The Claimants Unions of the 1970s and recent trade union struggles against the decline in public services exemplify community groups operating according to this model (Rose, 1973; Munro, 2001). Forming alliances to achieve a better life carries risks including losing the capacity to set specific agendas (Bishop, 1994; Kettle, 1998; Munro, 2001). British working-class activists have ignored this limitation to secure compromises that attract the labour movement as a key ally. In these, class is a unitary aspect of identity and indivisible while fractures that occur along ethnic and gender lines are neglected.

Class-based community action begins locally, but is organisationally extended to regional and other levels to maximise its effectiveness. Class-oriented community action has been traditionally masculist in its theory and practice as class interests supersede those based on other social divisions including 'race' and gender. Most paid community work posts continue to be held by white men who play key roles in identifying the processes and targets for action (Glen et al, 2004). Their methods, behaviour and analyses of social problems have often alienated women (Dixon et al, 1982) and black people (Ohri and

Manning, 1982; Babacan and Gopalkrishnan, 2001). Drawing on the women's movement and black liberation movement, many women and black people initially involved in class-based action created their own respective forms of community action to cater specifically for their needs. Working-class activism received a critical blow under Thatcherism through changes in trade union and employment laws that reduced the scope for sympathy strikes and shows of solidarity. These seriously undermined trade union mobilisation after the miners' strike of 1984–85 and have impacted strongly on current union resistance to the deterioration in public sector services, pay and pensions (Munro, 2001).

Feminist community action, initiated by feminists active in the women's liberation movement to address quality of life issues that affected women, fostered equality, democracy, connectedness and inclusivity. They confronted masculist community work on theoretical and practical grounds. Focusing on gender as a crucial feature of collective action that takes place in the community, they harnessed its energies to promote social change and gender equality (Wilson, 1977a; Marchant and Wearing, 1986; Dominelli and McLeod, 1989; Dominelli, 2002a). In doing this, feminist community workers began to transform traditional community work theory and practice by addressing matters that affected people's daily lives. Feminists achieved this by challenging fundamentally the nature of capitalist patriarchal social relations between men and women, women and the state and adults and children, and rooting their change efforts in the everyday routines of life and active citizenship.

In highlighting the specific needs of women as people previously excluded in community work, feminists have developed its theory and practice, produced new understandings of the concept of 'community' and revealed the political nature of social relations embedded within it. Developing services for women exposed the politicised nature of power relations between men and women (Adamson et al, 1988; Lowndes, 2000) and transcended the boundaries of traditional community work in practice. By exposing the problematic nature of the concept 'community' from women's point of view, feminist community workers have revealed the extent to which it relies on exploiting women's energies for the 'common good' (Finch and Groves, 1983) and questioned prevailing definitions of what constituted appropriate subjects for community action (Curno et al, 1982; Shaw and Martin, 2000; Shiva, 2003).

Feminists have made gender the basis of a dialectical process of organisation (Brandwein, 1987), and challenged the division of society into the private domestic sphere outside public scrutiny that encompasses women's place in the community and male-dominated spheres in social, political and economic life. This delineation had been accepted by traditional and radical community workers alike (see Bailey and Brake, 1975; Leonard, 1975; Fellin, 2001). Feminists' redefinition of private lives and concern with women's emotional fulfilment as well as women's physical needs have enabled feminists to focus on domestic violence, child sexual abuse and other instances of injustice that affect women to develop forms of practice and resources that are run by women to better meet their needs (Mayo, 1977; Curno et al, 1982; Hanmer and Statham, 1988; Dominelli and McLeod, 1989; Dominelli, 2002a).

In tackling issues that community workers had previously shunned, feminists have:

- developed new methods of organisation, for example, consciousness-raising (Dreifus, 1973) and procedures for emotional healing (Bass and Davis, 1988);
- redefined private troubles as social problems that needed public solutions, for example, men assaulting women in the home (Dominelli, 1990; Mullender, 1997);
- demanded that power relationships between men and women move in more equal directions (Dominelli and McLeod, 1989);
- focused on sharing power according to 'win-win' principles in which everyone gains from conflict resolution rather than having one group lose power to a more powerful one (Brandwein, 1987);
- highlighted the need for the positive appraisal of the contribution that women make to society (Janssen-Jurreit, 1982);
- made connections between the different responsibilities that women carry when involved in unpaid domestic and waged work (Dominelli and McLeod, 1989);
- created services run for and by women;
- developed forms of community work that enhance the welfare of women, men and children (Brook and Davis, 1985; Marchant and Wearing, 1986; Hanmer and Statham, 1988; Dominelli, 2002a; Phillips, 2004); and
- highlighted the links between industrial pollution, uncontrolled development, environmental degradation, destruction of everyday life and the poor quality of the human condition (Roy, 1999; Shiva, 2003).

Feminists have stressed the impact that forms of oppression such as classism, racism, ageism and disablism have on women's lives and the divisions these create among women in practice contexts (Lorde, 1984; Bryan et al, 1985; Doress and Siegal, 1987; Davis, 1989; Morris, 1991; Wendell, 1996; Frankenburg, 1997). This has enabled black feminists to identify the failure of the women's liberation movement to be inclusive of all women (Lorde, 1984; Collins, 1991) despite its rallying slogan that 'sisterhood is universal' (Morgan, 1970, 1984; Adamson et al, 1988), and demand recognition of women's differentiated experiences of oppression while calling for alternatives to mainstream responses (Bhavani, 1993). Feminist community action became a vehicle for feminist ideology, theory and practice to elaborate the feminist view that the 'personal is political' (Dreifus, 1973) and 'politics is personal' (Ungerson, 1987) while attempting to enact egalitarian relations of empowerment among women engaged in collective action (Adamson et al, 1988; Ledwith and Asgill, 1998).

Some black women have rejected the applicability of the term 'feminist' to their struggles and prefer the word 'womanist' (Collins, 1991). Womanism is rooted in African American traditions that emphasise strong women acting as agents who create their own destiny (Hudson-Weems, 1993). Feminist community workers' emphasis on collective action in changing women's lives has been disputed by postmodern feminists who question the relevance of the category 'woman' (Nicholson, 1990), and disparage it as essentialist and incapable of altering existing power relations.

By celebrating decontextualised diversity among women and individualised decision making, postmodern feminism has intensified fragmentation within the women's movement and legitimated personal responses to social problems. It remains a contested approach heavily critiqued for its inability to suggest solutions to problems encountered by women throughout the world regardless of those aspects of identity that feature in their lives, for example, earning less than men who share all attributes other than gender; undertaking the bulk of domestic labour; and being over-represented among poor people (Wichterich, 2000). And, postmodern feminism has failed to engage with collective action through which many gains in women's rights have been won (Dominelli, 2004b).

Community action from a black perspective was developed by black people because community work organisations had failed to address racism as a specific issue and hindered the development of services that met black people's needs. Criticising the inappropriateness of community workers operating from a colourblind approach, they felt compelled to develop their own form of community action (Mullard, 1973; Ohri and Manning, 1982) and make the struggle for racial equality central to their work (Dominelli, 1988). Black community activists created a range of provisions to meet the needs of black people while simultaneously addressing problems that various social divisions created in their organisations (Sondhi, 1982). Their activities have included establishing anti-racist and anti-ageist provisions for their elders (ASRA, 1981); campaigns and networks to support individuals and groups tackling state institutionalised racism, particularly in social security and immigration regulations (Sondhi, 1982); services for women (Guru, 1987); and reforming childcare and welfare services (Small, 1984).

Black women have also developed facilities appropriate to their needs. These include black women's refuges (Guru, 1987), healthcare networks (Malek, 1985), childcare provisions (Farrah, 1986) and improving workplace relations (Rogaly, 1997). Black women have played a significant role in developing feminist theory and practice (hooks, 1984; Lorde, 1984; Bryan et al, 1985; Bhavani, 1993; Davis, 1989, 1995; Collins, 1991; Wilson, 1993). This has been especially evident in the development of more inclusive forms of practice and critiques of racism inherent in white feminist community work (Bhavani, 1993; Ledwith and Asgill, 1998).

Anti-racist feminist community work has drawn inspiration from black and white women committed to empowering people and developing facilities that eliminate racial and gender inequalities. They have eschewed the creation of hierarchies of oppression that prioritise one form of oppression over another and insisted that all types of inequality are tackled together (hooks, 1984, 2000; Lorde, 1984; Davis, 1989, 1995; Dominelli, 2002a). Generating 'black feminist thought' (Collins, 1991), they made black perspectives in community work gender sensitive (hooks, 1990, 2000).

Emerging forms of community work

Fundamental social, political and economic changes since I wrote the first edition of *Women and Community Action* in the late 1980s have impacted heavily on communities and people's responses to them. These include the increasing use of community action among middle- and upper-class residents to protect their quality of life and environment; deindustrialisation of working-class communities; consolidation of the 'new' social movements that existed earlier and the rise of new ones; growth of community action tackling environmental issues (Ife, 1997; Hillman, 2002); subordination of local social issues to economic globalisation; and growing fears about physical security and terrorist activities. These have been supplemented by concerns to address structural inequalities locally, nationally and internationally and to transform social relations through community work (Mayo, 2000; Reisch, 2004).

The issues raised have caused me to recast community action models and divide these into: corporate welfarist community work; protectionist community action; emancipatory community action; environmental community action; and global social activism. These may be supportive of the status quo, reformist or transformative depending on participants' values, ideology and goals. Their diversity also makes the direction that collective action takes less certain. So, change to improve the overall quality of life cannot be taken for granted.

Corporate welfarist community work has been utilised by the state to regenerate communities ravaged by deindustrialisation. It relies on partnerships between private sector entrepreneurs and local authorities and residents in rebuilding elements of the local economy, often with state largesse in the form of lucrative contracts for services, outright grants, infrastructural provisions like roads, tax exemptions and legislation that deregulates business activities while regulating or controlling workers (Barlett and Steele, 1998). This model conserves capitalist social relations by providing waged work opportunities and training facilities that reduce unemployment or people's reliance on the welfare state during hard times.

Public–private partnerships in community enterprises and the workfare state favoured by neoliberals seek to find solutions for these concerns. This model has been extensively developed in the US through attacks on welfare (Perlmutter, 1997; Zucchino, 1997) and in the UK under the New Deal, launched in 1998, to get people out of poverty through waged work, usually casual and poorly paid (GMLPU, 2004) or training for work (Blair, 1999; ODPM, 2004). It can also involve big business adding a 'community' dimension to its portfolio and using money to promote a kindly image, often under corporate control. Their activities can be tokenistic, for example, sponsoring rubbish bins or providing free Internet access to extend advertising space.

Protectionist community action aims to safeguard the interests of those privileged by existing social relations. It creates a binary dyad around belonging and entitlement that excludes and devalues difference and involves the exercise of agency. The model has become strategic in middle-class communities' efforts to retain enjoyed group or community privileges, especially those linked to holding on to quality space and place. They have used this approach effectively on a range of issues to protect neighbourhoods from undertakings that might reduce property values, for example, preventing people they consider 'deviant' such as mentally disordered offenders from becoming members of their communities, opposing unwanted facilities and rejecting road building and other industrialisation schemes that threaten their localities.

Poor people utilise this model to exclude those they deem outsiders from sharing what little they have. The British National Party (BNP) has successfully exploited white working-class fears of deteriorating living conditions by occupying the vacuum left by mainstream politicians' failure to deal with environmental degradation, job insecurities, housing shortages and an unequal distribution of power and resources in disadvantaged communities. In this, racialised deviation from a white Anglo-Saxon norm is configured as not belonging and not entitled to treatment reserved for the privileged group which is not thought of in racialised terms because it provides the yardstick or norm whereby others are judged. Competition for scarce resources is managed by excluding 'outsiders' rather than addressing the lack of social resources in a community and questioning the privileging of some at the expense of others.

Emancipatory community action is rooted in identity politics. It is often linked to the 'new' social movements and realisation of autonomy, human rights, social justice and citizenship. It encompasses feminist community action, community action from black perspectives, disability community action and gay and lesbian initiatives in community action. These models of community action are concerned primarily with changing social relations to include groups that are currently excluded from sharing power, resources and entitlements to social benefits on an equal basis with the 'normalised' dominant group that exists in a binary dyad with them.

For example, gay men and lesbian women have organised against discrimination and oppression on the basis of sexual orientation to argue for the same rights as heterosexual men and women; and disabled people seek similar entitlements as able-bodied people. Promoting these goals in Britain has produced legislative changes authorising civil partnerships and the 1995 Disability Discrimination Act. A danger of these state responses is that freeing an identity-group from a specific aspect of oppression leaves an inegalitarian social edifice unchanged as radical demands are incorporated into existing mainstream structures that are not transformed in the process. Yet, these may have already been found wanting by members within the dyad privileged by them. For example, by linking civil partnerships to hegemonic formulations of marriage, women's attempts to reform the institution through collective action have become marginalised or forgotten. This is likely to continue because marriage and its couple-oriented rules have acquired a new lease of life with little attention paid to the institution's existing inequalities. This is illustrated by the failed 'Dissaggregation Now' Campaign which demanded that taxation laws treat men and women as individuals, each having his or her own rights to wealth and income, rather than being a couple who shared resources in ways that benefited the man more than the woman (Pahl, 1981; Dominelli, 1991). And such mainstreaming leaves to one side the question of the dependency of children on adults and their rights to an independent income. Despite feminist challenges to men's power in the socioeconomic and political arenas and some gains made by women, men continue to dominate in the economy and government and to earn higher levels of pay (Norris, 2000), even in community work (Gathiram and Hemson, 2002; Community Regeneration Online, 2004; Glen et al, 2004).

Environmental community action is among the newer forms of community action that targets corporate globalisation and crosses political, economic, social and cultural barriers. It has a transnational reach that focuses on raising awareness of damage being wrought on the environment by capitalist forms of industrial development, economic processes, consumerist lifestyles and politics (Hillman, 2002; Shiva, 2003). Organisations like Greenpeace raise highly contentious issues caused by industrial processes and companies' pollution of the earth's land, air and water through hydrocarbon use, genetically modified food and radioactive energy emissions. Their action seldom pays specific attention to social divisions, but poor people can benefit from these activities because environmental degradation often occurs in their communities, for example, locating toxic waste disposal units and polluting factories in their space. Classic examples of such destruction are the Bhopal Disaster and Chernobyl which left poor people without adequate medical attention, housing or employment opportunities that took account of failing health.

Environmental community activists undertake direct action that ranges from occupying underground tunnels to oppose airport runways like 'Swampy' in Manchester, living in trees to protect virgin forests to resisting the testing of nuclear weapons (Bari, 1994). Activist environmental groups usually operate on the margins and seek to hold global corporations accountable for their actions by linking local concerns to global ones. Some of these have been partially mainstreamed after years of lobbying, for example, the Kyoto Agreement on climate change, the World Wildlife Fund and the International Rivers Network (Hillman, 2002). Feminists like Judi Bari (1994) argue that environmental issues used to divide workers from environmental activists can be redefined to enable the two groups to work collaboratively through non-violent direct grassroots action that protects jobs and the environment – both crucial to continued human existence and the reproduction of everyday life. The 1990 Redwood Summer Campaign of mass protest organised by Earth First!, where Judi Bari had a significant strategising role despite having been car-bombed in May 1990, mobilised thousands of protestors around forest activism. This led to the US Congress passing the 1993 Headwaters Forest Act and reducing over-logging in old-growth forests in California and Oregon. Bari's activism continued to bridge feminism and ecological activism through alliances with the labour movement until her death from cancer in 1997.

Global social activism consists of action around specific issues that cross borders via amorphous movements built on alliances of solidarity involving individuals working through civil society agencies such as non-governmental organisations (NGOs), for example, Amnesty International, Minority Rights Group, Human Rights Watch, ActionAid, the peace movement, Jubilee 2000 for the debt cancellation campaign (against Third World debt), Real World Coalition, World Social Forum, World March of Women and the 2005 Make Poverty History campaign. Global social activists subscribe to anti-capitalist critiques and an egalitarian world order rooted in fair trade, and equal sharing of resources and power (Prigoff, 2000). Their impact on existing social relations and the neoliberal global order has been limited.

These initiatives overlap with environmental movements, but have a broader remit rooted in critiquing neoliberal globalisation, promoting identity issues, eradicating social problems and engaging a wider range of people. These movements have no identified leaders, and participants define themselves as activists who (re)configure processes to redefine social power or unsettle hegemonic meanings (Escobar, 1998). Connections between individual participants occur in autonomous spaces, are ephemeral and often mediated through the new information technologies. Mobile phones and the Internet act as tools for mobilising people around key events that juxtapose marginalised people with powerful world leaders, especially those in the G8 Summit and international organisations such as the World Trade Organization (WTO) via targeted actions including email campaigns. Rulers use new technologies to control activists by surveillance and curtailing information flows (Babacan and Gopalkrishnan, 2001).

The politics of community work

The politics of community work revolve around ideas of inclusion and exclusion, privilege and disadvantage. The lack of attention to social divisions other than class in the traditional community work literature has neglected forms of oppression other than classism, and discounted initiatives undertaken by women and black people. Classic texts like *Reveille for Radicals* (Alinsky, 1969), *Community Work* (Twelvetrees, 1982, 1st edn) and *The Making of Community Work* (Thomas, 1983) virtually ignore the implications of gender and 'race'. Others such as *Political Issues in Community Work* (Curno, 1978) and *Community Against Government* (Loney, 1983) present more radical views but are both genderblind and colourblind. Some texts have sought to include identity issues but continue to marginalise these in 'added on' chapters or comments, as occurs in *Community Work and the State* (Craig et al, 1982; Craig, 1989), *Community Work in the 1990s* (Jacobs and Popple, 1994), *Analyzing Community Work* (Popple, 1995) or *Community Empowerment* (Craig and Mayo, 1995). Recent texts like *The Community and the Social Worker* (Fellin, 2001), *The Well-Connected Community* (Gilchrist, 2004), *The Handbook of Community Action* (Weil, 2004) and *Community Work* (Smith, 2005) make modest references to women and black people without a substantial focus on their roles as community workers or activists.

Books that have highlighted women's contributions to community work have generally been written by women. These include Marjorie Mayo's (1977) *Women in the Community* and *Women in Collective Action* (Curno et al, 1982). Although a few white women have attempted to include issues of 'race' and racism in their writing, as Margaret Ledwith (1997) has done, these issues remain under-explored. Similar points can be made about coverage of other social divisions such as disability, mental incapacity, age and sexual orientation. At the same time, key texts that address issues of 'race' and racism ignore gender and other social divisions, for example, *Community Work and Racism* (Ohri and Manning, 1982), and, more recently, Arshad's (1995) *Anti-Racist Community Work*. The capacity of the politics of practice in community work to detract from the promotion of gender equality appears intractable without concerted and targeted action that endeavours to establish egalitarian social relations.

Current literature on community work, community care, community organisation, community development and some community action models follow Alinsky (1971) to reveal the continued acceptability of depicting 'community' as a 'passive' unitary entity awaiting intervention from an expert 'outsider' before a programme of action is set in motion (see SEU, 1999, 2000). Portrayed as a 'neutral' apolitical individual, the 'community worker' is interested only in implementing the 'will of the people' or 'meeting their needs' (Calouste Gulbenkian Foundation, 1968, 1973; Kramer and Specht, 1969; Henderson et al, 1980, Twelvetrees, 1982/2002; Fellin, 2001; Henderson and Thomas, 2002).

Passive portrayals of communities obscure important political realities, mask diversity, hide the deeply political nature of community mobilisation, and endorse the status quo. Hidden in its recesses is another political fact − communities are not simply passive. People react to changes in their environment, adapt to forces that impact on their lives and alter these while being changed by them. Neutral views of the community ignore the direction that community activists adopt in responding to political and economic pressures beyond the control of the locality. By superficially examining society's unequal distribution of power and resources and neglecting its gendered and racially structured framework, neutral approaches to community work suggest that increasing 'participation' in decision-making bodies can put matters right (Fraser, 2005). But these do not address structural inequalities, scarcity or the inequitable distribution of resources that lie at the heart of many social problems, especially for working-class residents, white women and black people. Solutions that support existing social relations shift resources from those inadequately resourced to those unable to organise or advance their interests. Those who have assets can mobilise to retain relatively privileged positions and the opportunities accompanying them.

The picture portrayed in the dominant literature presupposes community work as pressure group politics within a basically sound system that has only a few 'wrinkles' to be ironed out. The proposition is difficult to uphold as it underpins a psychological view of individuals as inadequate or pathological while some wrinkles are indelibly embedded in the human condition. Absolving the state of inaction, this idea affirms Biddle and Biddle's (1965) claim that 'the poor and the alienated must overcome their inner handicap practically through the cultivation of their own initiatives'.

Conclusion

The class, 'race', gender and other biases of society remain hidden within traditional community work alongside the unequal distribution of power, resources and structural inequalities that give rise to poverty and other forms of oppression. The amassing of riches and power at one end of the social spectrum continues unabated while misery and poverty have become the lot of the majority at the other. Since the 1960s, poverty has increased within countries and between them, leaving 2.3 billion people surviving on less than $2 per day (Wichterich, 2000). Even before the dotcom revolution, 387 individuals, mainly men, owned 45% of the world's wealth (UNDP, 1996), a situation that remains roughly unchanged (Hocking, 2003). Of the early models described above, only the community action model examines critically the nature of capitalist social relations that bolster poverty or other structural inequalities in contemporary communities in both industrialised and industrialising countries[2].

The concern to address structural inequalities features strongly in the community action oriented focus of this book. This is not to suggest an unproblematic response to community issues. For the failure of many community endeavours to reverse poverty affirms Marris and Rein's (1974) contention that, 'far from challenging established power, community action turned out to be merely another instrument of social services, essentially patronising and conservative'. Responding to this challenge is integral to the emancipatory, environmental and global social activism models of community action (Hocking, 2003). The future will tell whether new developments in reaching out to broader communities through activities like those embodied in the Make Poverty History campaign of 2005, will achieve what other forms of social activism and demands for social justice have not.

Note

[1] In discussing the dynamics of racism, I use the terms 'black' and 'white' to indicate the socially constructed racialisation of people into those who are disadvantaged by racist dynamics (black people regardless of their ethnic origins or skin colour who are subjected to racist actions) and those who are privileged by it (white people regardless of their ethnic origins or skin colour). I do not see these categories or the diverse variety of identities encompassed by them as biologically determined nor do I suggest that they are without internal differentiation on the basis of many social divisions including gender, class, age, disability, 'race' and ethnicity.

2 Descriptions of countries as Third World, Two-Thirds World, developing countries and the South are problematic. They presuppose a dichotomous view of the world in which one is superior or more desirable as a site for human achievement, namely the First World, the One-Third World, developed countries, the North (or even the West). This is a questionable claim ignoring as it does differentiation and disadvantage within each category, and it underrates significant contributions to human heritage made by countries excluded by this terminology. I prefer the phrases 'industrialising' and 'industrialised' countries because these focus on levels of industrialisation as the key distinguishing feature between them.

TWO

Gendered communities

Introduction

Gender is a crucial element of socially constructed identities that rests on a binary dyad that constitutes and is constituted by men and women. Gender relations are enacted within communities to configure the categories of men and women in a binary dyad of superiority and inferiority that favours men and propagates a deficit model of women who are presented as lacking the positive attributes ascribed to men. This arrangement between men and women is taken as natural and immutable. Defining difference as inferior and acting on this presumption creates oppressive relations.

Some communities are defined as men-only or women-only spaces. Gendered relations in the UK assume a white, middle-class heterosexuality that privileges white men who subscribe to a hegemonic masculinity and accompanying subjugated femininity (Hearn, 1987; Pringle, 1995). Based on gender differentiation, it views divergence from a white male norm as deficient, pathological or inferior and includes men who are different, for example, black, gay or disabled men. Configured as having subjugated masculinities, these men rank above women in their own grouping (Whitehead, 2002). Both 'subjugated' men and women resist their depiction in these terms through actions aimed at assuming control and realising agency. Gendered relations in Western societies are contested, contradictory and, at times, divisive because at their heart lies an inegalitarian way of organising social relationships.

Traditional approaches to gender presume that men and women are different and unequal. Men are ascribed the dominant role, usually associated with being providers and revolving around men's capacity to earn a living wage for their family and to secure its material needs. A woman is gendered around having domestic responsibilities linked into her roles as wife, mother and carer, undertaking the bulk of caring work and housework within the household (Belotti, 1975; Walby, 1990, 1997). Women's bodies are gendered around their capacities to satisfy men's sexual appetites, to give birth, to raise children and to care for others. Gendered relationships assume women's passivity and victimhood within the low status private sphere in which the dominant ideology confines them. Walby (1990) calls this private patriarchy.

James (1992) argues that women's activities are 'outside the political world of citizenship and largely irrelevant to it'. However, women do not simply go along with this particular definition of the world. They can accept this world view, accommodate its various injunctions to behave in particular ways while changing it at the edges, or resist it by challenging its precepts and putting forward their own ideas to emphasise their agency and determination to control their own lives in a world free from violence and fear. In this chapter I consider how gendered relations articulate identity politics that are consistent with particular ideological approaches to gender and engage women in community action linked to these.

Within gendered social relations, women's bodies depict certain types of communities. These revolve around women providing traditional stability and continuity in social relations and culture through their caring roles. Women can resist these and affirm alternatives by undertaking social action that subverts the existing social order. Women's desire to assert agency in community settings forms a significant part of this chapter. Gendered communities act as barometers of women's place in society and underpin relationships between men and women that are accepted as 'normal' in a given culture. They also expose the position of men, highlight how gendered power relations situate men and women in opposition to each other and reveal that opportunities open to one grouping are systematically denied to the other.

Gendered social relations

Dominant images of traditional womanhood in Western and Eastern cultures draw on biological traits that are deemed fixed, immutable and linked to women's reproductive capacities (Eisenstein, 1979). Within this differentiation, gendered relations based on sexist views of the world (re)produce inequalities between men and women through a sexist dyad that privileges men. White Western feminists have called this rule by men 'patriarchy' (Foster, 1997), a system embedded in *sexism* or the oppression of women in a gendered society and firmly rooted in the family (Segal, 1983), claiming this was a universal condition (Morgan, 1970, 1984). Black feminists in the West have challenged the relevance of this analysis to them, seeing the family as a site of safety for black men and women living in white racist societies (Bryan et al, 1985; Collins, 1991).

Feminists now accept that women's experiences of gender oppression are differentiated by a range of social divisions such as ethnicity, class, disability and sexual orientation. Further differentiation occurs because gender interacts with and cuts across other social divisions such as 'race' and disability to produce complex differentiated experiences of gender that are unique to an individual while having elements shared by others with similar identity traits.

I (Dominelli, 2002a) define *sexism* as:

> ... a system of oppression based on the presumption of antagonistic relationships between men and women. In these, men exercise power over women and are privileged or deemed superior while women are cast as inferior. The system of organising social relations so that men can control and exploit women on the personal, institutional and cultural levels is called *patriarchy*. (p. 4)

Sexism is an ideology that devalues women's attributes and work while celebrating those associated with men and promoting *inequality* between genders. Sexist social relations have the following features. They:

- focus on 'differences' between men and women within a deficit framework;
- establish men as the norm;
- define what is accepted as 'normal' behaviour for men and women;
- legitimate and validate men's *power over* women;
- 'other' those who are different from white male norms; and
- have personal, institutional and cultural elements. These are the:
  - attitudes and beliefs which underpin personal sexism;
  - legislation, policies and routine practices that produce institutional sexism; and
  - taken-for-granted assumptions, values and norms that form cultural sexism.

Equality is a key value for eliminating gendered oppressions that bar women from accessing opportunities which will improve their situation and control oppressive processes, but making it permeate all aspects of social relations is difficult.

Oppression is the systematic denial of the individual and collective rights of people through relations of domination or inequality. These divide people into *binary dyads* in which one part is superior, the other inferior. They are locally and specifically configured through everyday interactions (Giddens, 1990). In gender dyads, men are deemed superior, women inferior. Maintaining these dyads relies on the use of *power over* others and *othering* their attributes. This ensures that those 'othered' are seen as deviant from the hegemonic norm and have 'deficits' in their make-up that have to be made good, an often impossible demand that is usually outside the capacity of an individual to change, for example, skin colour (although Michael Jackson has demonstrated that it can happen). Sex change operations and transvestism indicate that gender and sexuality can be altered with determination and the finances to access available opportunities.

I (Dominelli, 2002a, 2002b, 2002c, 2004a) define 'othering' as:

> ... an active process of interaction that relies on the (re)creation of dyadic social relations where one group is socially dominant and the others subordinate. In gendered othering, women's physical, social and cultural attributes are treated as signifiers of inferiority in social relations where social encounters perpetuate the domination of one group by another. During this interaction, the dominant group is constructed as 'subject', the oppressed group as 'object'. (Dominelli, 2002c, p 5)

Inegalitarian social relations rely on subject-to-object interactions in which the subject succeeds in either imposing his/her views of the world on the object or setting this world view as a natural state of affairs that need not and cannot be challenged. This dynamic is central in (re)producing oppressive relationships and forms a 'technology of the self' that Foucault (1980) considers essential in the internalisation of dominant norms and securing oppressed people's consent to their oppression (Dominelli, 2002a). In egalitarian relationships, interactions are based on both parties recognising their respective subject status. Having people act as subjects, that is, creators of their own realities, is central to anti-oppressive relationships.

Othering processes are important in configuring social relations that define roles, status and positions within particular communities. They are integral to the processes of social inclusion and exclusion in that they normalise particular values and patterns of behaviour and legitimate the allocation of social resources in a manner that is conducive to excluding 'others'. Othering processes:

- establish relationships of inequality;
- involve relations of domination, that is, the exercise of *power over* others;
- create 'them–us' interpersonal relationships;
- draw on processes of exclusion to deny access to social power and resources, and prevent people from participating in public spaces as active citizens;
- treat 'othered' individuals as less than human, that is, deprived of human dignity;
- legitimate acts of physical, sexual or emotional violence against the person(s) who is(are) othered;
- can encompass more than one social division. Gender, 'race', age, disability and sexual orientation can be 'othered' in any combination and are interactive; and
- are replicated through social interactions by being accepted or accommodated, but they can also be resisted.

Gendered relations of oppression are reproduced through social interactions in which men and women accept differences between them as signifying a hierarchy of value that privileges men. Women who accept men's superiority consider themselves subordinate and see little possibility of challenging their lower position or status and do not question the status quo. Men who endorse this world view may use violence to enforce women's subordination and perpetuate inegalitarianism in relating to women.

Men have various strategies that they use to impose their dominance. These are identified in Figure 2.1 below and indicate that there are several mechanisms that they employ. These range from psychological strategies that disempower women through acts of isolation and intimidation that draw on emotional, physical and sexual assaults to formal exclusion from friendships, social resources and institutions. A woman can situate herself, her partner and her children or close others at different points in the figure according to those elements that apply in her particular circumstances.

The patriarchal social relations that give rise to sexism and 'othering' draw upon power relations that are rooted in zero-sum notions of power in which one party to an interaction has power while the other does not (Parsons, 1957). It rests on the formation of 'power over' relations that favour one party at the expense of the other to create winners who grab all the power and losers who have none. 'Power over' relations form part of a world view that divides the world into unequal binary dyads that privilege one element over another. These

Figure 2.1: Gendered relations of oppression

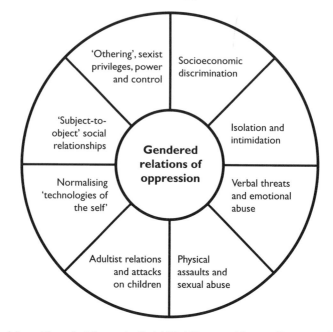

Source: Adapted from *Anti-Oppressive Social Work Theory and Practice* (Dominelli, 2002a)

underpin relations of domination and privilege members who belong to the hegemonic or normalising group.

Zero-sum views of power have been challenged by feminists such as Marilyn French (1985) who, like Foucault (1980), claim that power is multidimensional and formed through interpersonal interactions, that is, it is relational. French (1985) argues that there are other power relations, including the '*power to*' do something and '*power of*' particular groups to undertake collective action to pursue their own interests. Women can transform their positions by coming together to give force to the power of women in promoting the power to change their world in accordance with their own wishes. In Dominelli (1986a) I suggest that women can organise to expose the power of the powerless and powerlessness of the powerful. Power is both productive and coercive.

Gender relations impact on community work through:

• an ideology of caring as 'women's work';
• the composition of the workforce; and
• the unequal access to political structures and economic resources.

An ideology of caring as 'women's work' configures this activity as socially devalued while leaving those performing it in the background. Associated with tasks linked to the routines of everyday life, women undertake caring without pay in the privacy of their own homes. Caring work is considered second-rate work even when performed for a wage and is dogged by low pay. Community workers tend to see 'sociability work' (Daniels, 1985) or caring and routines of daily life as 'soft' issues that are the prerogative of women and preoccupy their energies in community action. Women community workers are involved in activities that promote personal and community well-being, for example, creating mothers and toddlers groups, forming play schemes for young children, cleaning up neighbourhoods and worrying about quality of life issues.

Men are deemed natural 'leaders' who manage projects (Grimwood and Popplestone, 1993; Hamd and Wright, 2001) and who are busy with the important 'hard' issues that constitute part of the public domain, for example, developing job opportunities in a community (Cowley et al, 1977). They often take women's contributions in daily community life for granted. While women are busy cultivating connections among community residents, promoting trust within networks of support, the men are doing the *real* business of the community. Women's networks are forms of 'social capital' (Putnam, 1993, 2000). Lowndes (2000) suggests that men appropriate the social capital women create in the community to advance their own positions in the public arena. Men's approaches to community matters have been quite different to those evident in initiatives identified as 'women only', such as the Greenham Common Women's Peace Movement (Cook and Kirk, 1983; Dominelli, 1986c). Men organise social action in ways that follow a 'strong strategic instrumentalist agenda' (Kenny, 2002, p 293), that requires people to take sides, to undertake specified acts, to obey instructions (Cook and Kirk, 1983) and to activate a top-down, hierarchical view of power in which those of higher status hold 'power over' others below them (Hamd and Wright, 2001).

Feminist community workers sought to eliminate sexist social relations in community work by identifying gender as a crucial feature in interactions between community members and professionals offering services to women. The alternative resources they created aimed to include women, to meet their specific needs as women and to be run by women. These endeavours were to ensure that authoritarian professional relationships were not reproduced in these facilities.

I define feminist community work as:

... a theory and practice of community intervention that takes women's experience of gendered oppression in community settings to challenge the lack of community provisions for women; poor quality of services women receive; unequal relationships between professionals and women; and unequal treatment of women workers. Feminist community work is collective action that aims to transform social relations in more egalitarian directions and alter both women's and men's behaviours alongside changing institutional policies and social norms. (Dominelli, 2002c, p. 5)

In responding to women's needs, feminist community work and social action has: enhanced understandings of women's position in society; improved services for women; re-theorised women's, men's and children's subjective experiences; and reoriented professional interventions towards women and children, notably in domestic violence and child sexual abuse situations. Feminist community work has: challenged the privileging of expert voices over those of women service users; redefined the meaning of professional practice in the public services; rooted change in women's experiences; and created new services for women, children and men.

Feminist challenges to traditional community work

Traditional community work had a number of objectives. Historically, these ranged from controlling insurgent populations to promoting social change. Community work in Northern Ireland was an example of the former (Griffiths, 1974a). The 'speak bitterness' meetings of the 1950s in which Chinese women challenged men's assaults on them in the home (Hinton, 1966) and mass campaigns that created the barefoot doctor system in China to deliver health services during the Cultural Revolution, epitomise the latter. Today's health campaigns and environmental activism indicate the significance of continued demands for transformational social change (Escobar, 1998).

Between these two extremes, community work in the UK, particularly its state-supported versions since the 1980s, has focused on improving the quality of daily life; fostering the formation of local caring networks; encouraging communities to take responsibility for their development; providing paid and unpaid work for groups and individuals; and encouraging community-oriented public–private partnerships (SEU, 2000). Women have been central to these initiatives, especially those relying on voluntary self-help initiatives that utilise their traditional skills to support hard-pressed individuals, supplementing resources provided by the state and replacing those eliminated by reduced public expenditures. Meals-on-Wheels, Community Care and Good Neighbour Schemes have traditionally typified these approaches.

Traditional community work focuses on reforming the status quo because it accepts that the basic organisation of society and distribution of power and resources are sound. It was challenged by the Community Development Projects (CDPs) (Loney, 1983) in turning to community action to highlight systemic economic decline and social disadvantage in impoverished communities. A reforming rather than transformative view of society continues in contemporary approaches to community work, including recent urban regeneration schemes and the New Deal for Communities (NDC) promoted by New Labour (ODPM, 2004). The NDC focuses on Local Strategic Partnerships (LSPs) as the government's key community-based approach for delivering resources to 88 of the most deprived local authority areas in Britain and renewing them.

In its early days, community action sought to change economic realities in deprived communities without acknowledging the specific needs of women, their contribution to community endeavours, or the diversity among women and their experiences of community. Elizabeth Wilson (1977a) deplored the lack of recognition of women's involvement in community life even when undertaken under the auspices of radical community workers. They were oblivious to the specific forms of oppression endured by women (Wilson, 1977b), the multiplicity of those experiences and their extensive diversity (Naples, 1998; Dominelli, 2002a). Privileging professional 'experts' over community activists and downplaying women's skills reinforced hierarchy (Hamd and Wright, 2001) and an oppressive top-down welfarism (Shaw and Martin, 2000).

Feminist community work developed as a reaction to community workers' neglect of women, despite the prevalence of the women's liberation movement. Feminist insights into gendered relations contributed to the feminist critique of traditional community work (Naples, 1998), especially those trends that rendered women invisible (Mayo, 1977, 1982) and controlled populations (Dominelli, 1990).

Gendering key concepts in community work

Community work has a number of key concepts that are helpful in understanding community dynamics and roles played by different actors. These include social exclusion, social capital, capacity building, participation, empowerment and agency (CRU, 2004). Experiences of these are gendered (Lowndes, 2000; Williams, C., 2004). Below, I use feminist research and scholarship to consider these from a gendered perspective that highlights women's strengths and resiliency. Each has been used at different points in time by policy makers to promote unitary views of communities that ignore social divisions, including the role of women in them. For example, undifferentiated participation ideologies have been central in mobilising residents through the idea that community groups can decide what will happen in their communities without acknowledging the diverse or conflicting interests of their constituents and specific contributions women make to community life. If not attended to, these conflicts can erupt into violence, as occurred during the riots in Lozells, Birmingham, in October 2005 when gendered and racialised ethnic relations collided and led to murder and massive damage to community relations and community resources (Dunton, 2005). Here, rumour of a woman of African heritage being raped by a gang of men of Asian descent spread through their respective communities and exacerbated existing tensions about the unequal distribution of resources between them.

Social exclusion

Poverty, as the outcome of personal and social circumstances, is a central ingredient in processes that result in social exclusion, although there are social, political and psychological forms of exclusion too. Social exclusion consists of processes of marginalisation and deprivation, primarily involving poor people, a disproportionately high number of whom are women. Community workers in deprived communities confront social exclusion daily in its many forms – individuals who feel demoralised and alienated from mainstream society, poverty, lack of social resources and poor physical environments. These are all signs of social exclusion or people's inability to participate actively as citizens in decision-making processes and representational forums and exploit the economic resources of a society. Community activists mobilise those living in exclusionary spaces, often with difficulty, to assert their rights and entitlements to the same assets as those who are socially included (Shaw and Martin, 2000; Goodman, 2004). Thus, social inclusion sits alongside social exclusion.

Despite the suggestion that social exclusion is a *structural* problem rooted in a particular type of social organisation, namely, the exploitation of social and physical resources for the profit of the few, key definitions of social exclusion focus on its personal dimensions. Duffy (1995, p 1) considers social exclusion as:

> ... the inability to participate effectively in economic, social, political and cultural life, and in some characterisations, alienation and distance from mainstream society.

De Haan and Maxwell (1998, p 2) give it a more narrow focus by suggesting that social exclusion is the 'failure or inability to participate in social and political activities'. These definitions ignore women's experiences of social exclusion while simultaneously emphasising its personal elements. The personal dimension of social exclusion is important, but highlighting the *personal* nature of social exclusion underplays the significance of structural inequalities and power relations that produce exclusionary outcomes. This is especially important for women because they are also *structurally excluded* from public positions by the current configuration of social relations. Personal inadequacy is a useful mechanism in blaming women for their plight and ignores structural deficiencies that also matter.

The concepts of social inclusion and exclusion became central aspects of European social policy, initially in France. It spread throughout Europe in response to the creation of a *single market* and a concern to improve *social cohesion* and productivity within European economies. The social objective of enhancing social cohesion was tied to economic exigencies, namely those of facilitating the capacity of goods, including units of labour, to move about the continent without hindrance. Linkage to the waged labour market and treatment of people as labour units to be deployed in the production cycle where and when needed, disadvantages women who are not equal participants in the waged labour market (ONS, 2004) and ignores domestic work.

This tendency has become more skewed by welfare benefits being tied to people's willingness to undertake paid work, the assumption being that only waged employment gets people out of poverty (David, 1999), devaluing unpaid work in the process. Thus, women's contribution to domestic labour and community activities become discounted as irrelevant to the grander project of participating in waged work, even if poorly paid. Discourses that divide society into two groups – those who are socially included and those who are not – axiomatic in policy debates, further embeds women's exclusion in low-waged labour because many of the jobs available in New Labour's booming economy are casual low-paid ones (Popple and Redmond, 2000).

Discourses about social exclusion draw on different theories of social solidarity, poverty and structural and/or individual inadequacies. Even when ignoring specific impacts on women, these discourses are gendered (Lowndes, 2000; Hocking, 2003). In the UK, social policy theorists worried that these two concepts would shift concern away from poverty (exclusion) and poor people's integration into society (inclusion) (David, 1999). Inclusion/exclusion and poverty/social divisions became contested concepts as marginalised groups rejected being integrated into mainstream society on the grounds that the forms advocated did not meet their needs, for example,, workfare-type programmes that locked women into poorly paid jobs (Popple and Redmond, 2000).

Social capital

Social capital has become a trendy word that describes the social resources that individuals bring to a community and which can be extended by collaborative relationships and interactions with others when lubricated by trust and reciprocity. The concept of social capital initially appeared in Lydia Judson Hanifan's (1916, 1920) writings. It was later picked up by Bourdieu (1986) and Coleman (1990). But it did not become popular coinage in public policy and community development discourses until Robert Putnam published his study on Italy in 1993 and used the term to refer to the decline in civic responsibilities in the US (1993, 2000). Putnam's concept fuses market discourses with those of social inclusion (Kenny, 2002). His analysis has been subjected to a number of critiques, not least from those who felt it ignored the significance of 'race' and ethnicity (Dhesi, 2000; Goulbourne and Solomos, 2003), gender (Lowndes, 2000; Ginn and Arber, 2002) and the development of new forms of social collaboration (Ladd, 1999). Catherine Campbell (2000, p 196) argues that 'our understanding of the role played by social capital in perpetuating unequal power relations is still in its infancy', but there is merit in looking at the points encapsulated by the term before considering its gendering, given the barriers that structural inequalities impose on the development of social capital (Dhesi, 2000).

Putnam (1993, 2000) suggests that social capital is embedded in trust, shared values, virtues, expectations, investing in social networks, reciprocal relationships and active connections with others (Gilchrist, 2000, 2004). Developing reciprocal relationships enriches the social capital of those involved (Putnam, 1993, 2000). Putnam subdivides it into two forms: 'bonding capital' and 'bridging capital'. Bonding capital is a property of tightly knit networks of support among fairly homogeneous groups, 'exclusive' in maintaining a particular group and inward-looking. Bridging capital is outward-looking and facilitates connections with others who are different. Woolcock (1998) adds 'linking' capital or capacity to develop relationships of trust and networks of reciprocity among community members to Putnam's classification. Women's caring and working through social networks are critical components of linking capital that increase a community's store of social capital, an aspect that Putnam neglects.

Putnam (2000) sees social capital declining in the US and blames American individualism for promoting solitary pursuits over social ones. But, as Ladd (1999) points out, people are participating in other forms of organisations, especially informal ones that rely on women. Putnam ignores the neoliberal context within which this decline appears. Under globalised neoliberalism, people have become individualised as fragmented consumers going to market to purchase the goods they need rather than developing these collectively. Rather than being pooled or socialised, risks have been personalised, thus exacerbating an individual's isolation (Dominelli, 2004b).

The personalisation of social capital has significant repercussions for women who not only have less access to formal social resources than men, but also have their stock of social capital appropriated by men, including at the individual level where they reap the benefits of 'gendered social capital' (Fine, 2001, p 123). Despite these structural inequalities, Sevenhuijsen (1998, p 148) argues that women's community networks are built on 'trusting connections' with others and caring for them. So, it is easier to engage women in transformative local politics and practice. Much of this interaction relies on informal networks. In this sense, women's skills and relationships form the social capital that lies at the centre of civic engagement, or creates the substance of community work. Stack's (1975) study reveals that black women living in extremely deprived circumstances use networking and caring skills to survive poverty and to carve out better lives for their children. This involves 'sociability work' in forming and sharing social capital in a community. Goulbourne and Solomos (2003) argue that ethnicity is a form of social capital, and so gender may be similarly considered. This does not mean that every woman has the same access to social capital or its reproduction. Structural inequalities along 'race', ethnicity, age, disability and other dimensions suggest differentiated experiences of and access to it (McLean, 2002; Hocking, 2003).

Lowndes (2000) argues that women and men have equal amounts of social capital as associational activities, but have different profiles. The social capital held by each gender is differently composed. Women's social capital is rooted more firmly in the private sphere while men's is located in the formal public arena, particularly in the organisations of representational politics within local authorities and the central state. Lowndes (2000) cites women's relative exclusion from political structures as indicative of this. Women know and trust their neighbours to a greater degree than men, have more contact with friends and relatives and access informal networks of support that are embedded in neighbourhood sociability more often. This insight carries implications for professional community workers working with women. They have strengths and resources that are useful in their mobilisation.

However, a stark division between the private and public domains can be misleading. For one thing, the boundaries between these two locations are becoming increasingly blurred, especially as more and more remunerated work is being conducted within the home and women participate more fully in waged work while retaining domestic responsibilities. A 'community', insofar as it exists, is configured by and configures both arenas. Women use community to mediate 'private' activities linked to the quality of life enjoyed (or not) by their families because this is impacted on by developments in the 'public' sphere through social policies, while treating the public domain as an object of community interventions. Community campaigns touch on all three spheres – the public, community and private. By embarking on community campaigns, women exchange and extend bonding capital and engage in the processes of creating bridging capital. Through these intercessions, women use strong bonding capital to create bridging capital and enact agency in forming 'a place of their own'. In my view, such action constitutes public associational activity.

Caution is required in applying the concept of social capital to women, especially black women, because they have been pathologised for relying on family-based community networks of social capital (Innerarity, 2003). Based on ethnicity, these are strengths (Goulbourne and Solomos, 2003) useful in resisting racism and ensuring survival. Strong social capital promotes local identity that fosters mutual support and trust among people, residents' belief in the local state's capacity to meet their needs and substantial involvement in informal and formal networks (McLean, 2002). McLean contextualises the formation and use of social capital as multidimensional and sited in several spheres. For McLean (2002), black women are strong in bonding capital, but weak in bridging capital. This view does not adequately represent their activities in the community because even those with strong bonding capital use it as linking capital to reach out to other women not necessarily in their particular ethnic or social group. For example, women connect with diverse members of a geographical community in developing action groups to improve the state of their neighbourhoods (Gittell et al, 1999). And so men's and women's different profiles of social capital can be reformulated to highlight *strengths* that women have in creating and extending the 'stock' of social capital in their society.

Capacity building

Capacity building refers to strengthening people's ability to improve their quality of life (Dominelli, 2004b). Capacity building involves a process of interaction that aims to develop people and their communities. This includes acquiring skills, forming community organisations and systems that enhance participation, engaging with more powerful others to create new resources or projects and to self-manage them (Skinner, 1997; LRN, 1999). It adds to a community's cache of social capital (Henderson and Salmon, 2001) at the personal, institutional and community levels. Skinner (1997), Henderson and Salmon (2001) barely focus on the gendered aspect of the concept. Development discourses conducted within the context of industrialising countries mention women as passive recipients of capacity building initiatives, often defined as education for women and girls to sustain a country's future reconstruction (Mizra, 1997). Women's role as active agents in community growth is downplayed. Skills they possess could be harnessed for developmental purposes but are cast aside to reveal the deficit model of gender relations within developmental configurations of social capital. The social development literature identifies women as 'saviours' of communities because they care about people. Many capacity building endeavours are aimed at women securing the future of a community – a concern traditionally linked to reproduction issues that primarily involve women. Centring women in building communities became an objective of the Beijing Declaration and Platform for Action (WEDO, 2005).

Participation

Participation is the act of engaging people in making decisions about matters that affect them or enabling people to take control of their situations. Participation can assume a number of forms and operate at different levels (Fraser, 2005). It is a major component of consultation processes that state officials use to discuss proposals with community members. *Consultative participation* is a top-down approach that can leave participants feeling excluded (Fraser, 2005). Phillips (2004, p 172) argues that regeneration boards favour 'upward' accountability procedures to 'downward' ones, and that this skews power-sharing endeavours between official representatives and community members, adults and children (Fraser, 2005). *Democratic participation* is a key ingredient in empowerment processes aimed at informing people of their options and helping them take responsibility for their behaviour (Goodman, 2004). Lister (1997) sees these processes as essential to becoming 'active citizens'.

Participation is gendered, with women more likely to engage in informal decision-making processes than formal ones, especially those that disparage experiential knowledge (Barnes, 1999) and enact bureaucratic requirements. Women face barriers to formal participation, for example, stressful domestic circumstances, financial limitations, lack of time (Reitsma-Street, in Reitsma-Street and Neysmith, 1999). Diversity within different groups of women has to be approached differently (Mizra, 1997) to engage them in formal initiatives. It cannot be assumed that all members in a group will participate on a uniform basis (Hobson and Beresford, 2001; Woodward, 2003). *Contingent participation*, where the limits to involvement are spelt out, will suit their positions better.

Empowerment

Empowerment is a subjectively experienced process of developing people's capacities to control their lives. Wallerstein and Bernstein (1994, p 198) define empowerment as:

> ... a social-action process that promotes participation of people, organisations and communities towards the goal of individual and community control, political efficacy, improved quality of community life and social justice.

Empowering practitioners treat users with respect and dignity, foster self-confidence, allow them to exercise *power over* their own affairs and understand complex social realities. Empowerment as the process of enabling people to act as subjects controlling their lives through relationships with others involve sharing power and working towards establishing egalitarian relations (Humphries, 1996). Thus, empowerment is interactive and negotiated. It is not a 'good' to be given (Oliver, 1990). Empowerment operates at both the individual and group level. Empowerment processes have to address 'race', gender and other social divisions in responding to the specificity of unique individuals while developing their full potential in organising collectively to eradicate oppression (Solomon, 1976). Empowering people in communities is integral to the processes of mobilisation.

Stuart Rees (1991) expects empowerment to reduce structural inequalities. He suggests that oppressed peoples redefine the problems they tackle to resist being pathologised and disempowered by professionals. Empowerment involves real shifts in power relations. It is not the act of clients signing a contract that assigns them tasks as occurs regularly in task-centred or contractual approaches to an intervention. By engaging in power shifts, people accessing services can (re)define their own needs, identify how professionals can help them and determine how their vision might be achieved. Agreements between them and practitioners have to address divergent priorities, different ideologies and specify what employing agencies deem affordable.

Empowerment has become another contested term. Oliver (1990) has argued that professionals cannot empower clients, but should focus instead on how not to disempower them. Initially referring to the process of enabling people to take control of their lives, particularly within community settings, it has been appropriated by politicians, commercial entrepreneurs and bureaucrats. Community work managers practising the 'new managerialism' have bureaucratised empowerment. Bureaucratic empowerment discourses are articulated through legislative and procedural means that commodify service users by turning them into agents of consumption (Dominelli, 2000, 2004b) and deprofessionalising working relations through procedural controls and performance indicators (Dominelli, 1996; Dominelli and Hoogvelt, 1996a).

Quality assurance is maintained through industry standards such as BS5759 or IS9001 and total quality management (TQM) systems that service providers have adopted as signifying quality that is ensured through bureaucratic means (Dominelli and Hoogvelt, 1996b). Commodified relations of empowerment create consumers who express power by exercising choices in the marketplace through what they buy. Resource restraints and lack of purchasing power severely restrict the options actualised by poor consumers, a majority of whom are women. Thus, market-based provisions can exacerbate women's exclusion from social resources.

Outside the marketplace, legal criteria of entitlement dictate the options open to service users as citizens and formal complaints procedures operationalise their rights to specific provisions if those they receive are not to their liking. Arrangements for processing complaints offer clients the possibility of refusing services that do not meet 'industry' standards. They are informed of their right to object through bureaucratic forms of empowerment like the Citizen's Charters. Complaints are made only after the fact and are defensive rather than proactive. These are unable to address resource constraints and formal litigation is too expensive for clients on limited incomes. Nor do they legitimate users' wishes to plan and create specific services. Bureaucratic empowerment cannot address the needs of people who want services that improve their quality of life, rather than choosing one product over another (Dominelli, 2000). Bureaucratic approaches cannot deal with structural inequalities, unequal organisational resources, legislative restrictions, resource constraints and power imbalances. These pose formidable obstacles to the processes of developing the capacities necessary to empower oneself and control one's life. Thus, empowerment can be experienced as tokenistic and disempowering (Dominelli, 2000, 2004b). Community workers should not treat empowerment as a trendy buzzword, but should explore the actual model being utilised in any intervention from the range available – tokenistic, bureaucratic, commodified or power sharing.

Agency

Agency is the capacity to take action as a subject, determining the direction of life and making decisions about it. Its enactment involves an interactive process whereby an individual is configured as the subject of an action rather than an object at the receiving end of another's behaviour, and is linked to empowerment that promotes egalitarian power relations. In egalitarian relations, all participants are subjects who interact with other subjects. In relations of domination, the privileged person is the subject while the other is constructed as an object or subjugated person. Agency also involves the processes of creating social structures that shape possibilities within which human behaviour occurs. Berger and Luckmann (1967) argue that people use agency to give their world meaning and, when institutionalised, it becomes part of a structure or meaning system that explains their world and shapes their engagement with it. It also affects their view of the possible – what they can or cannot do.

Agency is also gendered. Women are assumed to lack agency. Configuring women as passive victims of social forces denies them agency, discounts their capacity to become leaders defining the parameters within which action occurs and affirms their dependent status as victims. This makes it easier for men to assume leadership roles without having to justify doing so. Indeed, questioning men's right to be leaders rather than taking it for granted would be seen as unnatural.

Conclusion

Feminist community workers launched initiatives that have demanded that agendas for action include gender issues and have called for more fundamental forms of change than those involved in a simple redistribution of social power and resources among undifferentiated groups of people (Wilson and Weir, 1986). These steps, they thought, would provide new opportunities for women and enable them to create different paradigms of social action and to work within them. They demanded that the objectives, aims and techniques endorsed by community workers reflected egalitarian principles throughout their work rather than adding these on at the end of the process (Wandor, 1972), and acknowledged its relational dimensions (Gilligan, 1982).

Feminist community work differs from community work undertaken by women. The latter accepts the status quo and does not focus on women's specific needs as women or desire to transform their social position. Community initiatives undertaken by the Women's Institute illustrate community work undertaken by women. These contribute to community well-being but lack a feminist perspective and commitment to transformative change at individual and collective levels. They do not demand structural changes in society to ensure equality between women and men and are not embedded within a new vision of society, but simply rearrange players on a chessboard. Feminist community action has a critique that shows that community work can disguise the state's failure to address the needs of declining communities and tackle social problems that inhibit a community's capacity to become self-sustaining. And, feminist activists argue for processes that promote:

THREE

The state, social policy and communities

Introduction

The state has a vested interest in communities, often describing them in nostalgic terms as safe and harmonious havens. These definitions portray communities as unitary and essentialised. The state uses social policy to structure specific communities and to influence the expectations of those living within them. State policies have shaped with remarkable continuity the local, national and international positionality of communities, groupings formed as collective entities in the public sphere and the space that individuals inhabit within the private arena of the family.

In the current globalising world, the British state has adopted a neoliberal ideology and plays a key role in both fragmenting communities and encouraging social cohesion at the individual level to bring these together. Under neoliberalism, social solidarity is replaced by personal responsibility and market imperatives that advance profits at the expense of social inclusion. Social protections and supports that individuals might anticipate in relation to 'risks' that they are expected to overcome, especially those regarding social security, safety, environmental safeguards and peace, are often lacking. Their absence impinges on people's capacity to act as fully engaged citizens. Women, especially poor women, are badly affected by the withdrawal of social resources under the personal responsibility approach to the human condition (Zucchino, 1997). In this sense, the early part of the 21st century reflects continuities in social policies begun during the 1980s as a strong market-based individualist ethos has replaced the social democratic consensus of the 1970s.

In this chapter I consider the shifting role of the state in defining and redefining communities through social policies and expose continuities and discontinuities within it. Since the 1970s, different community work models[1] have gained government support. These vary as different policies have been enacted in response to specific socioeconomic formations and the social problems engendered. But there are remarkable continuities. Among these, I highlight the neglect of women's specific needs as women, and the belief that the community is a unitary entity in British state policies despite claims to the contrary.

Community work and the British state

Controlling communities by tackling deprivation

Economic crises in the late 1950s drew the postwar boom of the 'you have never had it so good' era to a close, and exposed social problems that shattered British complacency about unremitting economic progress through Keynesian economics. By the early 1960s, the 'rediscovery of poverty', a growing black activist movement resisting racial oppression, the 'breakdown of the family' and the rise of juvenile crime became major concerns for British policy makers. Conservative and Labour governments worried about the failure of the welfare state to meet the needs of both workers and capital. They commissioned numerous reports on these issues: *The Ingleby Report on Children and Young Persons* (Ingleby, 1960); *The Milner Holland Report on London Housing* (Milner and Holland, 1965); *The Plowden Report on Primary Education* (Plowden, 1967); and *The Seebohm Report on the Personal Social Services* (Seebohm, 1968). All pointed to the welfare state's failure to meet working-class needs.

These reports suggested that British people were generally doing well. The welfare state had eased many harsh realities of welfare inequality. But the reports revealed a country dotted with areas of 'special need' or 'pockets of deprivation' that required comprehensive policies to eradicate poverty ensconced within them. Their analyses claimed that areas of disadvantage existed because people did not know their rights or how to obtain services from the state. Social problems were blamed on poor people, who politicians assumed could not be bothered to work for their living or who had something wrong with them personally – a disability or lack of education that prevented them from being able to control their own lives. Pathologising individuals and communities for their poverty meant that social planners did not have to address structural inequalities, but could focus on tinkering with the outer margins of social organisation (CDP, 1977b).

Other reports, including the Home Office reports *Children, Family and Young Offenders* (1964) and *Children in Trouble* (1968) (referred to in Stewart and Tutt, 1987), also held the victims of poverty responsible for their plight, believing that the increase in divorce and single-parent families headed by women created the social problems enumerated above. Wage-earning mothers were perceived as precipitating juvenile delinquency by being away from home. The media deplored the high numbers of deprived 'latchkey' children this practice produced, and castigated working-class families for failing to raise law-abiding citizens. This concern persists, but has acquired a new twist in the 'absent father' ideology that continues to blame single mothers for alienating the men in their lives (Blankenhorn, 1995). Government sought to reduce welfare costs by reorganising the local state and introducing corporate management techniques to use material and human resources more effectively, a trend continued by 'new managerialism' (Clarke and Newman, 1997). These views underpin the philosophy of the New Deal promoted by New Labour to revive communities and people's roles in them (SEU, 1998, 1999).

The 20th-century state adopted a two-pronged strategy in tackling social problems: population control and community participation, an approach that has been retained in an updated form. Traditional population control methods drew on strengthening the 'law and order' apparatus – the police, magistrates' courts, prisons and the probation service (Buynan, 1977); restraining workforce activism by restricting trade union activity through legislation foreshadowed by *In Place of Strife* (Department of Employment and Productivity, 1969) but implemented under the 1971 Industrial Relations Act; regulating unemployed people (Castles and Kosack, 1972); and limiting black immigration beginning with the 1962 Commonwealth Immigration Act. The strategies of curtailing union activism and immigration flows have continued under Thatcherite and Blairite administrations as the postwar consensus on welfare evaporated and Conservative and New Labour policies converged around ideologies associated with neoliberalism (McGhee, 2005).

Key tenets in this neoliberal approach blame the state for failing to make people responsible for their behaviour, to stop criminal activities, to promote work as the way out of poverty, and to avoid a culture of 'welfare dependency' (Zucchino, 1997). By 2005, during the election that resulted in a third New Labour government, this convergence led the tabloid press to declare the Liberal Democrats, not noted for their socialist or leftwing leanings, the *left* party for advocating higher taxes and free personal care for older people. New Labour policies to counter social exclusion reaffirm deficit-oriented perceptions of poor people while emphasising personal responsibility and 'risk taking' in tackling the effects of structural inequalities (Fremeaux, 2005).

Despite extensive expenditures on them increasingly punitive 'law and order' measures, these proved inadequate under both Thatcher and Blair. The weakness of this element of the strategy led Bauman (2000) to recast the explosion in the prison population (now just under 80,000, a near doubling of the numbers incarcerated at the beginning of the 1990s) as the 'warehousing' of deviants in a bankrupt system that nonetheless provided profits for companies building and running the private prisons that secured state favour (Hencke, 2001). Nonetheless, the failure of this approach caused the state to formulate a 'softer' strategy aimed at gaining the consent of the governed and developing appropriate social structures. Community work became an indispensable tool of this approach. During the 1960s, it focused on promoting harmonious 'race relations' (Mullard, 1973) and urban regeneration. The bodies then formed to promote multiculturalism and community revival have undergone several changes, but persist today as the Commission for Racial Equality, community renewal schemes such as the New Deal for Communities (NDC) and partnerships that included private companies (Mizra, 1997). Today's Local Strategic Partnerships (LSPs) are expected to create an exclusion dividend that will overcome the lack of resources or exclusion deficit in deprived communities (Home Office, 2003). New Labour's policy of granting the corporate sector a greater role in community regeneration continues Thatcherite initiatives promoted under public–private partnerships (PPPs) and public–private finance (PPF) directives (Greer, 1994; Dominelli and Hoogvelt, 1996b; Fremeaux, 2005).

State attempts to satisfy the needs of both capital and labour were and are contradictory. Under capitalist social relations, the interests of one can only be promoted at the expense of the other. During the 1970s, the state's approach was compatible with social democratic ideologies that fired the imagination of the populace and legislators alike. This consensus fractured under Thatcherite neoliberalism while the thread that pathologises the casualties of economic exigencies for not exiting poverty through their own endeavours remains.

During the 1960s and 1970s, through the Rate Support Grant, the government targeted additional resources on deprived areas by introducing a 'needs' element for allocating funding to those with the greatest needs and fewest resources. Local authorities receiving this money distributed it locally. Their emphasis on areas of 'special need' furthered the employment of community workers charged with coordinating local authority work in specified areas. This strategy's popularity declined from the 1980s and by 2005 few municipalities employed community workers, and individuals rather than the state are responsible for meeting their own needs.

Community mechanisms were utilised to quell black community activism in decaying inner cities during the 1960s and 1970s. Racial tensions led the Home Office to launch the Urban Aid Programme (UAP) in 1968 in the aftermath of Enoch Powell's 'Rivers of Blood' speech in Birmingham. Bridges (1975) argues that the UAP was developed, not to attend to people's needs, but as a form of social control over black communities to ensure that these were policed more effectively. In theory, the UAP channelled money into needy areas. In practice, this did not happen as project rejection rates were high.

Powell's outburst as a government minister legitimated the view that harmonious race relations required restrictions in the numbers of black settlers in the UK. It subscribed to a 'social pathology' theory of poverty and continued the UAP strategy of action drawing on lessons from the American War on Poverty (CDP, 1977b) while sharing expenditures between the Home Office and relevant local authorities. Endorsing institutionalised racism, the UAP made individual racism respectable (CCCS, 1982). Decades later, the McPherson Report (1998) highlighted institutional racism as a contributory factor to racially motivated murder. Meanwhile, attacks on asylum seekers and refugees fan racist conceptualisations of difference (McGhee, 2005).

Following racist attacks in Notting Hill in 1958 community relations officers were appointed during the 1960s to address the racial dimensions of deprivation under a remit that incorporated black activists but pathologised black communities (Mullard, 1973). In 1981 riots took place in London, Bristol, Leicester, Liverpool, Leeds, Bradford and Tunbridge Wells. Further instances of social disorder followed. By 2001, racial tensions had erupted in smaller cities like Stoke, Bolton and Oldham. When white working-class Asian youths assaulted Walter Chamberlain, a 76-year-old white man in Oldham, the British National Party (BNP) used white supremacist ideologies to inflame the situation further. While men were at the forefront of these disturbances, women and children bore the brunt of the damage caused to their communities, but their roles in the events or cleaning up the mess remained invisible (see McGhee, 2005).

Black communities, along with their deprived white counterparts, continue to be pathologised and blamed for their plight while the structural causes of industrial decline are ignored. And the state cultivated the view that racism was the product of too many black people in the UK and introduced immigration controls to contain their numbers (Mullard, 1973; Sivanandan, 1976), an argument advanced today in restricting the numbers of asylum seekers and refugees entering the country (McGhee, 2005). Yet, primary immigration to the UK has been curtailed since the 1970s (Mullard, 1973). Black people have to deal with hardship produced by racist immigration legislation that denies admission to kin, divides families and excludes them from welfare state services through regulations that are racist in their impact, for example, the residency requirement for accessing council housing or child benefit (Bryan et al, 1985). Exacerbated since the 1980s, this approach is evident in current responses to asylum seekers and refugees as both Conservative and New Labour leaders have promised strong curbs on immigration. Immigration control initiatives include the dispersal of asylum seekers and refugees through the National Asylum Support Service (NASS), withdrawal of Income Support services to those awaiting decisions on their applications and threatened exclusion of unaccompanied children from the provisions of the 1989 Children Act (now the 2004 Children Act).

Local authorities assessed 'need' in deprived communities when bidding for government funding through indices of multiple deprivation, that encompassed:

- deficiencies in the environment, particularly housing;
- overcrowding;
- higher than average family size;
- persistent unemployment;
- a high proportion of children in trouble or in need of care; and
- high numbers of children requiring free school meals.

The number of indices has grown under New Labour while disadvantage and poverty persist even among target groups like children (SEU, 2004). These policies have had minimal impact on eliminating privation for women, black people or children.

Significant community initiatives

The Community Development Projects

Significant UAP initiatives included the Community Development Projects (CDPs) introduced in 1969 as community-based action-research projects through which the government hoped to engage voluntary agencies and community groups in tackling social problems. The Home Office authorised 12 CDPs, each having an action team to undertake community work and a university-based research team to monitor its activities. CDPs had the primary aim of alleviating poverty but lacked an analysis of its racialised or gendered impact and prevalence among lone mothers with children.

CDPs were locally based, but central control was retained by the Home Office sitting on management committees and approving funding for specific initiatives. The local authority where each CDP was located held day-to-day control of its programme of work and released social action funds for projects approved by a management committee that included its representatives. CDPs initially followed community organisation and development models of action. They assumed the overall system was basically sound and needed only piecemeal modifications to correct minor deficiencies. They emphasised a local community's role in meeting need through self-help endeavours and community participation. The government expected CDPs to:

> ... improve the efficiency of local government by co-ordinating service delivery and avoiding the unnecessary replication of services; affect local and central government policies through its research; and encourage local resident participation in policy formulation and service delivery through the establishment of self-help groups. (CDP, 1977c)

Promoted through the Seebohm (1968) and Skeffington (1969) Reports, the participation of citizens in community activities became trendy around this time and was linked to community work. Citizen participation became a tool used by a state following corporate management techniques to involve people in delivering services to residents in an efficient and cost-effective manner, to incorporate community energies in designing and delivering services and to spread its resources across wider groupings while retaining control of developments on the ground. This approach appears later in the NDC initiated at the end of the 20th century by Blair (ODPM, 2004).

CDPs soon exposed the contradictory assumptions underpinning UAP initiatives. Their activities revealed that a social pathology theory of poverty could not explain structurally induced poverty emanating from a declining industrial base as capital left a community for more favourable profit-making opportunities elsewhere, a trend intensified since then by globalisation (Wichterich, 2000). The work of CDPs demonstrated that structural change, not middle-level mismanagement, accounted for the failure of the welfare state to meet local needs (CDP, 1977a, b). This was not a message that the state wanted to hear, especially when coupled with the view that *poor people were necessary components in the cycle of capital accumulation.* This message continues to be advanced today by the global social activist movement (Edwards and Gaventa, 2001) in critiquing capitalist social relations promoted by neoliberal globalisation.

Sir Keith Joseph, Secretary of State for Health from 1972 to 1974, reaffirmed pathology-based explanations of poverty through his 'cycle of deprivation' theories. These countered the structural analyses of CDPs by focusing on generations of the same family being unable to exit the clutches of poverty. Joseph argued that this occurred because undesirable traits such as refusing to work were passed from one generation to another. He ignored opposing research that indicated that once caught in the poverty trap in declining communities without the prospect of well-paid work, poor adults could not access opportunities to rise from the bottom of the socio-economic hierarchy to better jobs, and thereby enhance their children's well-being. Joseph also blamed single-parent families, primarily women, for these social ills, a theme subsequently popularised by Peter Lilley during the 1980s.

These views acquired a new twist through the 'absent father' thesis promulgated in the 1990s. This blamed women for alienating men from the family circle without examining how men literally left women holding the baby when relationships broke down. By then, New Right ideologues pathologised poor people and blamed the state for promoting a 'culture of dependency' that encouraged people to live off benefits rather than work for their keep (Murray, 1990), and produced a special category of 'sponger' that abused the welfare system, the 'welfare queen' (Zucchino, 1997). New Labour grasped this nettle by promulgating the 'New Deal' to substantially reduce unemployment figures by encouraging people to undertake training and work their way out of poverty. New Deal measures encompass unemployed persons, young people, single mothers and older people (Millar, 2000). But the jobs on offer were low-paid casualised ones that failed to meet aspirations for a better life (Dominelli, 2003).

The state in the 1970s had been monitoring the results achieved by CDPs closely and found these wanting. The failure of CDPs to meet the objectives of the state, alongside their radical message, led the state to close problematic CDPs such as Cleator Moor and Batley, and ultimately to terminate funding for all CDP projects. Its alternative approaches to community work promoted state control of workers' activities, trends that continue today. Bureaucratic means and funding arrangements became key instruments that left radical approaches to community work in the cold (Loney, 1983), hijacked its language for ensuing decades (Mayo, 1994; Dominelli, 2004b), promoted top-down models of community intervention (Robson, 2000; Phillips, 2004; Mowbray, 2005) and integrated community organisations into market mechanisms (Hoatson, 2001).

CDPs had their own internal contradictions. Operating on genderblind and colourblind bases that treated everyone the same, their failure to deal with 'race' and gender divisions was central to these. Assuming that people had identical needs, CDP workers gave these forms of oppression scant attention. Few black people occupied positions as either paid community workers or team leaders, even when projects were based in black communities. Women community workers and secretaries were expected to make the tea and service area teams. Women workers were located primarily in the lower level ranks of the paid workforce regardless of qualifications. The few women who held positions as team leaders did not receive the same levels of pay as their male colleagues. No account was taken of the dual career burden that women carried to participate in waged employment. Gendered and racial dynamics in the organisation of paid work persist, but are at least being questioned by the government's Women and Equality Unit. The unit is arguing for a work–family balance (WEU, 2003), although this framing reaffirms the notions of domestic labour as not work.

CDPs attempted to tackle sexism and racism. The Working Women's Charter, promoted by the labour and women's movements of the early 1970s, encouraged a group of CDP women to examine the failure of CDPs to address gender inequalities in their own ranks. The late Jeanette Mitchell, Penny Remfry and I were among those who attended the few meetings that took place before CDPs, including the Central Office, were disbanded. We were struck by the irony of ignoring gender oppression within CDPs' own structures while trying to address it in the wider community.

The difficulties in forming a national organisation of CDP women were many. Meetings to discuss gender inequalities were additional to already heavy workloads. Uncovering the specifics of women's position in CDPs by examining pay scales, the position of secretaries and roles that women community workers occupied had to be completed on top of a full day's work. CDPs were nationally dispersed, with only a few women in any one project. It was time consuming and expensive for us to travel regularly to one location to meet, even if the venue was rotated. Women were supported in improving their position in waged work by strengthened union activity in workplaces predominantly hiring women. But their specific needs as women workers with family and workplace commitments were disregarded. Demands to schedule meetings to facilitate women's attendance were ignored, and women had to pay for childcare arrangements in order to be able to participate in meetings and activities outside office hours.

The work of CDPs with women in the community initially followed traditional lines (Remfry, 1979). Women were organised into women's groups to tackle issues related to motherwork, for example, childcare provision. There was no attempt to make these activities relevant to and involving men. Feminist community work prospered in certain CDPs towards the end of their existence. North Tyneside, for instance, vigorously addressed issues that impacted on women's lives as women, for example, domestic violence. Some of these initiatives have survived the demise of CDPs.

CDPs' record on combating racism was only marginally better. Several CDPs working with black communities sought to address this problem, for example, Saltley and Batley. They exposed institutionalised racist practices that hindered developments in these communities. The 'redlining' of black communities for mortgage purposes illustrated this problem (CDP, 1977c). 'Redlining' referred to the practice of defining certain communities as 'high risk' and unsuitable for lending purposes. Building societies and banks refused to lend money to applicants living in these areas, inhabited mainly by black (would-be) borrowers, a concern that remains current today.

Racist social relations permeated interactions between CDPs' black community workers and their white colleagues. Black employees often had the responsibility for eliminating racism in various communities dumped on their shoulders. They were usually hired at lower levels, although the work they were expected to undertake was more complex than that of white workers. Often living in black communities, black workers were accessible to residents requiring help round the clock.

In working with black women, white women community workers' attempts to counter the dynamics of racism and sexism were often mishandled, despite a commitment to being sensitive to black women's needs and position (Parmar, 1986). Benevolent paternalism pervaded these relationships, for example, the assumption that Mirpuri or Gujarati women needed white women's intervention and mediation with black men controlling their communities to form women's groups. CDPs held a radical reputation, but their contributions to eliminating gender or racial oppression did not merit it.

Fragmented state community initiatives

The Community Programmes Department, established in 1971, followed a community organisation model of community work and launched a number of programmes which, unlike those originating under the UAP, concentrated resources in small areas, for example, Neighbourhood Schemes in Liverpool and Teesside. Community Programmes focused on coordinating activities and improving service delivery without emphasising local participation. Women contributed resources by providing informal care. Competition between different community groups for scarce state funding ensued, an issue that continues to bedevil community groups (Diamond, 2004).

Other government departments staked out their turf and fragmented community interventions. In 1973, the Department of the Environment entered the arena through the Inner Area Studies in Oldham, Rotherham, Sunderland, Birmingham, Liverpool and London, engaging local authorities and councillors in eliminating urban deprivation. Undertaken by private management and economic planning *consultants* rather than grassroots-oriented community workers, the work emphasised bureaucratic professional expertise, a trend now evident in the NDC (Diamond, 2004). These arrangements addressed neither the needs of women and black people nor their exclusion from political processes.

The Department of the Environment added the Area Management Trials in Dudley and Haringey. These projects required area managers to coordinate policies, to act as access points for local groups and to ensure that resources were better managed, leaving little scope for direct community participation. Endorsing community organisation principles of action, these relied on 'experts' who issued directives to 'passive' urban communities. Their net effect was to curtail public participation in their localities and to 'depoliticise' community issues (Mowbray, 2005), turning them into neutral technical problems that could be most appropriately handled by technicians bringing their expertise to bear, an approach that has become finely honed under the NDC (Diamond, 2004). Women and black people, rarely found in managerial positions, had little input in the formulation of these directives, a form of exclusion that remains today.

The proliferation of 'community work' initiatives across government departments and community groups worried the Treasury who wanted to curb expenditure and ensure CDPs' experience of community workers going their own way was not repeated. The Urban Deprivation Unit (UDU) was created in 1973 to coordinate all programmes addressing urban deprivation through community organisation models of community work. It formulated Comprehensive Community Programmes (CCPs) in small areas of need to operate on managerialist lines without grassroots involvement (CDP, 1977b).

CCPs were launched in Bradford, Gateshead, the Wirral and deprived parts of Greater London – Spitalfields, Tower Hamlets, Henley Road, Islington and Wandsworth. These aimed to coordinate all existing action on deprivation in a locality and to expose gaps in existing programmes. Emphasising targeted interventions, applications for funding were restricted to areas *most* in need. This strategy did not appeal to local authorities who felt that their entire jurisdiction needed resources to help a specific needy area. Centralised control of community regeneration initiatives continues with the Office of the Deputy Prime Minister (ODPM) now having oversight of these.

By 1976, the UDU's initiatives were formalised in Labour's Policies for Inner Cities through the Inner Area Partnership Schemes (IAPS), which became strategic in handling urban poverty. Stressing 'self-help' and community development, IAPS held that economic decline was partly responsible for urban deprivation and stressed partnerships involving the central state, local authorities and entrepreneurs. This approach to resourcing community regeneration is evident in 'Third Way' social policies (Jordan, 2000) that acknowledge structural issues while favouring solutions that reside in individual actions replicated across a community (Kenny, 2002).

IAPS attracted private industry into designated areas via special concessions, subsidies and publicly funded infrastructures such as roads and communication networks. Its structures excluded women and black people who rarely had the resources to launch entrepreneurial initiatives. Local authorities having high levels of deprivation within their borders were annoyed when denied partnership status. Government control over IAPS allocated funds disproportionately to schemes with a traditional service orientation at the expense of community action and housing action projects. Radical community initiatives in Leeds, Leicester and Liverpool were hard hit by this policy (Armstrong, 1977). As feminist initiatives and community action from a black perspective secured little of the IAPS funding, a period of decline in their fortunes followed. Radical community groups continue to receive few state funds.

In 1980, Labour's IAPS scheme was reinvented by the Conservatives as the Free Enterprise Zones (FEZs) to encourage private industry's investment in inner-city areas. It extended concessions to private firms and eliminated many planning regulations that entrepreneurs disliked, an approach later promoted by New Labour. Deregulation enabled FEZ firms to penetrate declining communities without being held accountable for casualties created en route. The FEZ strategy excluded residents from decision-making processes and did not directly tackle racial or gender inequalities. White women and black people, largely excluded from the 'cut and thrust' of free enterprise, played virtually no part in corporate investment decisions. IAPS and FEZ had limited impact in stemming inner-city decay, a failure evident in the NDC (Diamond, 2004).

The rebellion of young black people in London, Liverpool, Birmingham, Leeds, Leicester and Bristol in the summer of 1981 testified to the failure of IAPS and FEZ in meeting their needs. Since then, precarious employment prospects, increasing losses in manufacturing jobs, continued deprivation in Britain's inner cities and a rise in racist attacks have demonstrated the bankruptcy of free enterprise initiatives in revitalising inner cities. Even the strategy of developing a sizeable black middle-class along the lines of the American experience has not reduced inner-city poverty. Hidden for many years, poverty in rural communities (Francis and Henderson, 1992) has now reached the public agenda and is particularly acute for older women (Chapman et al, 1998) and black people (Chakraborti and Garland, 2004).

Linking community work to social work

Despite the antipathy of community workers to social work in the 1970s, the local state's utilisation of community work within social services departments pre-dated Thatcher – in the Seebohm reorganisation of the 1970s. The Seebohm Report (1968) had laid the basis for a community work dimension in social services through the concept of the area team (Leissner and Joslin, 1974). The realisation that 60% of social work cases involved low income and bad housing (Seebohm, 1968) underpinned the impetus for 'patch-based' neighbourhood work within locality-based area teams. This facilitated the development of a 'comprehensive area team approach' to provide 'an effective family social service'. Experience and training were to make these teams 'skilled at working in and with the community'.

The opening provided by Seebohm was widened by the Barclay Report (1982), which encouraged local authorities to develop community social work. Community social work aimed to increase social workers' effectiveness in the community and reduce costs by covering more people more effectively with the same resources

(Cockburn, 1977a, b). The Wagner Report (1988) endorsed these proposals to create facilities more relevant to users' needs (Ungerson, 1987, 1990). The Griffiths Report (1988) assumed women's labour would underpin community-based healthcare.

These reports did not acknowledge the centrality of women's unpaid contribution to the viability of proposed schemes, but assumed it in their costings. This confirmed Elizabeth Wilson's (1982) view that 'community is an ideological portmanteau word for a reactionary, conservative ideology that oppresses women by silently confining them to the private sphere without so much as mentioning them'. Yet women bear a personal cost in terms of a fraught existence and foregone opportunities by putting their labour at the disposal of others (Ashurst and Hall, 1989).

The forms of community work endorsed by Barclay (1982), Wagner (1988) and Griffiths (1988) redefined community work away from mobilising people and towards servicing activities controlled by local authorities, an approach familiar to community workers today (Mowbray, 2005). This was achieved by focusing on job functions that emphasise the role of community workers in elaborating government policy and managing limited financial resources and buildings. The position of workers is contradictory, full of potential and limitations. Space for community workers to manoeuvre within this restricted position (LEWRG, 1979) hinges on residents' hopes of moving in progressive directions and their willingness to engage in external action. The capacity of community workers to utilise these spaces creatively depends on their ability to organise a strong power base among constituents. Griffiths's interventions laid the basis for a formal policy of community care under the 1990 National Health Service and Community Care Act and advanced the cause for private entrepreneurial activity in the welfare arena, a policy that continues today.

Community regeneration to curb welfare demands

Thatcherite welfare interventions to mitigate the damage done to people thrown on the 'scrap heap' through economic decline occurred within the context of severely curtailed welfare funding (Iliffe, 1985; Loney, 1983). Thatcher's public expenditure cuts severely undermined welfare state provisions in housing, education, social security, health and personal social services and marked the central state's decision to refrain from filling a 'bottomless pit of need'. Thatcherite responses culminated in the 1986 Social Security Act that excluded more client groups from coverage: 16- to 18-year-olds from supplementary benefits, women from the previously universal maternity grant and all client groups seeking Income Support from special needs payments, which were abolished (LSCC, 1986). This reality continues today. Besides depriving women of benefits by revising social security, the government's welfare strategy called on women to provide unpaid informal caring and to do low-paid welfare work. However, allowing women to access benefits in their own right provided a change that favoured women.

Limited public expenditure became crucial to imposing an efficient use of resources on the welfare bureaucracy. Thatcher sought to limit commitments to open-ended welfare expenditure by forcing people off welfare and into low-paid work. These initiatives favoured 'community work' controlled by the state, a policy continued by New Labour (Diamond, 2004; Mowbray, 2005). Growing numbers of economic casualties stretched limited resources. The then National Training Board (later the Manpower Services Commission) was crucial in providing community-based training and retraining schemes in partnership with employers and trade unions to absorb casualties of deindustrialisation and refit them for new employment (Finn, 1985).

The voluntary sector, women's unpaid domestic caring work and private enterprise became attractive resources for a government developing strategies to reach additional resources at no extra cost to it (Iliffe, 1985). The state's twin need to be both controlling and cost-effective surfaced anew at the local level, exacerbating the detrimental impact of industrial decline on individuals, particularly women and black people, who experienced the loss of services and poverty most.

Good Neighbour Schemes, community care schemes, voluntary self-help initiatives and 'patch-based' community social work have legitimised community work within such parameters (Wolfenberger, 1977; Barclay, 1982; Hadley et al, 1987; Griffiths, 1988; Wagner, 1988). The burden of care forced onto women in their waged and unwaged capacities has added to their overall caring workload. The state acts as if it provides the bulk of care for older people and children, but this is not so. The majority of older people and children are cared for in the private sphere of the home by women who receive little or no state support (Higgins, 1989; Twigg and Atkin, 1994).

With the exception of low-paid part-time work attracting women with childcare duties (Segal, 1987), few jobs materialised for men or women and unemployment levels remained high under Thatcher, reaching 3 million at its height in the mid-1980s. Matters became so serious that at one point training resources were rationed by excluding married women from Community Programme projects aimed at attracting long-term unemployed people into temporary work. Projects in this scheme were part-time community work ones, so the ruling had serious implications for women. Yet the state declared that costs for providing vast numbers of people with welfare resources exceeded existing priorities. This policy has been reversed, but the position of poor women in the labour market has changed little and they struggle to earn enough to meet family needs (DWP, 2004).

'Cuts' in welfare services for older people and disabled people prompted the creation of 'self-help' groups to cushion the effects of withdrawn state resources. Self-help organisations, private entrepreneurs and unpaid domestic work provided by women in the home have reduced the resulting gaps. The closure of residential homes and day centres has released users into communities with few provisions catering for their needs, a trend that has intensified as the government continues to limit direct state funding for personal social services (Batty, 2002).

Community work as community development became useful in rationing resources, an approach that had been facilitated by the retreat of state-funded community action critical of state responses to deprived areas, exemplified by the CDPs. The departure of the CDPs had left a vacuum that the state filled by maintaining community workers in voluntary settings using 'self-help' principles and employing them in statutory settings where managers could direct their labour through tight job descriptions.

Local authorities found that they could control the performance of community workers through bureaucratic devices that drew tight boundaries around their work. State-employed community workers were used to demonstrate the state's desire to curb the impact of deprivation on poor people, collect information on how deprived communities coped with economic decline and fragmented social lives and develop better policies for deploying limited state resources. New Labour has not altered this approach, with community work having increasingly bureaucratic and centralised forms of control running alongside demands that practitioners become professionally competent and endorse social justice by working in partnership with others (Murphy, 2002).

Blairite community initiatives

The control of community workers through job descriptions, financing and specified interventions constrained radical approaches to community mobilisation. Begun under Thatcher, this approach continues in New Labour's regeneration measures for revitalising deprived urban communities. John Major's emphasis on public–private partnerships in the City Challenge and Single Regeneration Budgets (SRBs) of the 1990s favouring private investment for economic growth has been retained in the NDC of 1998 and the National Strategy for Neighbourhood Renewal of 2001. Public–private partnerships pulled together Blair's concern to tackle social exclusion, especially that linked to poverty (SEU, 1999).

The SRB began in 1994 to streamline fragmented government assistance to poor communities. It became a national programme of seven years' duration to revitalise deprived communities through local regeneration partnerships composed of local businesses, voluntary sector players, residents and public authorities. Large sums were appropriated for this purpose through public sector, private sector and European Union monies. SRBs created projects to enhance the quality of life by reducing the gap between deprived communities and affluent areas. They focused on local circumstances to tackle worklessness, to provide employment, to raise skills and educational levels among residents, to reduce crime by eliminating drug abuse and social exclusion, to improve housing, to enhance health and to build sustainable environments (Anastacio et al, 2000). Projects were evaluated according to outcomes or set targets that were monitored. The SRBs continued under New Labour, initially through the Department of Trade and Industry. To curb fragmentation, they were subsumed under Regional Development Agencies in the Single Programme in 2002, under the aegis of the ODPM.

Working according to central government directives, 'partnership working' and 'capacity building' were to resolve structural problems in contemporary Britain (Diamond, 2004; Williams, C., 2004). Regenerating communities by multiagency working enables community professionals to participate in activities in this predefined agenda. Community development processes were truncated by bureaucratised state controls imposed on how projects were run, the types of participation endorsed, innovative changes and strong central control, which became endemic to modernising the public services under New Labour (Barnes, 1999; Kenny, 2002; Gilchrist, 2003).

Earlier problems such as the proliferation of departments controlling different aspects of community development remain under New Labour despite a commitment to 'joined-up' government. The Social Exclusion Unit (SEU), which undertook initial research and prepared the grand plan for communities, began life in 1997 in the Cabinet Office under the eye of Prime Minister Blair. It has been transferred to the ODPM that now houses the Neighbourhood Renewal Unit (NRU) and plays a key role in community regeneration. Meanwhile, the Home Office retains an interest through the Civil Renewal Unit (CRU) and Community Unit (CU).

The ODPM's vision is encapsulated in the features guiding Community Cohesion and Conflict Resolution. These are: a common vision; sense of belonging; valuing diversity; equal life chances; and positive relationships among diverse peoples. Interestingly, these cover the workplace, school and neighbourhood, but not the family. The NRU hosts three community programmes – Community Chests, Community Learning Chests and the Community Empowerment Fund. These have now merged into the Single Community Programme to enable NRU funding to better meet local needs in 88 Neighbourhood Renewal Areas. The NRU has a Community Forum to include grassroots perspectives in national neighbourhood renewal policies. From January 2005, the Community Forum's remit was extended to encompass the Tackling Disadvantage Group to address homelessness, housing and social exclusion.

The NDC started as 39 projects under the aegis of the Department for Transport, Local Government and the Regions (DTLR), but relocated to the ODPM in 2002 with 38 authorised projects costing £1.9 billion over 10 years. The NRU acquired 18 Policy Action Teams (PATs) in 2001, charged with implementing the Action Plan for the National Strategy. Local authorities work with business, voluntary agencies and residents to realise the government's plans via Local Strategic Partnerships that encourage people to collaborate in solving deep-seated, complex problems.

Blair's commitment to create 'sustainable communities', to end social exclusion and to promote 'active citizenship' are new (SEU, 1998). So is the rhetoric: 'building a safe, just and tolerant society' from the Home Office, 'a prosperous and sustainable community for the 21st century' by the ODPM and 'people and government solving problems together' at the CRU. Despite fine words, research by Purdue et al (2000) and Anastacio et al (2000) indicates that local participants in these schemes feel sidelined by the experts who retain control. By focusing on unitary communities, diversity and equality in general, the specific needs of and roles played by women and marginalised others merge into the background (Fremeaux, 2005).

Community work, corporate management and restructuring hierarchical institutions

The voluntary sector claims that the absence of corporate management structures accords it greater freedom in developing more appropriate forms of practice (Ng, 1988). Viewing the voluntary sector as autonomous ignores the constraints of insecure funding and a reliance on government contracts (Barnes, 1999). The state funded voluntary initiatives to integrate them more securely into capitalist social relations (Cockburn, 1977b; Ng, 1988; Wistow et al, 1994; Barnes and Prior, 2000) and impose 'contract government' on them (Dominelli and Hoogvelt, 1996b; Kenny, 2002). Funding restructures the relationship between the state and voluntary organisations, legitimates certain activities while excluding others and alters the internal relationships and dynamics of voluntary groups (Ng, 1988; Ng et al, 1989). These effects are very problematic for feminist community groups attempting to work in non-hierarchical ways (Ng, 1988). The women's movement and black community activists have developed autonomous alternative forms of practice by drawing largely on their own resources, for example, Incest Survivor Groups and refuges (Binney et al, 1981; Mama, 1989a, b; Wilson, 1993) and filling gaps in services left by the state (SWAF, 1980; Gilroy, 1987; Bhatti-Sinclair, 1994; Naples, 1998).

The drive to 'modernise' or raise efficiency in the public services continues to draw heavily on restructuring the welfare state (Blair, 1999), and returning caring responsibilities to 'the family', that is, women (Glazer, 1988; Twigg and Atkin, 1994). The 'new managerialism' that accompanies these initiatives favours lines of accountability that rely on hierarchical structures (Ng, 1988), specified procedures and intensified bureaucratic controls over state employees (Dominelli and Hoogvelt, 1996b; Clarke and Newman, 1997), and promotes 'instrumentally based interactions, rather than social relations based on political solidarity, civic virtue or dependency' (Kenny, 2002, p 294). Public expenditure cuts and restructured state services that accord with neoliberal ideologies have accelerated the effects of corporate management on welfare provision and the evolution of community work in the public sector. Corporate management practices have assumed a significant role in restructuring the labour process, reorganising social services (Cockburn, 1977a, b) and reshaping training (Dominelli, 2004a; FCDL, 2004). By 2005, corporate management in the public sector had introduced techniques developed in industry to make more efficient use of labour power and resources and to shift the balance of power in workplace relations towards management.

These have increased managerial control over day-to-day decision making in areas once within the realms of professional autonomy, for example, managerial directives on the handling of child abuse, prescribed ways of advising 13- to 19-year-olds in Connexions and national occupational standards for community work. And they favour 'contractual reciprocity based on individualistic and instrumental approach to social relations' (Kenny, 2002, p 294).

This erosion of professional power could be more easily countenanced had it empowered service users. But it has not. Managerial control of practitioners has strengthened the hand of bureaucratic experts, fragmented professional labour processes and transformed the nature of decision making (Dominelli, 2004a). Decisions about the allocation of resources are no longer political questions but technical ones. Instead of focusing on the political question of *why* resources have been allocated in particular ways, workers become bogged down in answering the technical question of *how* to distribute available resources to specific users within given constraints (Dominelli and Hoogvelt, 1996b). Its impact on women has been quite serious. Managerialising decision making has weighted the process in favour of men (Howe, 1986; Coyle, 1989; Grimwood and Popplestone, 1993) and whittled away frontline practitioners' space for manoeuvre (Dominelli, 1997, 2002a). Men managing women frontline workers have not worked with service users and have little appreciation of the complex realities they handle daily. Restrictions in shaping working plans with people who access services has made women workers party to bureaucratic and remote forms of service delivery that have increasingly alienated both users and workers. A social worker that I asked about the subject said:

> I feel that managerialism and market forces within a supposedly mixed economy of welfare are destroying professional social work practice. Increasingly the organisation is driven towards creating an expensive, callous bureaucracy which prides itself on delivering resource-led policies as prime measures of its effectiveness and efficiency. Not content with deskilling a professional workforce, the organisation appears to have effectively distanced itself from being accountable or responsible.... Social services departments are usually predominantly managed by white middle class men. This perpetuates the patriarchal, conservative nature of the organisation. (Dominelli, 2004a, p 160)

Organising tips

Questions to help overcome the constraints of hierarchy:

1. What hierarchical constraints apply in a specific situation?
2. What action(s) is (are) required to overcome them?
3. What resources are required to implement the action(s)?
4. What support groups/alliances can help overturn the constraints of hierarchy?

Community action within a social services setting: the 'patch' system

The attempt to bring community empowering techniques into social work as the 'patch' system occupied a moment in its history. Its significance as an initiative that brought new insights into the profession and lessons to be learnt from its failure have led me to retain it here. The understandings of community development theory and practice might reinvigorate social work. Social workers' growing disillusionment with their failure to offer clients a meaningful service in the context of public expenditure cuts and dismantling of the welfare state of the 1980s increased their interest in the possibilities contained within community work (Hadley and McGrath, 1980; Hadley and Hatch, 1981). This concern coincided with the state's desire to improve the delivery of personal social services to the community without increasing costs and to contain community action within acceptable parameters. The state tried to meet this objective by employing community workers within social services departments. These ambitions became encapsulated in a short-lived initiative known as the 'patch' system (Cooper, 1980).

Several local authorities pioneered the integration of community work techniques with casework ones, and switched teams over to the patch system during the 1980s, for example, Birmingham, Nottingham and Wakefield. These sought to increase community participation in planning services (Cooper, 1980). Convincing opponents of its viability made establishing a patch system problematic. Opposition emanated from within the social services department, beginning with social services committee members and ending with practitioners in district teams. Before enacting the programme, a lengthy process of education had to be undertaken to convince people of its advantages. Carrying this out required the development of links with councillors, senior and middle management, trade unions, fieldworkers and users. Convincing councillors of the appropriateness of such action was not easy. The process was often protracted, with the final outcome being one or two councillors endorsing the patch system (Cockburn, 1977b). Their support could facilitate its realisation by getting the social services committee to encourage the input of the district team into innovative and preventative work instead of simply responding to crises.

Middle management's backing for a grassroots proposal could facilitate its progress through the bureaucratic machinery of social services. Trade union support could also prove helpful. Current legislation restricts industrial action for such initiatives, but if they take such possibilities on board, trade unionists can put pressure on employers through negotiations and shift their stance from opposing community workers' proposals to favouring them (Joyce et al, 1987; Munro, 2001). Union solidarity can also protect workers' career prospects if caught in disputes caused by implementation.

Patch-based community workers were technically part of a social services team. They have been used in a variety of settings to offer a range of services including community directories, projects for older people, childcare resources, facilities and jobs for young people and community newspapers. A geographically based patch system relies on unitary depictions of community. The district team, located in a given section of a community, is responsible for addressing all the problems arising in a particular neighbourhood (Rosenthal, 1983). The patch system offered social workers and users the opportunity to influence policy formation and service delivery by engaging with communities and forming alliances. The task of patch social workers was to get to know the community – its problems and resources, both formal and informal – and to maximise the use of existing resources. So it lies within the community organisation mould of community work. Patch workers are expected to become acquainted with all residents, the informal networks and organisations, including voluntary and statutory ones, operating within the area. The converse is also true: people become familiar with the community workers. Through time, workers become recognised and more accessible to the community.

Patch workers operated in the community. Their restricted contact with district teams proved deleterious to its aim of changing mainstream practice as patch workers had little impact on office-based social workers. But, as community workers, they were aware of residents' hostility and frustration with social services' inadequate responses to their plight. The patch system was initially envisaged as a means of developing more relevant services for users. It aimed to reduce the dichotomy between 'expert' professional and 'dependent' client by fostering existing or new self-help groups. Self-help groups can become dependent on practitioners acting as initiators of action and gatekeepers of resources (Davies, 1982). Practitioners acting as patch leaders can devalue the contributions of locally recruited volunteers who assume subordinate roles as patch workers simply backing professional interventions.

Enabling deprived working-class communities to procure additional resources, patch systems act as mechanisms for social services departments to co-opt community resources and to compensate for deficiencies in service delivery, itself a worrying development. One reason for unbalanced relationships between formal agencies and community groups is that patch-based social work was presented to communities in a passive consultation mode. The community was asked to ratify a patch plan by using it and providing the human and material resources required for implementation.

The diminution of community involvement through oppressive decision-making hierarchies intensifies the exploitation of residents' labour whether unpaid, voluntary or low paid. Home helps, street wardens and other ancillary and domestic workers are the backbone of the 'patch' system and constitute the bulk of its low-paid echelons who are primarily women. Besides using volunteers as workers, the patch system draws lay members of the community, professionals and councillors into its ranks.

Patch leaders must ensure close liaison and consultation between local participants and members of the social services team and use both community and departmental resources in the most effective manner when meeting identified needs. The priorities that guide a patch leader allocating resources place utilising informal support networks, self-help groups and voluntary groups before using statutory resources. This policy meant that rationing social services could continue unnoticed as long as community resources procured by the state were either free or affordable.

Some patch systems have attempted to reduce the powers of professional workers through a Social Care Assembly (SCA), in which community participants are drawn into decision-making processes. Usually formulated on non-sectarian and non-political bases, an SCA can mystify the power relations that permeate the patch system. By involving local residents in decision making on day-to-day matters, the political realities shaping the overall allocation of resources can be ignored. Such participation can give people a false sense of power in which determination of a part is assumed to be the whole. The mystification of these power relations is conducive to retaining the status quo and represents a political stance. It also masks the ultimate veto that professionals hold in matters encompassed by day-to-day decision-making processes. The SCA exists because workers have decided that it will and consultation processes occur because people are willing to listen.

Consultation falls far short of holding full and equal power. Patch system workers engage the community to a certain extent, but its involvement falls short of the principle aim of community action, that of redistributing power and resources in favour of powerless people. For full participation to occur, communities must become full partners in the patch system with the power to determine key decisions affecting policy formulation and the allocation of resources as well as day-to-day concerns. Hierarchical differentiation and its role in retaining community participants in subordinate positions should be questioned.

A measure of worker equality among social workers operating a patch system takes place through genericism or assigning a number of tasks to each worker and expecting the worker to know all aspects of the work. Status inequalities can be perpetuated if one specialism is valued over others. A career structure must be incorporated into the patch system to overcome disparities between patch workers and those in the office and to address gender and 'race' inequalities. Professional differentiation is reinforced through remuneration systems that are predicated on workers' previous classification (Cooper, 1980), and privileges men who receive higher starting salaries. Without a career structure, the patch system in a social services department penalises the internal promotion prospects of patch employees. Patch workers often leave to be promoted.

Within the patch system, women support informal, unpaid care by keeping an eye on their neighbours and looking after kin. Women's commitment to seeing people receive the care they need is presumed. They are expected to provide the necessary care without formal external backing. Women pay a price for being overburdened with caring work (Burden and Gottlieb, 1987): mental illness, tranquillisers to see them through the day and simple frustration at being at everyone's beck and call (Ashurst and Hall, 1989; Bondi and Burman, 2001). Institutional racism and the lack of resources to meet black people's needs intensify the caring burden borne by black women and increase the pressures operating against their well-being (Malek, 1985).

Women are central to the 'patch' system as both paid and unpaid workers. Many support services and voluntary tasks are performed by women. The work allotted to them has increased in complexity and changed from being simply about physical care to providing advice and making preliminary assessments of need. If paid, their wages do not reflect the level of responsibility they hold. Changes in the labour process at the lower level of the social services hierarchy reflect the system's concern with making maximum use of resources, even if it means exploiting women's labour to assure the well-being of others. Meanwhile, the posts at the upper reaches of the social work profession are held primarily by men (Coyle, 1989; Grimwood and Popplestone, 1993; EOC, 2004), although by 2005 more women had entered managerial ranks (ONS, 2004). The degradation of professional labour, indicated by increased bureaucratisation and technocratisation through the 'new managerialism', has brought more women into these posts as men leave them for more favourable options, a trend also evident in community work (Glen et al, 2004). A survey of community development workers undertaken by the Community Development Foundation during 2002 and 2003 found that, compared to men, women community workers are located in lower pay scales, more likely than men to work on shorter contracts and twice as likely to hold part-time posts (Glen et al, 2004).

Feminist community workers in patch systems can identify inequalities stemming from various social divisions including 'race', and can initiate organisational changes that more effectively meet the interests of women service users and workers. They can develop feminist services, networks and support groups among women in the community and establish groups to monitor the impact of the patch system on services in the community to identify and advocate on behalf of excluded members.

Patch workers have also taken on board changing contexts. The government no longer favours social work-based interventions in the community. They prefer 'social care', with its apolitical and technical connotations, rather than either social work or community work. Many people now working in the community, organising and mobilising people under the New Deal flag, are called anything but social workers or community workers. Personal advisors, Sure Start workers and similar titles are more popular although occasionally they may be referred to as community development workers. Despite not being oriented towards transformative change, they undertake work in the community that requires people's participation, organisation and mobilisation. This indicates the increasingly fragmented nature of state interventions in communities and the restructuring of 'the social'.

The patch system relied heavily on state inputs and the centrality of workers directly employed by it. Alongside fear of the radical potential of workers working out of their office and acceptability to local residents, other key factors accounting for the decline in the popularity of the patch system in the government's repertoire was its penchant for public–private partnerships and technological orientation of professional work under the 'new managerialism'.

Power sharing in hierarchical institutions

Consumer participation and the direct involvement of basic grade social workers in decision making within social services departments are of interest to practitioners keen to democratise services and managers aiming to reduce costs. Managers' and workers' interests converge around employment initiatives in hierarchical institutions. Community work insights can assist in democratising services. Social workers' day-to-day knowledge of client needs and responses are relevant in determining policy issues but the institutional mechanisms for inserting these understandings into policy making are lacking. Some social workers resent their powerlessness and inability to influence decision makers because they often implement policies developed without consulting them and that they oppose. As a social worker in a community care team in Dominelli (2004a, p 162) claimed:

> Resource-led assessments – not needs-led. I am compelled
> to adopt this 'value' rather than adopt it voluntarily.

Users are also excluded from policy making except at the point of casting a vote during electoral processes that brings a particular political party to power or complaining about a poorly delivered service.

Middle level managers instructed to respond to political directives emanating from a central government that does not seek their advice also feel disempowered. They are caught between the pressures of grassroots consumers and workers pushing for increased and better services and political masters demanding cuts in them. This untenable and contradictory position opens the possibility of alliances to improve service delivery involving middle managers, practitioners and service users (Dominelli and Leonard, 1982). Power-sharing alliances across differences (Bishop, 1994) pose the question of how to engage consumers in decisions that promote their welfare within hierarchical institutions such as social services departments, and make these organisations the object of transformative community actions.

Democratising decision making within hierarchical institutions is a difficult process. It involves making alliances with individuals and groups within organisations and outside it. These include service users, community groups, trade unionists, professional associations, the women's movement, black activists, other practitioners (Kettle, 1998), policy makers, academics and consultants sympathetic to its aims and objectives. Formed into a supportive network, these groupings can increase social capital in a community by providing practical help and leverage in promoting a cause, offering advice and giving theoretical direction.

Social workers embarking on a process of democratising the workplace take risks. Community-based professionals whose position differs from their employers are wise to take precautionary measures before embarking on democratising services if their managers hold opposing views. Measures that safeguard users' interests before forming alliances with management are also advisable (Dominelli and Leonard, 1982; Dominelli, 2004b). If working outside their office, workers should ensure that employers provide cover during their absence. This frees workers to engage in community work, acknowledges time spent developing these links as part of normal workloads and ensures that democratising efforts do not facilitate 'cuts' in services or become incorporated in serving the status quo. Engaging in democratising activities can inflict damage on workers' promotion prospects and subject them to disciplinary procedures or dismissal if their support for service users conflicts with employers' interests. They may have to form alliances that reduce the power of employers to activate adverse judgements about them for favouring community group positions.

Agreeing the following principles before embarking on community-based action helps establish a degree of parity between workers and management:

- confidentiality of proceedings within the group;
- mutual accountability;
- developing power bases within the department and in the community; and
- undertaking collective action.

Adhering to these principles sustains the momentum of collaborative work and counters division and suspicion in groups endeavouring to share power (Dominelli and Leonard, 1982). Achieving these in practice will be difficult if the privileging of professional knowledge continues and multiple levels of diversity are not addressed.

To facilitate this work, workers have found it useful to know the institutions they seek to change, to understand the people they are dealing with, to clarify the organisational features they aim to transform and share as their unifying goals, to obtain the factual information they require and to identify available resources. They should become familiar with power structures and the political alignments of the people involved, and understand the organisations that they seek to influence. Much of this information is easily accessible, but people may have difficulty bringing it together and using it to influence organisational processes, other professionals and the community.

Social workers and middle managers attempting to push back the boundaries of hierarchical decision-making structures through community action have developed support groups to promote their democratisation efforts and implement the strategy and tactics entailed in doing so. This has also meant forming alliances outside social services departments to encompass users, tenants, trade unions and community groups. When embarking on social change of this nature, women have formed autonomous women-only support groups to identify their particular needs and interests, to develop confidence in their own abilities and ideas and to establish wider networks (Dreifus, 1973; BWHC, 1979; Stanley and Wise, 1983, 1997; hooks, 1984; Hanmer and Statham, 1988; Dominelli, 2002a).

Once embarked on the process of altering decision making within their employing agencies, participants may confront a mixture of advances and reverses in realising their goals. Being prepared for messy results makes it easier for those involved to cope with them. They have to face the possibility of total failure and dismissal from their posts. Support groups can facilitate the process of grieving over frustrated ambitions and learning from experience. Collective action can take time to develop and, in the interim period, as women have discovered, it is important to retain a sense of humour, radical perspective and patience. That means recognising that working with groups also involves emotional work of both a positive and negative nature.

Black people have developed autonomous support groups to develop capacities that promote their interests and development (hooks, 1984, 2000; Lorde, 1984; Malek, 1985; Rooney, 1987; Collins, 1991). Black activists and disabled people seeking to democratise hierarchical institutions have created support groups and networks while simultaneously organising their own demands and monitoring services that social workers place at their disposal (see Rooney, 1987; Barnes, 2003). Their formation has been crucial in strengthening social inclusion and solidarity among community groups and getting community backing for their endeavours (Hudson-Weems, 1993).

Conclusion

The state uses social policies to promote particular conceptualisations of community, usually unitary ones. The trends these portray have been remarkably consistent since the 1960s – shifting responsibility for people's well-being onto individuals and communities and involving the private sector more closely in providing welfare services. A community's social capital has provided the means whereby the state assumes control over a multiplicity of institutions. Legislation and policies coordinate the activities of ruling with linking the private and public spheres and reconfigure social relations within neoliberal frameworks that shift responsibility for welfare provisions onto individuals while enhancing the market's capacity to provide services to individual consumers with money. These initiatives have generally failed to empower communities except in bureaucratic ways. Nor have they taken account of the unpaid contributions that women make when actualising community services while women in paid work occupy the lower levels of the labour hierarchy and pay (Hallett, 1991).

Note

[1] This book is primarily about community action. I use the term 'community work' when commenting on the profession in general or when I do not wish to distinguish between the different models that it encompasses. In this chapter I take a historical approach to community work to highlight continuities and discontinuities in policy that continue to disadvantage women and poor people, black and white.

FOUR

Feminist challenges to community work

Introduction

The unpaid contributions of women to community care and place in the community have been assumed for several decades. Care given by kin is extended through Neighbourhood Schemes and various forms of community care to encompass other residents. Women's unpaid contribution to the national economy is usually invisible (Hirst, 1999), but it costs money to provide this care through the welfare state, even if it is undervalued and social care workers are among the lowest paid in the country. Canadians have measured women's domestic work in a shadow economy and found its value equivalent to that of the manufacturing industry (Status of Women, 2001).

Feminists have critiqued community workers for failing to take seriously how gendered relations are played out in all models of community work. Their analyses have shown that women are usually left in supporting roles while men take the leading ones, even in cases where the majority of activists are women. There have been some changes in community work approaches to women since Marjorie Mayo first identified, questioned and theorised this neglect. Yet gender relations that disadvantage women persist and play significant roles in community work. Feminists have challenged how women are conceptualised as not being knowledgeable and reformulated contemporary definitions of professionalism (Belenky et al, 1997).

In this chapter I consider feminist challenges to negative images of women in the community, their contribution to its overall work (paid and unpaid), feminist theorisation of it and attempts to make it more appreciated and valued. In reflecting on these issues, I ask why, despite endeavours aimed at altering this situation, change has been so limited. In other words, why have feminist approaches to the subject failed to gain the prominence they deserve?

Women as knowledgeable beings

Women's engagement in daily life and social relations in communities have been identified as important components of their knowledge-based capacities. These have featured the different bases on which women take action to promote community well-being and become politicised by participating in community activities. Gilligan's (1982) analysis of women's action being motivated by connections to others rather than concerns for procedural justice that guide men has been evidenced by feminist social action such as that of the Women's Peace Camp at Greenham Common (Cook and Kirk, 1983) and feminist environmental movements (Shiva, 2003). Feminists have focused on differences that configure gendered relationships in men's and women's lives, and highlighted the separate ontological domains that each gender occupies. These have been questioned on essentialist grounds, but they indicate that women can use knowledge acquired through interactions with each other to build personal self-esteem, question existing social structures, unpack many forms of oppression and develop alternative services based on their insights, even if these are highly embedded in community-based relationships. Yet women ignore their involvement in these locations by claiming they are 'just housewives doing housework' (Gavron, 1966), and discounting caring for others as contributions to civil society (Cohen, 1999).

Feminist social action has been central in redefining women as subjects, validating and valuing women's knowledge, developing new forms of knowledge, challenging professionalism, highlighting the existence of multiple truths, arguing to resolve contradictory situations by embracing ambiguity, creating win–win opportunities and demonstrating the capacities of women as active beings who both think and do. In creating feminist social action (Weir and Wilson, 1984) and mobilising women, feminists also created new areas of contestation rather than simply dissolving existing contradictions.

Women have used the law in mobilising communities and creating alternative spaces for women (Naples, 1998). These have been instigated after critiquing existing provisions, whether provided by the state or private sector. Challenging laws that configured women and children as men's property subjected to reasonable violence symbolise this approach (Mullender, 1997). The 'education over-campaign' in Massachusetts, USA, of the late 1990s also exemplifies this. Opposing Proposition 2½ which limited tax rises to 2.5% per annum unless approved by referendum because state schools would be underfunded, it highlighted the diverse mobilisation tactics utilised by different social classes (Howe, 1998). Working-class mothers with children in state schools defending their right to a decent education through grassroots collective action contrasted with the individualistic mobilisation white middle-class businessmen and politicians utilised. Using the artefacts of everyday life to which they had access, working-class women organised a 'school phone tree' as a key mechanism in connecting parents interested in getting public funds into state schools. Its more empowering structure encouraged people not usually involved in political processes to participate. While successfully opposing Proposition 2½, this school-based strategy failed to transform the white power elite structures that governed local politics (Howe, 1998). This illustrates strengths and weaknesses in women's campaigns: change in one area, the status quo in a key other.

Domestic work as women's unvalued contribution to community well-being

Feminist social action and scholarship has been crucial in unpacking the significance of women's role in the domestic sphere and their participation in public life, including the community, by focusing on the impact of gendered relations in the interstices of daily life and exposing how these are taken for granted in configuring how things are done. Women's work in the home remains under-appreciated. Although men now do more than previously, the bulk of domestic work is still performed by women (Grenier and Wright, 2001). Given as a 'labour of love' (Graham, 1983) to family members, voluntary work undertaken in communities extends it to other people. This contribution, formally unmeasured, is considerable (Hirst, 1999), and presumed available in government policies such as Neighbourhood Schemes and community care initiatives.

Feminists identified women as time and leisure poor (Balbo, 1987), but, along with the rest of the population, ignored the impact of lack of time on motherwork. Men have on average 50 minutes more leisure time per day and three times more time for socialising while women spend four times longer on domestic work than men (Gershung and Fisher, cited in Grenier and Wright, 2001). This has implications for women's capacity to build social capital and to participate in formal community endeavours.

Women in waged work

The gender gap in waged work still disadvantages women. Men earn more than 15% than women on average and control the economy's most important and well-paid positions. Men's median hourly pay is £11.04 hourly, while women's is £9.46 (ONS, 2004). In the private sector, the City is dominated by men and the top managerial jobs are held by them. In government, key posts are occupied by men, even though the number of women currently in Parliament has never been higher (Norris, 2000). Women's different but unequal social position has meant that only 28% of councillors are women compared with 72% of men. Although the Blair administrations have had the highest number of women members, the 1997 victory still resulted in only 18% of MPs being women (Norris, 2000). In the public sector, including social and community work, the majority of managers are men. Women dominate at the lower levels of the managerial ranks (ONS, 2004). Women seem to assume social services director posts when men find better alternatives. And, 'failing' authorities led by men have had women take over, for example, Hackney.

Women's contributions to community life

In community work, leadership roles are assumed by men while women adopt the supporting ones (Dominelli, 1990; Lowndes, 2000). This pattern persists (Glen et al, 2004). Gaskin and Davis Smith (1995) found that men are more likely to occupy committee posts while women do the befriending activities. Hood and Woods (1994) have shown that women who founded community groups such as tenants' associations have given way to male leaders when they came on the scene, and their involvement is reduced as organisations become more formal and bureaucratic. Geddes (1997) found few women on community partnership boards in urban regeneration schemes. Vincent and Martin (2000) emphasise women's 'support' roles and fund-raising capacities.

Women continue to mobilise and be mobilised around caring responsibilities. Hall (1999) argues that women's contributions to community life have sustained social capital in the UK and that their involvement in community associations has risen at a higher rate than men's. In highlighting women's caring capacities, feminists have made visible women's contribution to public social capital. This has highlighted that women's caring work, including forming tenants' groups around housing issues and creating playgroups to develop resources for children, belongs in the public arena and acknowledged activities carried out in the home or informal networking, not as private matters, but as part of the wider civil society that is embedded in communities. This approach counters the devaluation of women's contribution to social capital (Hall, 1999) and Walby's (1997) separation of public and private patriarchy.

The fracturing of the women's movement

Third wave feminism

Olive Banks (1981) divided feminist activism into first and second waves. Some now refer to a third or post-feminist wave (Friedlin, 2002). The first wave focused on realising women's political rights. The second one fought collective campaigns to actualise women's social and economic rights. The third wave takes as given the gains of the second, especially in employment rights. It centres on personal freedoms for individual women and is more actively discussed in the US. Here, the Veteran Feminists of America express concern at the fracturing of the movement, loss of solidarity among women and taken-for-grantedness of earlier feminist achievements and social justice claims that have yet to be fully realised (Friedlin, 2002).

Given continued gendered inequalities that primarily disadvantage women, earlier gains are far from being firmly embedded in society, making this post-feminist view of the world overly optimistic. Already, third wave feminism has made discourses on gender relations focus less on women's overall position in society and more on personal concerns, particularly sexual expression. This may render women's specific interests as women invisible and fragment feminist social action. Still in its early days, third wave feminism carries implications for mobilising women in future, not least by creating generational divisions linked to particular periods of activism among women. Third wave feminists like Jennifer Baumgardner argue that their innovations are more person-focused than those of the second wave, but as socially significant (Baumgardner and Richards, 2000), for example, abortion fund-raisers.

The Third Wave Foundation that supports young women in their late teens to early thirties argues that the movement is set in a more diffuse range of issues with women as both subjects and objects of social activism. It presents 'girlie power' as real feminism and rejects the feminist label as it is associated with hostility against women and conformity to feminist stereotypes (Baumgardner and Richards, 2000;

Friedlin, 2002). The third wave's strength is viewing feminism as specific to each individual woman who attaches the term 'feminist' to herself. These feminists reinvent themselves by redrawing the boundaries between the personal and political, the private and public, and theorising from daily routines. As Jennifer Baumgardner said, 'we are private citizens who have the same rights as yesterday's public heroines' (Baumgardner and Richards, 2000, p 2).

Fragmentation within the women's movement is not new. The unitary movement that women thought they had formed in the 1960s and 1970s has fragmented, although its unity was always an illusion. Working-class women, black women, disabled women and older women consistently felt their interests ignored by a white middle-class women's movement that grabbed media headlines and defined the broader movement (hooks, 1984; Collins, 1991; Dominelli, 2002a). Particularly hard to bear was white women's implication in racism and imperialist ventures that oppressed black women and the realisation that being oppressed did not inoculate women against oppressing other women. The movement's fragmentation began to be theorised by Rowbotham et al (1980), who felt that the disintegrating unity among women and between women and the Left would reduce their capacity to improve substantially women's lives or make achieved gains durable. Attempts to move 'Beyond the Fragments' have not yielded the desired results and women still struggle to meet the demands of unpaid motherwork, housework, caring work and waged work.

Postmodern feminists' focus on individual identities has strengthened women's ability to address identity politics and celebrate diversity, but it has hastened the loss of the strategic essentialism initiated by the women's movement to forge unity and execute social change. New ways of addressing this issue effectively have yet to be devised. Meanwhile, those wishing to reverse feminist gains have benefited from this fragmentation. For example, white men in the US have challenged affirmative action as discriminatory to their interests (Cahn, 1995), without acknowledging the privileging that they previously enjoyed at the expense of women and black people, who were simply excluded from participating in the employment arena on an equal basis before its promulgation. The 'cultural wars' can be depicted as attempts to reassert taken-for-granted privileging by favoured groups.

In making this interpretation of events, feminists should not assume that there are no conflicts of interests either between men and women or among women when addressing historical wrongs. Nor should they be frightened of seeing these as destructive of cooperation between and among diverse ranges of women. These differences have to be confronted directly and creatively within mobilising processes if feminists are not to reinforce power over relations of domination that replace one select group by another. And it complicates the range of concerns to be taken into account when devising win–win situations through consensual agreements. Third wave feminists have sought to address ambiguities and multiple positioning at the individual level rather than suppress these in the interests of a forced or false unity.

Third wave feminists embark on constant and unfinished processes of becoming rather than reaching an end point, and engage in negotiating differences to rethink meanings of identity and community. Holding and negotiating contradictory positions in the desire to accommodate and resist oppression is indicative of third wave feminist struggles, although I would argue that those of us classified as second wave feminists by virtue of our age, but who did not hold white middle-class Anglo-Saxon upbringings, did likewise long before third wave feminists claimed this as their territory, a point made by Angela Davis (1995) and Catherine Orr (1997). The use of alternative media such as the Internet, websites, emails, blogs, ezines and music to portray their views helps third wave feminists spread their messages and access audiences left out by earlier generations of feminists who were dependent on the commercial media and printed word. The Riot Grrrl movement of the 1990s was a powerful proponent of this approach to producing and expressing transgressive cultures and ideas.

Women's reproductive rights provide another arena for the backlash against feminist gains. Recent feminist theorising on women's bodies has identified women's inability to self-define these except in limited circumstances. Women's reproductive rights, an arena of important feminist social action that enabled women to control their own fertility during the 1970s, are highly contested, particularly those related to giving birth (Steinberg, 1997). Women's demands for reproductive rights initially focused on abortion. These became redefined as women's rights to choose in response to black women's critique of the enforced sterilisation imposed on them (Sidel, 1986). Third wave feminists have added to these concerns women's right to choose when and where to have abortions so as to avoid the 'factory' atmosphere of abortion clinics, suggesting involving midwives or having home abortions, and offering post-abortion grief counselling for every woman (Baumgardner and Richards, 2000). Feminists are now demanding that new reproductive technologies including in vitro fertilisation and surrogacy are given to women who want them under their control (Steinberg, 1997; Dominelli, 2002b). Third wave feminists build on the gains of the second wave while seeking ways of working together 'without sacrificing their identities' (Siegal, 1997).

Women's control over their bodies is being challenged by discourses that configure a foetus as a human being with full rights from the moment of conception when it is a few cells and pitting the 'rights of the unborn child' against the mother's. Debates on removing women's right to retain control of their reproductive capacities are currently acquiring strength in both the UK and the US as men's interests in the birth process and childrearing are being realigned. These discourses are dominated by men including religious leaders who argue that women have secured too many rights (Farrell, 1994). Another site of contestation involves women's rights to influence the socialisation of children. These are being questioned by part of the men's movement that is organising to affirm fathers' rights at the expense of women (Russo, 1978; Fathers 4 Justice, 2005), and indicates the creation of another binary dyad that pits men's and women's interests against each other to undermine women's hard-won freedoms.

Fathers 4 Justice (2005) set up the dyad of powerful women abusing powerless men by stating that women exclude men from being involved with children when relationships end, and that this contributes to youth offending, while ignoring the damage that fathers do when they are violent or abuse power within the family. Their stances downplay the complex issues and power relations that skew interactions between adult men and women. Simplistically portrayed, this neglects situations where men have abused women and children, are unable to undertake the required childcare, or only want to be 'good-time dads'. This approach is no more acceptable than the unwarranted exclusion of fathers seeking contact with children. Fathers 4 Justice are creating another oppositional binary dyad while feminists demand that men take a full share of childcare responsibilities. Polarising men's and women's rights in this way means that the issues of proportionality and equality in childcare are avoided.

The position of black men is even more complicated (Staples, 1988). They have a lengthy history of being denied access to children, often under explicit social policies that have banned them from contributing to childrearing, for example, the American 'man about the house' rule that cast them in the provider role and made them economically responsible for dependants while they were being excluded from well-paid jobs by racism. Working alongside black women they are reclaiming a place in their families and communities (Staples, 1988; Connell, 1995).

Women's position as signifiers of the nation is being reaffirmed as a site of women's oppression. In this configuration, women's role is neither self-defined, nor reached through negotiations that involve women as equal partners in defining their role and position in society. Nira Yuval-Davis (1997) has argued that women's bodies are inscribed by men while women play an active role in reinforcing what is presented as a natural state of affairs. Feminists have challenged this depiction of women through campaigns highlighting women's right to self-realisation.

The backlash has been accompanied by a counter-struggle as women continue to insist that egalitarian relations will better serve the interests of all people – children, men and women. Its holistic approach to social issues has placed social justice, democracy and inclusion on the public agenda, encouraged humanity to care for the environment and to end industrial forms of production that degrade it to enrich the few (Shiva, 2003).

Firing the public's imagination

Feminists have successfully put gender on the map, but gender oppression remains strong throughout the world. The United Nations (UN) began to profile women's issues in the mid-1970s and championed their rights in political and social arenas. Progress in actualising these has been slow. Over the years, women's rights were redefined as human rights for women, a position adopted at the UN Fourth World Conference on Women in Beijing (more commonly known as Beijing Conference) in 1995 in the hope of making more rapid movement on the matter globally (WEDO, 2005). The UN's Commission on the Status of Women at a meeting in New York in March 2005 commented on the long road that has to be travelled before women will be able to gain equality in both private and public spheres. And so women's activism on this front continues.

Feminist endeavours have involved women in redefining communities in ways that challenge the exclusion of women from the public sphere. Key challenges to traditional community work have been feminists' insistence on recognising women's strengths, responding to their needs and ensuring that these occupy a central place in community action. To achieve these objectives, feminists have sought to understand how power relations shape community dynamics to privilege men's position, skills and attributes, identify women's talents, celebrate their contributions to community life and assert women's rightful place in it. Knowing the roles that women play in communities, the resources they have at their disposal and having others willing to assist in these tasks helped feminists to progress their interventions, fire the public's imagination and to secure change. Crucial to this have been negotiated interactions that fully involve women in identifying issues, skills, resources and actors that could engage in social action involving communities. Developing a community's profile provides women with a holistic picture of this site and is important in forming mobilisation strategies. I consider this aspect of their work below.

Building a picture of a community: the community profile

A community profile is a comprehensive picture of a community that provides baseline data for action that enhances the well-being of all. It can be conceptualised as a detailed audit that is produced and controlled by a community. The knowledge it contains is a prerequisite for effective feminist community campaigns and for acquiring external support for particular activities because a profile reveals the people, attitudes, skills and resources that exist in an area. It can be used to assess needs, plan action in meeting them, identify allies and monitor change. A community profile is compiled on both informal and formal bases, so data have to be interpreted carefully. Amassing the profile draws on knowledge already within a community and accessible to groups wishing to raise consciousness about issues. Interactive exchanges or dialogue with community members enrich data collection. Women are a rich source of community 'facts'. A lot of their knowledge cannot be obtained through formal information gathering, storage and dissemination outlets. This is because women use their sociability to explore fluid relationships that structure their communities (Daniels, 1985). Trust between people acts as a lubricant in gathering data and evaluating the worth of what is collected. Mistrust of those excluded from the community has to be transcended for they are also important sources of knowledge, expertise and abilities. Yet their views and insights may often be ignored (Chakraborti and Garland, 2004).

Community activists collect details on a community when identifying the economic, political, social and environmental needs of a particular area and resources that local inhabitants have. Whether working solely with women or in mixed groups, feminist community workers try to ensure that data collection follows feminist principles of leaving control over the use of information with those providing it; sharing information and the skills entailed in collecting it among group members; highlighting the significance of gender during data collection, dissemination and use; and utilising findings to improve the position of women (see Roberts, 1982; Stanley and Wise, 1983, 1997; Eichler, 1988; Kelly, 1988; Dominelli, 2005).

Having collected the information, community activists must then assess its accuracy, the support they can achieve by forming groups around specified problems and should then check out people's opinions and willingness to take action. The methods used for gauging support for their cause can range from word of mouth to administering formal surveys. People will have varying degrees of commitment, ranging from agreeing to vote in favour of an action or writing a letter of complaint to occupying a building.

A community profile can identify opposition to a plan of action and reveal people's vested interests in adopting particular positions. Knowing the group's opponents can facilitate planning for action, monitoring change and assessing outcomes. It can help formulate counter-arguments to those voiced by opponents and form support groups.

Some of the major aims, objectives and items to be covered in a community profile involve a lengthy process which never really ends since the information which is held collectively by the group must be continually updated. This task may be made easier if the information is computerised, but it has to comply with the requirements of the 1998 Data Protection Act. Some information is already publicly available; some will have to be unearthed by the group. It is important that data in the community profile are easily accessible to members and supportive community groups. Ensuring the accessibility of the profile requires the group to consider how the information can be regularly updated, distributed, used and stored. Improving women's access to data exposes the politics of information collection and retrieval, enhances manoeuvrability in ensuing power struggles and strengthens women's willingness to redress the current lack of information and resultant powerlessness (Adamson et al, 1988; Scott, 2001). The new information technologies can be used to improve a regular updating of a community profile. Spreadsheets and other software can be used to analyse the data in increasingly complex and refined ways (Clarke, 2004).

Compiling a community profile

A community profile aims to:

- identify community needs (where resources are available or required);
- identify organisational, material, human and other resources available in the community on both formal and informal levels; and
- use data to enhance the well-being of children, women and men.

A community profile is used to:

- provide information about a community, including its resource base;
- organise people to change their community in accordance with their needs; and
- redistribute power and resources in egalitarian directions.

The major items to be covered in a community profile are as follows.

Physical and environmental description of the area

Once the data are collected, the ensuing community profile may be presented in paper or audio–visual format, for example, a map or project website. Questions to be asked include:

- Where is the community physically located?
- How many people live there?
- What general description would you give it (include the 'feel' of an area, general appearance and environment)?
- What industries, enterprises, factories, offices, workplaces are there and where are they located?
- What shopping facilities are there and where are they located?
- What recreational or leisure facilities are there and where are they located?
- How is land used (include recreational land)?
- What major roads and natural barriers divide the area, for example, rivers?
- Are there empty properties in the area?
  - Where are these located?
  - Who owns them?
  - Are there people living in allegedly empty properties?
    If yes, who are they?
    How many people are in them?

- What types of housing are there?
  - According to tenure:
    Council tenanted
    Housing association
    Private tenanted
    Owner-occupied
- What is the distribution of housing according to social divisions?
  - Class
  - 'Race'
  - Ethnicity
  - Gender
  - Age
  - Disability
  - Sexual orientation (if appropriate)
- What type of housing construction is there?
  - Houses with gardens:
    Detached houses
    Semi-detached houses
    Terraced houses
    Town houses
    Maisonettes
  - Houses without gardens:
    Detached houses
    Semi-detached houses
    Terraced houses
    Maisonettes
  - Low-rise flats
  - Tower blocks
  - Communal living arrangements
  - Sheltered housing
- Where is each type of housing located?
- What amenities do the different types of houses have?
- Is there overcrowding in the houses? If yes, which ones and where are they?
- What community halls, churches, pubs, social clubs and other social buildings are there?
- What statutory services are found in the area and where are they located?
  - Government offices
  - Health
  - Education
  - Personal social services

  - Housing
  - Police
- What transportation networks (sea, land, rail, air) are there?
  - What is the frequency of these services?
  - How much do these services cost?
  - What is the quality of these services?
  - Who uses these services?
- What (current and future) plans does the local authority have for the area?
  - Zoning changes
  - New developments, especially in housing, road and other infrastructural construction including airports and telecommunications, and commercial ventures including business parks.

Demographic description of the area

- What is the gender distribution of the area and what roles does each gender play?
- What is its ethnic distribution and what roles do each ethnic grouping play?
- What is its age distribution?
- What is the income distribution of residents (include inheritances, Income Support, pensions, unemployment benefits, disability allowances, wages)?
- What occupations do its residents follow?
- How many multi-household/single-parent household dwellings are there?
- What religious practices/faiths are observed by its residents?
- What are the 'travel-to-work journey' distances (local working or commuting)?
- How do people use their leisure time? What hobbies do they have?

Economic description

- Who are the employers in the area?
  - Where do they live?
  - Where are their headquarters located?
  - What lifestyles do they have?
- How many employees does each employer have?
  - Are they organised in trade unions, company associations or unorganised?

- What are the employers' attitudes to these organisations?
- Are the employers making a profit?
- What plans do they have for remaining in the area?
  - What attracted them to the area in the first instance (for example, subsidies, available labour, cheap land, cheap premises, unprotected and deregulated labour)?
- What future plans for developing the local economy are there (in the public, commercial, voluntary and domestic sectors)?
- Are new employers coming into the area?
  - Where?
  - How many jobs do they offer and how many are taken up by local people?
  - Where do these employers come from (they often disinvest in other deprived areas to go to one which offers more profit-making incentives including public subsidies and cheap labour)?
- What do councillors and government officers think of these developments?
- Can the local authority and central state take a more interventionist role in promoting the community's future well-being?
  - At what points?
  - For what purposes?
  - How?

Political description

- Which political parties/organisations are involved in the community?
  - How does this compare to their involvement in other parts of the area?
  - What have they done (not done) for the community and when?
- What resources do these political parties and organisations have?
- What is the relationship between these organisations and residents like (include their power base and number of supporters they have)?
  - How can you gain their support for your group's activities?
- Which trade unions are active in the area, how do they involve the community and engage with it?
  - What resources do they have at their disposal?
  - Are these available to the community?
  - How can you gain their support for your group's activities?
- Which community groups and organisations are there?
  - How many people does each of these contain?
  - What policies do they hold?

- What campaigns have they had?
- Who leads them or organises their activities?
- What resources do they have?
- How can you gain their support for your group's activities?
• Which feminist organisations, campaigns and networks can you identify?
- What resources do they have available?
- Are there any specific services earmarked for women?
- How can you gain their support for your group's activities?

Informal networks

Knowing about informal networks is very important for women as these act as sites where women exchange, extend and create social capital. Points to cover include:

• Who is looked up to for advice/opinion formation?
• What is their power base and its extent (it may be formal or informal)?
• What views do they hold strongly?
• Who is the neighbourhood 'gossip' and why?
• Who is the neighbourhood 'scapegoat' and why?
• What voluntary organisations are there, for example, churches, charities?
• What specialist groups are there, for example, groups for elders, single parents, disabled people and unemployed people?
- Who runs these groups?
- What resources do they have?
- What activities do they support?
- Who are their supporters?
- What views or opinions do they endorse?
- How easy is it for new members to join?
- How can you gain their support for your group's activities?
• Are there any informal 'helping' networks, for example, helping the old, the sick?
- Are these individual or group networks?
- Who does the helping?
- Who runs the groups?
- Which groups of residents do they help?
- How do they help these groups?
- Where do the helpers and the people they help live?
- What occupations do they follow?

- What are their demographic characteristics, for example, age, gender, ethnicity?
- What, if any, formal structures are there in these networks?

Organising tips

Information collection

Collecting information about communities is necessary for community activists to:

- become accepted as organisers;
- understand a community;
- become involved in organising that community; and
- engage in action in that community.

Information may be collected in a variety of ways. Some of these include:

Impressionistic enquiry: this is most useful for community activists wanting an easily and quickly obtained impression of the community. It is the cheapest method of information collection and draws on women's capacities to network and connect with others. The method is largely informal and relies on activists talking to, listening to and watching community residents, groups or organisations with which they interact. At this point, community activists are 'sussing out' the community, getting to know it and trying to establish a relationship of trust with its members. The community is simultaneously becoming informed about them. The main drawbacks in this method are:

- the community worker's dependence on items people will reveal to an 'outsider'; and
- the community activist's skills and powers of observation introducing bias by ignoring important subtleties in data collected.

The 'impressions' obtained may be fragmented and lack a coherent structure for recognising significant processes operating in a situation. The interaction between community activists and the community can become one-dimensional. A key advantage of an impressionistic enquiry is that a 'picture' of the community can be developed in a relatively short time. It is a cheap method to finance, few resource commitments are necessary and it relies on community activists utilising their intuitive capacities, exercising judgement judiciously and forming relationships with community residents. It is, however, time consuming.

Opinion surveys: questionnaires or interviews are useful in ascertaining people's views and opinions on issues. Feminists have varied traditional approaches to these by including women and intensively exploring issues with small in-depth interviews. A main weakness of small-scale research stems from its lack of generalisability. In these, a researcher uses her experience as a woman to develop rapport with women interviewees (Stanley and Wise, 1983, 1997) and yield insights not accessed by traditional approaches. The women being interviewed are involved in controlling how to use the results of the research to promote women's interests (Kelly, 1988), equalise power relations and inclusivity in research (Dominelli, 2005).

Feminists may use traditional survey methods, but omit their most sexist elements by introducing gender as an explicit variable (Eichler, 1988). Sensitivity to gender issues and an awareness of the different ways in which gender affects men and women make feminist approaches to research in the community valid for both men and women. Feminists do not administer opinion surveys in a vacuum, but as part of a contextualised programme of action aimed at improving the quality of women's lives. Surveys may reflect people's attitudes at the time of the study, but these may undergo change as other variables in the situation alter. The basis on which the survey sample is selected introduces its own limitations. Yet opinion surveys enable community activists to test reactions to proposed programmes. They act as a means of obtaining suggestions for programmes of action before plans are fully formulated and implemented. In developing community profiles, community activists need research skills that enable them to use available resources sensitively for collecting information on who interacts with whom, in which locations and for what purposes.

Local sources of information: these are varied and numerous, but include the following:

- *Local libraries* are useful in providing histories of an area. Information on the role of local firms and politicians in developing the local socioeconomic system can be found here. The material may exclude women's contribution and activists may need to rely on oral histories, particularly for working-class and black women. However, local libraries are closing, thus limiting women's access to information, especially if they work in the home and are unable to access other libraries through employment or education.

- *Local community groups* often have a lot of useful information on local personalities and community perceptions of them.
- *Local newspapers* reveal community interactions, not just in feature articles, but in the small items. These can indicate local networks of social contact. A systematic collection of this information enables community activists to construct patterns of interactions that can inform their activities.
- *Websites* can reveal much information about specific communities, the people, businesses and organisations within it. Computers and broadband may be costly and limit women's individual access to these, but some community groups and local Internet cafes may make these available to them.

Formal sources of information: these involve pursuing information that is often held formally in specific institutions and questions of access can arise. These include:

- *Census data.*
- *Town plans.*
- *Company reports, company papers and company officers* can provide details on company organisation, including subsidiary companies, investment policies, employment policies and decision-making mechanisms. Useful quotes may be gleaned while compiling information. Public relations officers at the local level and head office are other informative sources.
- *Companies House, the Registrar of Friendly Societies and the Charities Commission* can supply the minimal information that commercial enterprises and registered charities are legally required to divulge. Information obtained from their records must be treated carefully since it is incomplete. Omissions can be as important as revelations. Additional information on commercial enterprises, their nature and activities in which they are involved can be acquired from these other sources:
  - *Who Owns Whom*
  - *UK Compass*
  - *Register of British Industry and Commerce*
  - *Moodie Cards (Moodie's Company Service)*
  - *Kelly's Directory*
  - *Register of Business Names*
  - *Stock Exchange Register of Defunct Companies*

     – *Extel Book of New Issues (Stocks)*
     – *Company websites*

Community activists must be able to develop a coherent analysis of the community from the extensive, but often fragmented information collected. Feminist community workers use a feminist perspective in making sense of this data; other community workers rely on their political philosophies. The compilers' perspectives provide the spine that structures information into a rational narrative that is then used in campaigning around particular issues.

Use of information: producing a report based on the information gathered and not followed by action is of limited relevance to a community group. Information, especially material countering that provided by the media and official bureaucracy, can be critical in a community's struggle to fulfil perceived needs. In writing a pamphlet or report, community activists have to consider the audiences they will address. An expensively produced, highly abstract or technological (jargonistic) pamphlet will not motivate local community organisations to read it or involve themselves in action predicated on it. Publications must speak the readers' language and address their realities in concrete terms to become effective means of communicating and galvanising action.

    The tactical use of the information collected requires serious consideration. The type of community being addressed and group purpose will affect decisions about how it is used and handled. Some situations call for the slow release of data to get the other side to provide further details of its activities. Others demand immediate release of information collected. In any event, utilising information becomes a political act. Politically used information can become a threat to the status quo. Thus, community activists must ensure the accuracy of their 'facts' and be thoroughly aware of the communities they seek to influence. Otherwise, the whole weight of the legal apparatus, pertaining to libel and slander, may be brought to bear against their group, or they may find both they and their group lack credibility.

Conclusion

Feminists have challenged traditional community work's neglect of women and demanded that women's contributions to the well-being of their communities and the activities they carry out within them be made visible and valued. Women use their status and position in communities to act within them and build alliances with others to change their world. Campaigns that focus on women's strengths and commitments to collective action based on egalitarian social relations are crucial in achieving this goal. Using information and the relevant technologies politically becomes a crucial factor in these endeavours and its collection enables women to identify allies and resources for their struggles as well as recognise their opponents. Feminist gains in improving women's lives are vulnerable and traditional community activists can do more in safeguarding these by forming alliances with women to enhance the well-being of all. But this will require working with women on an egalitarian basis.

FIVE

Feminist campaigns and networks

Introduction

Feminist social action has drawn on collective forms of organisation, such as campaigns and networks, as primary vehicles for ameliorating the position of women. Crucial to this has been redefining social problems, reconfiguring them as public issues for society to address rather than being personal woes to be forgotten unless individuals solved them. Feminists have targeted public policies, legislation, policy makers and general public attitudes of indifference to get women's stories of private misery heard, demonstrate that these could be retold by women everywhere and demand social change. Feminist social activists did not wait for others to produce new provisions for them. Women with personal experiences of issues they sought to remedy embarked on actions that developed new services that were created by and run for women.

In this chapter I focus on examples of feminist social action as a form of community work that brought women and their supporters together in campaigns and networks of collaboration to change social attitudes about men's and women's roles in society, obtain women-friendly legislation and develop alternative provisions for women. I consider feminist campaigning to highlight techniques and forms of organising that women use to overcome isolation and secure change. Women's gains are vulnerable. Thus, understanding their origins and defending them from current attacks remain contemporary feminist concerns.

I examine feminist campaigns and networks in terms of the processes through which feminist community workers identify problems that need to be addressed, the ways in which women organise collectively and difficulties they have to resolve if they are successfully to involve women in collective action in the community. I scrutinise feminist campaigns around childcare, violence to women and children in the home, child sexual abuse, peace and environmental issues. I show that feminist community activists use 'the personal is political' as a central organising principle to redefine matters that society relegates to the private realm and beyond social intervention as issues that affect everyone. I reveal that women refocus the techniques and skills required for redefining problems in feminist directions by drawing on feminist principles. These include: probing feminist attempts to introduce non-hierarchical ways of working, developing support networks and using their experiences as women in relating to other women. And I reflect on concerns that women share regardless of their status in the labour market.

Feminist campaigns have introduced new features to community action. Foremost among these have been: recognising interdependence between people (Dominelli, 2002a); developing inclusion and solidarity among women; extending the subjects covered by community action; creating novel forms of community organisation (Adamson et al, 1988); and valuing women's knowledge (Belenky et al, 1997). Women involved in feminist campaigns provide evidence that women can organise effectively to improve conditions around specific issues such as prostitution or defend hard-earned gains, for example, reproductive rights. Through their actions, the myth of female passivity has received a hard knock.

Changing the world for women, men and children

Feminist campaigns and networks began as social action to tackle women's inequality in all areas of life. Feminist social activists had a vision of a better world that would materialise as a result of eliminating the oppression of a majority (not minority) of the population. Experience in the field revealed that this goal was more difficult to achieve than envisaged, and that it was not enough simply to change women and their position in society. It became increasingly clear that the roles and status of men and women had to change for egalitarian social relations to be realised. The interdependence of men, women and children required change in all their lives to ensure social justice and active citizenship for all. The links between people and the physical environment meant that the well-being of humans also required a healthy planet. And so the change effort today encompasses the entire world, even if it begins with women's issues.

Changing the world for women

Feminist campaigns and networks have been crucial vehicles of social action that create spaces for women and promote their human, political, economic and social rights. Furthering these objectives has yielded innovative forms of community work. Feminist campaigns and networks take women's gender-based oppression as their starting point, set about eradicating it by changing social relations in practice and make these the basis of feminist community work.

Important feminist campaigns that challenge existing configurations of social relations have included abortion issues through the National Abortion Campaign (NAC) (Greenwood and Young, 1976); reproductive rights through the Reproductive Rights Campaign (RRC) (Frankfort, 1972; Davis et al, 1988); decriminalising prostitution via the Programme for the Reform of the Law on Soliciting (PROS) (McLeod, 1982; Dominelli, 1986a); eliminating domestic violence and assaults on women in the home (SWAF, 1980; Binney et al, 1981; Wilson, 1983; Mullender, 1997; McClennen, 2005) with campaigns organised largely by the National Women's Aid Federation (NWAF); campaigning to acknowledge women's specific health needs and secure better health facilities for them (Ruzek, 1978, 1986; Doyal, 1983); campaigns for peace (Cook and Kirk, 1983; Dominelli, 1986c); and environmental campaigns (Mies and Shiva, 1993). Gains made in these areas cannot be assumed to last forever. For example, the reproductive rights of women in the US are currently being threatened by the appointment of conservative judges to its Supreme Court who might further undermine the provisions of *Rowe versus Wade*, a court decision that made abortion legal in the USA.

In mounting feminist campaigns and networks, women have had to redefine individual social problems as social issues. In doing so, feminists have placed at the top of the agenda for change the role of men in creating difficulties for women and children. For instance, the NWAF campaign against men's violence in intimate relationships has revealed that the acceptance of social attitudes that condone men's prerogative in disciplining women legitimates their violence, physical and emotional abuse in domestic settings. Furthermore, NWAF has revealed that women have been unable to leave violent partners not because they are mentally defective, as some theorists suggest, but because the necessary material conditions for leaving, for example, jobs, housing and money, have simply been unavailable (SWAF, 1980). Women's lack of access to resources continues to be a problem (Mullender, 1997).

Women Against Violence Against Women (WAVAW) mounted a more general attack on male violence. Arguing that the violence ranges from pornography to rape, WAVAW's position encouraged people to think about male aggression in a new light (Lederer, 1982; McNeil and Rhodes, 1985; MacKinnon, 1993). Some of WAVAW's initiatives were innovative, for example, one called for a male curfew when the Yorkshire Ripper stalked women on the streets of Leeds. Their Women Reclaim the Night demonstrations reinforced the message that women have the right to go about their business as they see fit. Their approach assumed women's experiences of gender oppression were unitary and by marching through black neighbourhoods ignored the impact of racism on these communities (Bishop, 1994). This fed into popular characterisations of black men as sexual predators and prompted black women to demand specific action to counter this (hooks, 1984; Bryan et al, 1985).

By participating in feminist campaigns and networks, women who had not previously engaged in public affairs acquired the confidence and skills needed to challenge hegemonic definitions of their realities and to confront powerful people. For instance, women in PROS ran publicity campaigns that debunked hardened police chiefs' definition of prostitution as a social evil by claiming it was a job with validity and social usefulness (McLeod, 1982). This definition is by no means accepted by all, but PROS has succeeded in providing an alternative view of prostitution and *redefining an allegedly personal problem as a social issue.*

Another important feature of feminist campaigns has been the commitment of women to raising public consciousness. This has involved women in forming alliances and achieving a broad base of support for their activities, calling on trade unions and professional organisations to endorse their demands (Bishop, 1994). Activating such support has required women to organise within these organisations over a period of time. Their local efforts ultimately coalesced in securing national trade union support for their struggles through the Trade Unions Congress (TUC), for example, the homeworkers' campaign (Hopkins, 1982), the RRC and campaigns for equal pay (Munro, 2001). Feminists have succeeded in getting male trade unionists, especially those in public sector unions where female membership is high, to acknowledge the impact of women's lack of control over their fertility on their employment prospects and its role in undermining equal opportunities and career prospects for women in the workplace (Kettle, 1998).

Women's interests have come to the fore, primarily because feminists have organised to ensure this happens. Feminist social action in promoting women's well-being has demonstrated that the welfare of children and men is badly served by current social arrangements. Thus, marital violence has been exposed as damaging the emotional existence of children, men and women. Feminists' work on this score has highlighted the urgency of challenging male stereotypes and providing men with the help and support networks necessary for them to break the confines of their oppressing and oppressive roles (Dominelli, 1982, 2002a). So, feminists redefined issues previously deemed private troubles as social ones and secured other forms of support, for example, state concern over the extreme overcrowding in British prisons has contributed towards the acceptability of PROS's decriminalisation campaign, and public anxieties about the welfare and rights of children has affected people's views on domestic violence.

Feminist campaigns seeking social justice for women carry implications for all those abhorring injustice, wherever it occurs. The moral case for these campaigns has provided opportunities for feminists to obtain further resources for their campaigns and has been a decisive factor in securing support and sympathy from individuals and organisations not predominantly feminist in their orientation. These supporters are part of a campaign's broader network that covers feminist and non-feminist groups.

The broad-ranging nature of these support networks enhances the possibility that the social change engendered by campaigns encompass more than women's concerns. But expanding their support networks has also held back feminists' challenges, and instead of transforming social relations, their campaigns have resulted in piecemeal reforms that leave the status quo intact. For example, American feminists have discovered that changing legislation regarding abortion began working against the interests of women when doctors found that enormous profits could be made from providing these abortions (Frankfort, 1972). Abortion clinics have turned abortion into a commodity and initiated a process of medical treatment that has left women feeling powerless and exploited (Worcester and Whatley, 1988; Friedlin, 2002). Yet those opposed to women's reproductive rights have launched vociferous and, at times, violent attacks on these gains and succeeded in introducing counter-legislation.

By privatising public provisions, the private sector is given opportunities for making profits. In the UK, trade in public services has been estimated to net private sector providers with £30 billion per year. Health and education services that represent 13% of Gross Domestic Product (GDP) in the UK make ripe pickings for private entrepreneurs. Moreover, the state, in privatising public assets through its connections to private business, underplays women's role in creating their own realities as control goes over to men (Sale, 2005).

Some feminist changes, such as social services departments, residential homes and probation services, have permeated hierarchical institutions to challenge organisational structures and practice (McLeod, 1982). NWAF's work on domestic violence has exposed social services departments' relative neglect and lack of understanding of the needs of women recovering from domestic violence and compelled them to provide resources for abused women, including refuges. NWAF's stance on women's self-determination and democratic decision making for those living in refuges has promoted the adoption of these practices in local authority refuges. These practices contrast with the authoritarian manner formerly used in these facilities. NWAF refuges reveal that women stigmatised as clients can organise their own lives if given the opportunity and necessary resources (Binney et al, 1981), an issue that the government has incorporated into recent guidelines on supporting women in domestic violence situations (Home Office, 2004).

Community workers, social workers and probation officers who became involved in feminist campaigns have developed internal support groups and networks among colleagues and sympathetic managerial staff within their employing authorities. Such support has been essential, not only for furthering campaign objectives, but to ease the sense of isolation and despair workers have felt when facing organisational intransigence and resistance to demands for change (McLeod, 1982). Allies can also be crucial in providing personal support for professional workers (Bishop, 1994).

Characteristics of feminist campaigns and networks

Feminist campaigns and networks have featured significantly in the feminist political landscape and played a key role in establishing feminist community work. As major forms of feminist collective organisation, feminist campaigns and networks are fluid entities structured around a group or groups of women working to change a particular aspect of their reality as part of the process of eradicating sexist oppression. Feminist campaigns are normally issue-based forms of direct action including demonstrations and mass movements. They may be small localised affairs in which a group of women offer each other support and seek specific resources for their cause such as the Southwark Asian Women's Aid (Malek, 1985), or national or international endeavours such as the Women's Peace Movement (Cook and Kirk, 1983). Feminist networks can also be ad hoc support groups that enable women to connect with each other. At times, the distinction between a campaign and a network may be blurred, for example, NWAF is a campaigning organisation that has a national network of refuges women can draw on. Feminist campaigns and networks form part of the process of feminist activity that transforms social relations. The campaigns and networks begin with a redefinition of social problems (Dominelli and McLeod, 1989).

Redefining social problems

A key understanding of the feminist movement is that relationships between individuals are imbued with power relations rooted in the ideology of female subordination and male supremacy. This has given rise to the often quoted phrase, 'the personal is political', as shorthand, standing for the sexual politics that pervade every aspect of women's lives, from the most intimate to the most distant (Millet, 1969). Sexual politics are about power, the socially legitimised power of men to control women and the unacknowledged power of women to resist that control and to assert their right to live according to egalitarian principles that do not presuppose the subjugation of others. Feminists have reached this awareness collectively by examining their individual experiences as women and comparing these with other women in similar situations. Such insights initially arose in fairly loose, unstructured meetings between women who came together to make sense of their position. Gatherings of this nature were to become more widespread and to address women's issues more systematically. These get-togethers have provided the basis of consciousness-raising groups that have featured strongly in feminist organisational repertoires (Dreifus, 1973). These groups are currently used by third wave feminists to theorise from their experiences and to validate diversity and difference as the basis for feminist action, even if this occurs at the individual level (Siegal, 1997).

   Redefining social problems from a feminist perspective is crucial to challenging prevailing definitions of issues and developing feminist consciousness. It is also a preliminary step in the formation of feminist campaigns and networks. Redefining social problems from a feminist perspective demystifies social relations and reveals the extent to which these subordinate women in the public arena and work to their detriment. Some of the earliest feminist campaigns and networks have been developed by radical feminists tackling male violence, particularly men's physical violence against and rape of women in the home. This has entailed redefining the issue from a personal problem between individual men and women, to a social matter involving all men and women, because such assaults are sanctioned by configuring women in subordinate positions (Brownmiller, 1976).

   Since then, other forms of male violence, such as pornography, rape in marriage, environmental degradation and global nuclear threat, have been addressed. Feminist analyses have demonstrated how the pattern of male violence, which begins with men showing contempt for women by calling them derogatory names such as 'bitch', 'broad' and 'whore', and denying their human rights and dignity, ends in a deep-seated hatred of women, legitimising rape or murder. This was exemplified on 6 December 1989 when a man walked into the University of Montreal, Canada, and committed femicide. The man gunned down 14 female engineering students, who represented the feminists he hated, because they had dared to enter a man's world by becoming engineers. He was making the point that the place of women in the community was not in the public world of waged work but in the privacy of the home, ministering to men's needs. It is precisely these definitions of the position and role of women in society that feminists challenge.

In redefining society's understanding of male violence against women, feminists have focused on the social construction of masculinity and femininity rather than biological attributes (Brownmiller, 1976; Lederer, 1982; Gordon, 1988; Babacan and Gopalkrishnan, 2001) and highlighted the significance of the following elements:

- *gender:* men violate women's rights to a safe environment through assault;
- *gender-neutral language:* using gender-neutral language masks gender power relations, obscuring the fact that men are the attackers and women their victims;
- *power:* men's sexual attacks on women are about power, not sex, nor men's biological urges;
- *control:* in sanctioning men's right to control women, society legitimates men's use of violence against and abuse of women;
- *normality:* men who attack women are 'normal' men, not psychopaths;
- *misogyny:* personal sexism is rooted in an individual man's hatred of and contempt for women;
- *institutional sexism:* society's treatment of women victims of men's physical and sexual aggression reinforces the abuse of women. The police, judiciary, courts and public contribute by holding women responsible for these attacks;
- *subordination of women:* women's subordinate social position endorses men's belief in their right to force women to comply with their wishes;

- *women's strength:* women's strengths facilitate survival during harrowing ordeals and moving from victim to survivor. Thriving is next on the agenda; and
- *women's voice:* feminist theory and practice is based on women's own accounts of their experiences, thereby giving women a voice rather than conceding expertise on their condition to professionals.

Unearthing the dynamics of male violence, bringing these into public consciousness and strengthening the capacities of women who have been attacked to survive, form the basis of feminist campaigns and networks on these issues. This began when American feminists in the anti-rape movement organised a Rape Speak-Out in New York in 1971. These events provided women with a forum that broke the isolation and fear that had prevented them from placing their ordeals in the public arena, and began the process of educating Americans to the realities of rape (Davis, 1989). Feminists in Berkeley, California, set up a community-based 24-hour crisis line known as the Bay Area Women Against Rape that same year. This became the crisis centre that has since formed the model for rape crisis centres feminists created later in the rest of America and other countries (Davis, 1989). These centres support women struggling to transcend the pain and disability engendered by assaults on their person and for those women feeling able to do so, to report these crimes and proceed with court cases (MacKinnon, 1993). Moving from victim to survivor to thriver requires such support.

Since those days, feminists have uncovered the extent of sexual assaults against female children, within the alleged sanctity of the family, and the institutional abuse caused by the professionals responsible for them (Hooper, 1992). They have developed networks of Incest Survivor Groups to support the healing processes (Dominelli, 1989; Armstrong, 1988; Kelly, 1988). Feminist social action on sexual violence has also revealed that young boys are physically and sexually abused by adult men (Russell, 1984). They have highlighted the problematic nature of the dominant ideology of masculinity (McLeod, 1982; Dominelli, 1989, 2002a) and the pressures society places on men to conform to the unfeeling, aggressive, macho stereotypical man (see Festau, 1975; Tolson, 1977; Bowl, 1985; Hearn, 1987; Pringle, 1995). Anti-sexist men have taken up issues raised by feminists (see Hearn, 1987; Connell, 1995). Feminists have begun the process of eliminating sexist oppression by focusing on women, but their work has exposed the stunted emotional development of children and men and promoted action aimed at ensuring their well-being. Eliminating sexism will enhance the quality of life for children, women and men (Dominelli and McLeod, 1989; Dominelli, 2002a).

There are dangers in redefining social problems without taking account of other social divisions. If feminists do not successfully avoid these hazards, they reinforce other forms of oppression and undermine their struggle to eradicate gender inequality, for example, ignoring the interconnectedness of racism and sexism in sexual violence debates has meant that white radical feminists in the UK and America inadvertently confirmed racist views of black men as the main assailants (hooks, 1984; Bryan et al, 1985; Davis, 1989). Black feminists have pointed out that without including racism in their analyses, white feminists' actions on rape fed racist myths of black men's criminality and sexual appetites and disregarded facts. Most rapes are committed by white men who are more likely to rape black women than black men raping white women (Davis, 1989). White feminists are beginning to respond to their critiques and becoming more sensitive to the interaction between racism and sexism (Barrett and McIntosh, 1985; Bhavani, 1993). Black feminists' demands have furthered the development of white feminist principles, for example, listening to other women's accounts of their experiences and using these to develop less oppressive forms of social action. Reflexivity in handling criticism has enabled feminists to engage in the processes of adapting to new insights and understandings, thereby giving feminism an open and unfinished character (Dominelli, 2002a).

Consciousness-raising groups

Consciousness-raising groups are another tool feminists use when working with women. These have enabled women to come together as women, to talk about their lives and organise to change them. Women have drawn on personal experiences to understand gender oppression as it impacts on them and other women and to uncover its social causation (Morgan, 1970). In the early days of the women's liberation movement, white middle-class women in consciousness-raising groups analysed their own experiences and concluded that women's oppression featured universally in women's lives (Friedan, 1963). These insights have been extended to encompass older women as activists themselves aged (see Friedan, 1993; Greer, 1993).

At first, other social divisions through which oppression occurs were neglected as feminists subsumed the experience of all women under their own (see Freidan, 1963). Lesbian, working-class and black women have rejected these analyses (see Davis, 1981; Carby, 1982; Amos and

Parmar, 1984; hooks, 1984; Lorde, 1984) and highlighted differences arising from women's sexual orientation, class, 'race', age and physical and mental impairment (Wilson, 1993). These highlight women's experience of oppression as complex and varied (Wilson, 1996). Postmodern feminists have taken this further to emphasise the uniqueness of experience and to question the relevance of the category 'woman' (Nicholson, 1990; Collins, 1991). From these insights, it follows that sisterhood is something that has to be worked for rather than assumed. Nonetheless, women's experience of oppression as women has been crucial in redefining social problems in ways that expose the gendered impact of social relations (Morgan, 1970) and its social construction (Dominelli, 2002a).

Feminists have brought women together in groups to discuss issues and to raise consciousness about them. By sharing personal experiences, women have identified common problems (Dreifus, 1973). Seeing that they were experiencing similar problems in somewhat different circumstances enabled women to challenge the view that they had precipitated problems by their (in)action and inadequacies and to realise that their predicament had social bases. Continuing discussions to understand their situations and to develop strategies for changing them gave these groups a crucial role in fostering women's confidence and self-esteem (Curno et al, 1982). These have in turn empowered women to speak out publicly with their stories and experiences, to challenge accepted definitions of their problems and stereotypes about the passivity of women in the process (SWAT, 1982), and to take action to remedy their position themselves (Walker and Hennessy, 2004). Care must be taken not to exaggerate commonalities that have been identified in these sessions. In the process, women asked the crucial questions listed below.

Organising tips

Problem (re)definition

1. Who defines the problem?
2. For whom is it a problem?
3. What is the problem?
4. How can we address the problem?

Collective organisation

Feminist community workers have drawn on women's individual experience of oppression to identify issues that needed to be addressed through collective action. By bringing women together in groups, feminist community workers have worked with women to highlight the structural dimensions of oppression, to redefine social problems and to undermine the individualising and pathologising approaches to women's issues that prevailed in traditional community work practice. Crucial to their challenge has been undoing the division of social problems into private matters requiring individual or family solutions and public ones in which a range of formal agencies, the state and public intervene. A focus on the structural nature of women's oppression reveals the socially transformative potential of feminist social action. Actualising it requires collective action and widespread support for feminist goals. This gives feminist community activists the enormous task of raising consciousness among the broader public including non-feminist women and men.

Organising collectively has given women the courage to validate personal knowledge, to speak out and to get their voices heard and suffering known. Violence to women in the home exemplifies a key phenomenon that was treated as a private matter until feminist campaigns of the early 1970s revealed that the definition of domestic violence as a private issue legitimised its continued occurrence, blamed women who were caught within its web and left women who wished to escape it without access to the resources necessary for this to happen (SWAF, 1980). Feminist campaigns have made domestic violence a social issue and established a network of refuges that support women leaving violent partners. Feminist analyses of domestic violence have revealed how social definitions of masculinity and femininity presuppose women's subordinate position and underwrite the acceptability of men using force to control women. This makes every member of society responsible both for the perpetuation of domestic violence and its elimination. The approach has borne fruit in social policies that endorse the view that domestic violence is a crime of assault (Mullender, 1997), but gains in eliminating it have been few. Feminist insights have also been used to develop resources for men engaging in nurturing relationships (Pringle, 1995).

Childcare has been another arena in which feminists have undermined the view that it is a private task to be undertaken by women in the home. I am not saying, however, that feminists are demanding that the state becomes an instrument for the surveillance of family life, but that society acknowledges children as a social responsibility and grants them rights of their own rather than seeing them as puppets parents dangle on a string. Social resources should provide unstigmatised and stimulating childcare for *all* children, and childcare should cease being the sole responsibility of women (David and New, 1985). Although unsuccessful in securing publicly funded child-centred childcare for all children in the UK, the National Childcare Campaign (NCC) has enabled women to make connections between their low status in the home and low pay in the workforce (NCC, 1984, 1985). Employers still assume that women will work for short periods before leaving the workforce to start a family and deny them access to update skills, train or do more prestigious work (Aldred, 1981; Armstrong and Connelly, 1997; GMLPU, 2004). New Labour has, without success, recently promoted a National Childcare Strategy to provide places for poor children so that mothers can assume their position in the workforce (David, 1999). And even in 2004, when women constitute 45% of the workforce and 55% of women with children under five hold waged employment, women can still face dismissal for being pregnant (Frean, 2004; Hinsliff, 2004).

Identifying which problems feminists should address

The issues women seek to address in transforming private woes into social concerns are related to their experience of gender oppression. There are no areas of life, private or public, outside feminists' remit. So far, feminists have tackled issues ranging from physical and sexual assaults against women in the home to the militarisation of the world (Davis, 1989) and its environmental degradation (Mies and Shiva, 1993; Shiva, 2003). The specificity of gender oppression suggests that the types of issues that are taken on board will depend on the context and women involved. Some problems have now acquired a global dimension and foreshadow an internationalisation of gender oppression that can hinder women's progress in divesting themselves of it, for example, trafficking women has exacerbated the sexual exploitation of women and children (Moosa-Mitha, 2003). Eliminating this form of exploitation requires links among women with different origins, resources and expectations as well as between women and the 'law and order' professionals, on a global basis.

Feminists have shown that women actively create history. Women are neither robots dancing to men's tunes nor passive victims in a historic process. Feminists have described the impact of material circumstances on women's oppression and its contribution in preventing their becoming free of it, for example, women remain with violent men because they realise that without adequate housing and an income of their own, they are vulnerable outside the relationship. In redefining social problems, feminists have revealed women's resistance to oppression in countless ways. Some is public, some private, some effective, some ineffective. Even within violent relationships, women actively take steps to minimise the violence perpetrated against them. Not annoying a partner or overtly challenging his views are parts of a strategy to secure their safety. Similar difficulties are encountered by women experiencing same-gender violence. But there are also differences between these groups of women. These include lesbian women's fear of being 'outed', disbelief by outsiders and shame and stigma associated with being assaulted by another woman (McClennen, 2005).

The women's movement has consisted of diverse initiatives ranging from a woman writing from her own experience through to a couple of women getting together to talk about their lives and larger groups organising mass campaigns around community issues. This provides feminism with a rich variety of organisational forms, while increasing its fragmented appearance. Fragmentation may be a weakness in certain situations like organising women nationally and internationally (Wilson and Weir, 1986). But locally it is a strength that helps women to create spaces for pursuing their interests in appropriate ways (Segal, 1987; Collins, 1991).

Eschewing dogma is a central tenet of feminist theory and action. Women developing forms of organisation best suited to their purposes facilitate adherence to this principle in practice. Issues raised by the Working Women's Charter (Wilson and Weir, 1986; Segal, 1987) readily attracted support from a cross-section of women while others have required more sustained action before becoming popularly recognised, for example, women's right to publicly express sexual attraction for other women (Hunt, 1990). Some concerns have initially been addressed by a small group of women who have relied on other women to join their efforts and subsequently achieve widespread support. This has occurred for feminist social workers who had to overcome societal denial of child sexual abuse while tackling it (see Bass and Davis, 1988; Bell, 1988).

The feminist movement has been castigated for presenting as the property of white middle-class feminists (hooks, 1984; Bryan et al, 1985). An examination of struggles women have undertaken in the community reveals that feminist activities have encompassed a variety of women – working class, middle class, black, white, older, disabled and lesbian. Each of these groups has highlighted and devoted its energies to different issues. One group's definition of and approach to a problem could estrange others (see Wilson, 1993). White feminists' call for 'abortion on demand' alienated black women who pointed out that their problem was that abortions and sterilisations were being forced on them (hooks, 1984; Bryan et al, 1985). This led to a more acceptable redefinition of the problem as a woman's right to control her own fertility in the manner most appropriate for her and campaigns against sterilisation abuse (Sidel, 1986). The propensity of feminist action tackling one problem to uncover others portrays reflexivity in the feminist movement (Dominelli and McLeod, 1989).

Feminists have to beware of minimising or ignoring the struggles of women lacking access to the media and publishers (Hunt, 1990). Appreciating this pitfall is vital if working-class and black women's struggles for a better life are not to be devalued and made invisible. In an era of mass communications women keyed into communication networks can define the terrain of the women's movement simply because in the eyes of the media their concerns make better copy. Women without access to such resources also struggle to improve their conditions. Their efforts may be unsung, but they exist nonetheless and can be uncovered at the local level of communities.

Examples of this are working-class and black feminist struggles to survive, to secure decent housing, childcare provisions and equality at work and to rescind racist immigration policies and practices. These issues continue to engage black women activists. Working-class and black feminists use workplace-based organisations such as trade unions to gain rights in waged employment, while simultaneously challenging their racist and sexist nature. During these struggles, they have made connections between their positions in the workforce and community. Historically, black women seeking employment equality at Mansfield Hosiery and Grunwick, and more recently at Gateway Gourmet, have drawn heavily on community support networks nurtured over the years to sustain them in protracted battles with recalcitrant employers. In the strike at Mansfield Hosiery, the trade union concerned was a major obstacle to black women achieving equality in waged work (CIR, 1973). At Grunwick, the trade union movement adopted a more enlightened position, but failed to support women by endorsing anti-sexist and anti-racist practices (Rogaly, 1977). Women workers at Grunwick used community pressure to shift the trade union movement from sexist and racist positions that excluded them from becoming full members of it because they were Asian women, and to convince their families of their 'right to join the picket line' (Lane, 2005). While the Gateway Gourmet dispute disrupted British Airways flights in 2005, the Transport and General Workers Union recognised racialised social relations and supported Asian women in ethnically sensitive ways (SchNEWS, 2005).

Women getting in touch with other women by organising

Forming networks is a crucial ingredient in facilitating the processes whereby women make contact with and secure support from other women. Gilchrist (2000, p 271) defines networking as a skilled 'process by which relationships and contacts between people or organisations are established, nurtured and utilised for mutual benefit' and as central in 'reducing uncertainty'. Networking enables women to stay connected and may be formal or informal. If informal, it may simply involve women asking other women they know to join them in examining and making sense of an issue (Curno et al, 1982). These women then ask other women to come along and a loose group or network is formed. This approach adds a personal dimension to networking, making women feel more comfortable when discussing issues than if facing a group of strangers. Establishing a trusting and relaxed atmosphere is crucial for women to feel free to be frank in sharing their experiences and forming or extending social capital.

More formal approaches include women putting up notices of meetings in places frequented by women, for example, local shops, laundrettes, doctors' surgeries and washrooms. Women may print leaflets calling other women to join their group in a specific activity. Or they may use community newspapers to run feature articles on their work and invite women to join them. Their oppression as women links group members together and enables them to empathise with the plight of other women when they may not have undergone that particular experience of it (Dreifus, 1973). Empathising may fall short of truly understanding a given instance of oppression and feminists desist from speaking on behalf of other women. The World Wide Web constitutes a forum through which women can reach one another and secure support for their issues, even among people they do not know and may never meet. The World March of Women uses the web published in three languages to create solidarity among women worldwide and to demand changes in the position of women globally (see www.marchemondiale.org).

Women's participation in these activities is often squeezed between their domestic commitments and waged work. Women can run considerable risks to participate in feminist campaigns. Many women have to surmount considerable hostility from male partners who resent their taking an interest in feminist activities, and may require support in handling conflict within intimate relationships (SWAT, 1982; Finn, 2001; Hoong Sin, 2002). The following account explains the fears of a woman involved in occupying Afan Council Offices:

> Ceri started to cry. She said she didn't want to go home but she'd got to. She hadn't told her husband she was going to the sit-in. She'd just told him she was going to a meeting. She said that she hadn't dared tell him she was going to stay out all night (let alone three nights!) because he would have stopped her going. Now, she thought, he's bound to beat her up. (SWAT, 1982, p 25)

Ceri's husband surprises her by admiring her stance because she had appeared on TV. The episode forced this women's group to reappraise its work, tactics and achievements and to consider the link between personal relations and political activism. It also highlights the importance of integrating theory and practice and learning from personal experience. Being fearful of having a hard time as a consequence of taking action may arise when employers resent women who tackle inequalities and sexist practices in the workplace. Women's role in public space continues to be contested, as traditional practices, some affirmed by religious and cultural beliefs, become challenged through women's actions (Hoong Sin, 2002; Lahiri-Dutt and Samanta, 2002; Williams, L., 2004) and men's expectations about them (Finn, 2001). In the process, women have subverted their images as wives and mothers and shifted them towards becoming iconic community builders (Finn, 2001).

Feminist groups take account of women's social roles in particular communities through the ways in which they intervene in them and the kinds of support they provide to facilitate women's involvement in collective action. Women's domestic responsibilities are catered for by providing childminding facilities and timing meetings appropriately. Making connections between the different spheres within which women operate is essential if more women are to be drawn into feminist campaigns and networks. Having services that ease women's participation in feminist activities is in keeping with the feminist principle that 'the personal is political'. Reducing power differentials between women and making it possible for more women to attend and contribute to a group's business are other important dimensions of this. This might mean sharing accessed resources differentially to cater for women's diverse social positions in achieving equality. Redefining power differentials between women responds to these concerns. Egalitarianism has to permeate all relationships within a group. Valuing women's personal knowledge is a crucial aspect of group interaction and feminists have to ensure that women's experiential knowledge is appreciated and celebrated alongside their professional expertise.

Feminists have tried to reduce the power that emanates from formal positions within groups by eliminating powerful roles through flatter decision-making structures or by sharing or rotating these so that all women gain the skills of the job and no one holds a post long enough to form a clique that bolsters individual power (TRCCC, 1982). Also, women share the power that is derived from expertise by sharing knowledge with each other. Reducing inegalitarian relationships within groups is not easy. In pursuing equality, feminists have to beware of the 'false equality trap' (Barker, 1986; Dominelli, 2002a). This perpetuates the *illusion* of equality but reproduces practices of inequality by assuming that all women have similar experiences of oppression, are at the same starting point, have access to the same resources and can participate in the same actions. In other words, the false equality trap normalises all women within the hegemonic feminine experience of white middle-class women (Dominelli, 2002a).

Despite brave attempts to counter hierarchical relationships, these can creep into feminist organisations. Working-class women have complained that processes organised by middle-class women favour more articulate women familiar with expressing themselves verbally (Finch, 1983; Davis, 1988). Middle-class women have access to resources that promote participation in group activities (Torkington, 1981). These are denied working-class women and can engender hierarchy by excluding women who cannot purchase them. Money creates a hierarchy that gives middle-class women a voice while denying working-class and black women theirs. An example of this is evident in feminist academic conferences that charge high fees and prevent women with low incomes from joining them.

Fees on a sliding scale do not solve this problem because poor women cannot afford these, travel, accommodation and subsistence costs. So their voices are marginalised if not totally excluded, for example, the Fourth International Congress on Women, scheduled at Hunter College in New York, charged between $US200 and $US275 in conference fees alone. High costs at the 1995 Beijing Conference on Women excluded poor women and privileged the attendance of better-off women from each country and so they were over-represented among delegates. Limited access to the new information technologies restricts poor women's capacity to engage in many of the online discussions on the ensuing Platform for Action (WEDO, 2005). On the local level, high transportation costs inhibit poor women from participating in feminist activities. Here, middle-class women have attempted to be more inclusive by subsidising working-class women's participation in groups by providing transportation and paying for telephone calls and stationery (Torkington, 1981). In sharing resources, women have drawn on their ingenuity, persistence and organisational skills to reinforce solidarity and 'sociability' in supporting others (Daniels, 1985).

Feminist campaigns and networks have featured strongly in the women's health movement. In this, women have shared medical knowledge to reduce the power hierarchy that is derived from doctors' control of medical information, which, if accessible to patients, would facilitate their taking a more active role in their treatment (Ruzek, 1978; Doyal, 1983; Foster, 1989). Many feminist innovations have now been incorporated into the National Health Service (NHS), for example, Well-Women Clinics and midwives in hospital. Feminist demands for preventative medical care have also been taken on board in part, for example, breast and cervical screening. Women have been crucial to extending demands for innovations that take account of new medical developments, for example, Karen Gibson, Barbara Clark and Elaine Barber have campaigned to have all women facing breast cancer access expensive drugs like Herceptin that the National Institute for Clinical Excellence (NICE) had limited to a few women on the basis of costs. Women have been arguing that a recently developed vaccine that could reduce 70% of cases of cervical cancer is made available to all young women. These endeavours also indicate the unfinished nature of feminist social action that has to constantly reinvent itself to take account of new developments, resources and knowledge and challenge health inequalities that have not disappeared with the passage of time. Feminist initiatives have been thwarted by multinational corporations seeking to maximise profit-making opportunities in the healthcare arena and the unwillingness of governments to spend even more public money on drugs.

Feminist groups have organised around social policies that affect women's everyday lives to demonstrate that 'the political is personal', for example, social security regulations such as the British 'cohabitation rule' and American 'man about the house rule' assume women's financial dependency on men (Land, 1976; Sidel, 1986). In the UK, Special

Claims Squads (SCS) forced single-parent women having any contact with men to become financially dependent on the men and intimidated women into dropping social security claims. They also prompted feminists to organise in defence of women. The Women's Right to Income Group challenged the activities of the SCS by redefining the problem as one of ensuring women's right to an independent income (Torkington, 1981). These activities reveal that while the personal is political, the political is also personal, and led to some changes in social security law, for example, the 1986 Social Security Act that allowed women to claim benefits for their family.

However, rather than eliminating women's financial dependency on men, the 1986 changes in British social security legislation shifted the problem to enforcing dependency within the family by aggregating men's and women's incomes and holding them responsible for each other and their children. The Child Support Agency replicates these assumptions today. These outcomes are also the result of the failure of the 'Disaggregation Now' Campaign to be accepted by government. In it, feminists argued for women's right to an independent income rather than their income being treated as part of the family's, especially as women have a smaller share of its resources than men. The state's response incorporated women's demands for change while ignoring their lesser access to so-called 'family' resources. The 1986 Social Security Act also removed the right of 16- to 18-year-olds to independently access social security by insisting that their families support them. This has created difficulties for young people who do not get along with their parents and have left the family home. It also discounts their poverty and lesser access to resources within families even when they live at home.

Campaigning aids, techniques and tips

In organising terms, feminists working with women in a community have sought to uphold principles of social justice, equality, women's control over their lives, interdependence and democratic decision making in their practice. These concerns have concentrated feminists' energies on sharing skills and knowledge with other women, acquiring and retaining control of their organisations, building women's confidence, reducing conflict between workers and users of facilities and developing strategies that seek consensual 'win-win' solutions to problems (Brandwein, 1987).

Besides redefining social problems, feminist campaigns and networks have brought centre stage the *processes* whereby issues are tackled and highlighted the relationships that community workers establish with community group members. I cover intragroup dynamics and consciousness-raising techniques in the following chapters by drawing on the principles, techniques and skills that feminists use in campaigning activities. These provide organising tips for social workers and community workers of both genders to use when adopting practices consistent with feminist organisational principles in reaching constituents.

Campaigning requires specific organisational skills to mobilise people and generate support for a cause, to gather the information necessary to identify an issue and present it to others, to procure the material and human resources needed to mount a campaign and to ensure that action remains under the direction of the campaigning group. Implementing these tasks effectively involves communicative, organisational, political and interpersonal know-how. Obtaining resources and support requires groups to consider the questions identified below.

Forming support groups and alliances to realise an agreed strategy

- What kind of support does the group need?
- What groups/individuals can it call on to provide this support?
- At what point does the group ask for external support?
- What compromises will the group make to obtain this support?
- How long does the group require this support?

Resources required in implementing an action plan

- What resources are required?
  - personnel
  - material including financial and organisational
- Where can these resources come from?
  - groups
  - supporters
  - public agencies
  - commercial bodies
  - others
- How much money is required to obtain these resources?
- For what period of time are these resources required?

Running facilities for women

- What kind of facility is needed?
- What are the aims of the facility?
  - What do community workers hope to achieve?
  - What do users want to achieve?
    confidence and self-esteem
    independence in women and the capacity to stand up for their rights
    services to meet the needs of diverse women, for example, black women, lesbian women, older women, disabled women, mentally ill women.
  - What does the group hope to achieve in its interaction with the public?
    use consciousness-raising, political education and animation techniques to change attitudes and behaviour towards women.
- Who will make decisions in the group and how?
  - distinguish between collective decisions and individual ones
  - develop ways of combating hierarchy and promoting equality
  - endorse democratic decision making and consensus building
  - adopt policies that do not discriminate against other women, for example, black women, lesbian women, older women, disabled women, mentally ill women.
- Keep records of the facility's activities, resources, funds and expenditures.
- What facilities will be available to women?
- Where will these facilities be located?
- Who will have access to the facility?
  - access by users, workers and those they invite
  - protection for users and workers (very important if the facility is a refuge). The issue of access (or not) by men also has to be considered
  - ensure that the facility is accessible to women with disabilities, that it meets fire, building, health, safety and other regulations
  - ensure that those using facilities relate to other users in anti-oppressive ways.
- Who will be the users of the facility?
  - how will they find out about the facility?
  - will they self-refer or be referred by others?
  - how will they be involved in running the facility?
- What skills sharing, formal advice services, professional services and educative functions will the facility offer users?

– What support services will the facility offer women?
consider childminding provisions, recreational services, meeting rooms, privacy within the facility.
– What training facilities, housing, employment and other services will women require that may have to be provided by others outside the facility?
Who will provide these?
How will they be accessed?
Who will pay for them?

• How will the facility be funded, repaired and maintained?
• What attitudes and policies will the facility adopt towards male visitors?
– for example, excluding violent partners from refuges may be necessary to protect women from further assaults, but it may conflict with women's wish to develop future relationships with them, or enable their children to do so.
• What relationships will the facility develop with other agencies in the voluntary, state and commercial sectors?
• What supports does the group expect from the public?
– target the groups it intends to reach
– identify women and men sympathetic to the cause
– consider political organisations and parties, especially women's sections, women's groups, feminist and non-feminist community groups, labour organisations, environmental groups, women sharing the experiences of the group setting up the facility and other groups.
• Ensure that relationships with supporters do not endanger egalitarian group processes and dynamics in a facility by ceding control of the action to them.
• Methods of reaching the public include leafleting, commercial, newspapers, public meetings, established media coverage (television, radio), articles, lectures, the Internet, demonstrations, lobbying, squatting and occupations.
• Maintaining group morale.

Public meetings

Public meetings continue to be important in the community activists' repertoire for explaining actions to the public and involving it in their activities, particularly if it is unaware of a group's existence. These gatherings can promote community participation initiatives by conveying information, mobilising support for a proposed plan of action, facilitating the acquisition of information not known to organisers and forming an umbrella organisation that organises action around particular issues.

Public meetings can be important vehicles for communicating to mass audiences but they can easily go awry. Careful thought on handling the meeting, preparing for it in advance and allocating tasks to different group members are essential in ensuring that:

- people are notified about the meeting;
- the meeting is well-organised and run; and
- the meeting achieves the group's aims and objectives.

Identifying a minute-taker helps obtain an accurate recording of the proceedings for use in future deliberations. If the subject under discussion is serious or controversial, create a relaxed but sober start to the meeting. After welcoming all those present, the chairperson should explain the purpose of the meeting and how they intend to run it. If the meeting is primarily a social occasion, ensure that it is an enjoyable one.

The chairperson for the meeting is a significant and powerful figure. The group should carefully consider who it wants in this position. They must be able to control the meeting and apply rules of order so that it runs smoothly, give people on any presentation panel the opportunity to present their messages to those attending and facilitate members of the audience in gaining the floor. This includes enabling those supporting and those opposing particular proposals to speak in an orderly fashion and to suggest alternative motions to those considered by the organisers, even if these are controversial. They also have to be prepared to deal with hecklers and others disrupting the proceedings. The group may wish to role-play such situations in advance to empower the chairperson in handling actual ones. The group may need to consider other ways of supporting the chairperson in controlling disruptive behaviour. The role should be rotated regularly to ensure that the skills in chairing meetings are acquired by others in the group and that no one person usurps the position and enhances personal power.

Speakers should be given specific guidance about what they should discuss and how long they may speak. Wherever possible, they should be given advance notice to prepare themselves fully for the task. Some women will be daunted by the prospect of speaking at a public meeting. The chairperson may have to help them deal with their nervousness. Group role-plays can assist in reducing it. Speakers may supplement their contributions by using films, videos, slides, computers or other aids to present messages more interestingly and effectively. Organisers should ensure that the equipment needed is in working order. Testing it beforehand is a good idea.

In planning the end of the meeting, designate a person responsible for summarising the main points of the meeting and make sure someone is allocated the task of placing suggestions and motions before participants. Calls for action, appeals for cash and details of future meetings should be made at this point. Recruiting new members can be an inordinately long process. Women will leave before the meeting finishes if they are bored or have other commitments to fulfil. Start on time and finish on time. If the group has previously decided it is appropriate to do so, the chairperson may invite those wishing to remain once the meeting ends to chat informally over refreshments. This can be a productive way of continuing discussions among those who are particularly committed to a cause.

Leaflets

Leaflets are useful vehicles for communication between an action group and the community because these are relatively cheap and easy to produce in a variety of formats. Leaflets can provide residents with the group's views on specific issues and give them up-to-date information on controversial matters. Since leaflets are intended to communicate with people, they should look well-produced and give a clear and concise message. The presentation and organisation of a leaflet should attract the reader's attention and hold it while the leaflet is being read. It should be interesting without either sensationalising issues or degrading women. The following points may act as minimal guides in the production of leaflets:

- *Be informative:* decide on the issue to be addressed, what the group wants to say about it and to whom it should be said. Leaflets should provide people with the following information:
  - What is happening?
  - Who is doing it?
  - Where is it happening?
  - Why is it happening?
  - When is it happening?

- *Get the 'facts' right:* accuracy in the information released is essential if the group is not to lose credibility.

- *Make the leaflet interesting:* the leaflet should attract readers through its presentation as well as by what it says on specific issues. It should use several techniques in its layout to provide variety. It should be easily recognisable as standing for the group. An attractive symbol, memorable abbreviation or catchy name can imprint its particular message in readers' minds. Headings can highlight key points or signal transitions between one message and others. Cartoons and pictures can present the group's message more graphically.

- *Producing the leaflet:* make a mock-up of the leaflet. This gives the group the opportunity to see how it looks and reads. It can also help spot errors before printing – commercial printing can be an expensive process. Choose a method that is appropriate to the group's budget. Offset litho may look very professional, but can the group handle the costs? If a computer is available, can it be published using that? Photocopying is cheaper, but equipment for good copy may be expensive. Investigate the different options available for printing before committing to a particular method. This is highly relevant in a context of desktop publishing and computerised technologies that make previously complex and expensive printing functions available to small groups that have access to computers and desktop publishing software (CWIT, 2005).

- *Distributing the leaflet:* distributing leaflets can be expensive unless done by volunteers. The group needs to decide who is to receive them and whether there will be a charge. Women's limited access to financial resources could be decisive here. Considerations will be affected by the audience, its relationship to the group and the group's resources. People distributing the leaflet should be familiar with its contents and be prepared to answer questions on its contents.

- *Have a contact person:* the leaflet should have the name, address and telephone number of someone who is available to answer questions about the group and its position on a given matter. In the UK, the name and address of the person(s) or organisation(s) printing and publishing the leaflet is a legal requirement.

- *Take heed of libel and copyright laws:* the laws against slandering individuals apply to leaflets as to any other medium of communication. Make sure that these are not infringed. Getting the facts about any issue correct is invaluable in keeping the group out of the courts and maintaining its credibility.

Community newspapers

Producing a community newspaper provides activists with the opportunity to use alternative methods of collecting, organising and disseminating information than those prevailing in the traditional commercial press nationally or locally. Feminists organise the production of community newspapers collectively. In these, editorial policy decisions about the newspaper's production, distribution and costs are made by an editorial collective working together on an egalitarian basis. Tasks are shared and individual women are encouraged to learn a range of skills. This form of operation contrasts with hierarchical structures under the authority of an editor guiding relationships among workers in the traditional press.

A feminist production embodies a different concept of news and what is newsworthy. Emphasis is placed on those affected by the event being involved in communicating it to others. An equally important feature is that those making the news also report and produce it in a form easily accessible to their audiences. The notion of dispassionate, neutral reporters presenting their case gives way to involved activist ones. The dissemination of information and what is considered newsworthy is neither constrained nor determined by the test of profitability. The question is what details women want to convey or require for taking action. Editorial collectives produce community newspapers noted for their consciousness–raising potential by providing controversial information and points of view not conveyed in traditional newspapers.

The high ideals of collectively produced, non–profit-oriented feminist community newspapers are difficult to realise. There are problems in sustaining continuity in an editorial collective over long periods of time, obtaining funds for launching the community newspaper and maintaining production in the long term, especially if the community newspaper is produced by unpaid, voluntary labour and distributed free. Despite these difficulties, there are successful ventures, including commercial ones, in the alternative feminist press that have consolidated their position and extended their operations for a considerable time, for example, Virago, the Women's Press, *Spare Rib* and *MS*. The first of these has been taken over by commercial publishers. *Spare Rib* folded in 1994, having disseminated feminist writings for many years. *MS*, *Affilia* and *Feminist Review* are being published with extended coverage, and new ones have been initiated to advance feminist scholarship, for example, *Gender and Social Policy*.

Points to consider in launching a community newspaper

- Who will be involved in producing the newspaper and what role will each participant play?
- How will the newspaper be produced?
  - Collectively or hierarchically under an editor?
- On what basis will the contents of the paper be decided?
- How often will the paper be printed?
- How will the paper be financed?
- Will there be a charge for the paper? If yes, how much (think of the implications of charging for accessibility for women on low incomes)?
- How will the newspaper be distributed? By whom (paid or unpaid workers)?
- How will women's involvement in producing the newspaper be maintained?
- Technical decisions:
  - What format will it have?
  - How will headings be used?
  - How will the front page be laid out?
  - What layout will be used?
  - What size of paper will be used?
  - How many pages will the newspaper have?
  - Will the paper contain photographs?
  - Will the paper use cartoons?
  - How will the paper be produced (offset litho, photocopying, desktop publishing)?
- How will tasks be allocated?
- What premises will be required to produce the paper?
- Provide the publishers'/printers' address on the newspaper.
- Beware:
  - libellous statements
  - inaccurate facts
  - copyright regulations.

Preparing videos/films/street theatre

Community groups are becoming more adventurous communicators as the price of equipment such as videos, digital cameras and computers drops, bringing new possibilities for getting messages across. These technologies can increase participation in a group's activities and empower people by utilising their experiential knowledge and giving expression to their voice. The production and distribution of materials have technical dimensions requiring specific training, but questions about what goes into them and who produces them will be similar to those encountered in producing leaflets and community newspapers (CWIT, 2005). Street theatre can be mounted with limited props and exploit dramatic effects to convey messages with power and force, giving powerful expression to communications by people unskilled in the written word. Videos and community art can empower previously marginalised groups and help people participate in regenerating their communities (Kay, 2000).

Handling the media

Handling the media effectively is critical for feminist community workers. Dealing with conventional media – television, newspapers, radio – demands that women community activists acquire important skills. These involve learning how to negotiate a path through the forest of distortion, sensationalism and ridicule facing those using traditional media to communicate radical viewpoints; to present their case accurately; and to deal with conflict and controversy. Feminists' desire to transform social relations makes feminism an anti-establishment philosophy unlikely to be treated sympathetically by the media. As third wave feminists argue, feminist perspectives can be trivialised or sensationalised to foster hostility to feminist causes.

Community groups have tried to deal with the dilemmas and contradictions posed by interactions with conventional media by developing alternative forms of dramatic communication, for example, street theatre, community video and alternative publications such as the now defunct *Spare Rib*. Vulnerable through lack of funding, these forms are important in their own right. The size of audience they reach compared to the mainstream media is small. The support systems and resources underwriting the messages that can be delivered efficiently through feminist ventures are also limited. Thus, community groups have to exploit both traditional and alternative media successfully.

Points to consider in dealing with the media

Handling the traditional media requires skill and considerable thought and preparation beforehand. Here are some useful tips for doing this:

- What is considered 'newsworthy'?
  - conflict

- hardship and danger to the community
- public scandal
- unusualness
- individualism.
- How does 'newsworthiness' affect the media's response to your cause?
  - Does it assist in conveying the group's message or hinder it?
- Press officer to handle publicity:
  - Rotate to enable all women to acquire the skills of the post.
  - Has the press officer been given clear guidelines on what to say about a particular campaign or action?
  - How does the group decide on its spokesperson for each occasion?
- Preparation (before interview/appearing on radio or television):
  - Collecting and verifying all the information needed.
  - Role-playing the interview with group members.
  - Is the timing of the interview suitable?
  - How will the group's or spokesperson's arrival at the interview be handled?
  - Make a note of the main points the group wishes to discuss.
  - Assess whether or not the reporter or interviewer will be sympathetic and how his/her hostility might be handled.
  - Ways of handling a reporter's hostility:
    refusing the interview (the group lose a chance to present its case);
    putting conditions on the interview and on how the information is going to be released (this keeps the initiative with the group);
    looking for other publicity (finding a sympathetic source).
- During the interview:
  - How do you maintain the initiative or control its direction?
  - Define which questions you are not prepared to answer and have your reasons for doing so available for presentation, for example, protecting a vulnerable person's identity; secrecy (relevant in protecting the group's action); accountability to your group (you are responsible to it for both your views and your behaviour); and bad taste (something being offensive or degrading).
  - Consider how information given might be used. Explain why you will not comment if this is so. Be positive in your approach and statements. Be professionally friendly when refusing to comment (this may be difficult).

- Beware of long questions that 'summarise' your position and require only a 'yes' or 'no' answer. These are likely to distort your group's case.
- Do not be pushed into giving answers to impromptu questions, particularly on the telephone, unless you are certain of the answer.
- Ask the reporter to call back later if necessary. Otherwise, you may reveal more information than your group intended you to give.
- Comments given 'off the record':
  - Such comments make reporters suspicious about what it is you are trying to hide, or may be taken out of context and misquoted, so avoid making them.
- If after giving an interview, you remember something else you want to say, go back to the reporter and tell him/her about it.
- Make a note of the main points of your conversation with the reporter afterwards. You may need it to check the article before/ when it appears.
- Follow-up after the interview:
  - Check what the reporter says about your case.
  - Ask for the right to reply if you feel your case is wrongly presented.
  - Check out the reactions of readers/supporters to the article(s), if possible.
- Do not go for publicity just for the sake of it. Use publicity to promote your case, not to detract from it.
- Ways of attracting publicity:
  - press release
  - letters to the editor
  - feature articles
  - taking action.

The press release

The press release is a springboard to publicity because it provides the group with an opportunity to present its arguments and views on a particular campaign or action as opposed to those items identified by the media. It is also easier for the group to control its contents. The press release is an important document and must be carefully prepared to attract interest in the group's cause. Once interest is secured, the group has further work to do with those responding positively if it wants further publicity. The group should ensure that contact details are contained within the press release for this to happen. Having a website with an email address can facilitate the exchange of views between the group and a broader audience (see www.-unix.umbc.edu).

Points to consider in preparing a press release:

- *Purpose:* what is the purpose of your press release?
  - background information
  - notice of event
  - report of meeting/event
  - details of interview
  - basis of interview.
- *Newsworthiness:* is what you have to say 'newsworthy'?
- *Style:* is your style suitable for the task?
  - use short, simple sentences
  - concentrate on the facts
  - use quotes from individuals involved in the campaign or work.
- *Essential information:* your information should cover the following questions:
  - What is happening?
  - Who is doing it?
  - Where is it happening?
  - When is it happening?
  - Why is it happening?
- *Length:* presentation and impact are affected by length:
  - try to stick to one sheet of paper
  - if possible, use headed paper; otherwise, have the name of your organisation on top of the page
  - give prominence to important aspects of what you are trying to say.
- *Release:* give the *date* of release clearly.
- *Embargo:* give the *date* that the story can be published if you wish the information to be held back until a particular date and time:
  - avoid having an embargo wherever possible; it is preferable for you to release the information later instead.
- *Headlines:* use headlines in presenting your information, but keep them short and simple.
- *First paragraph:* the first paragraph of your press release is crucial. It should:
  - attract the reader's attention
  - keep the reader's attention and interest in what the group is saying
  - set the tone of the release and be differentiated from following paragraphs.

- *Typing:* press releases should be typed wherever possible. It makes for easier reading and is more likely to be read.
- *End of the press release:* the end of the press release should be clearly marked 'ENDS'.
- *Contact person:* the name, address, telephone number and email address of the contact person should be provided at the end of the press release.
- *Photographs:* give details of whether or not photographs are available and if they can be used by the press.

The new information technologies

The new computer-assisted information technologies have opened new opportunities for women and community groups to network across time and space as geographical boundaries and time frames become irrelevant. Differential access to these carries the danger of reproducing existing inequalities among women and poor people, creating new generations of information-poor or marginalised people and exacerbating social exclusion (Babacan and Gopalkrishnan, 2001; Burrows et al, 2005; CWIT, 2005).

Creating a project website

The World Wide Web (WWW) has fostered a revolution in communication and enables people to communicate with each other rapidly and with few intermediaries. It is an invaluable site of information, ranging from informal anecdotal stories to sophisticated scientific journals. A website can be a popular way of communicating with people in informal, less controlled space. The possibility of forming chat rooms and discussion groups to convey one's own message without censorship is attractive, but there are dangers in creating and using such opportunities. Avoiding cyber-stalkers, remaining within lawful limits and communicating issues in an interesting manner apply to this domain as they do to more traditional communication venues. In creating a project website, computing expertise not within the group's capacity may have to be accessed (Scott, 2001; CWIT, 2005). Resources have to be found for it, but once acquired, all women in the group should learn computer skills so that over time they can engage in developing the website or creating a new one in future.

Points to bear in mind in creating a website:

- What do you want to communicate?
- Who is your audience?
- What facilities and information will you want on your website?
- How can you make your website user-friendly?
- How will your website be regularly updated and maintained?
  - Who will do this work?
  - How much will it cost?
  - How will you acquire the necessary resources?
- What guidelines will you have for users to follow so that they can be ethical about what goes on the website?
  - How will this be monitored and by whom?

Conclusion

Feminist campaigns and networks have been crucial in advancing women's concerns and in initiating social change. These have been diverse and have covered every aspect of women's lives – from reproductive rights to equality at work. Attention is also given to the processes whereby women organise and interact with other women. These activities should not essentialise women by treating all women the same. Women's experiences of oppression vary and so feminist campaigns and networks have to address this diversity among women to avoid oppressing other women in seeking to end their own oppression, even while organising collective action with them. At the same time, they have to find common goals and ties that will allow unity to be created among women. Communicating these objectives to others is a concern that feminist groups have to handle with sensitivity if they are not to perpetuate inegalitarian relations, especially those that are evident in reproducing 'false equality traps'.

SIX

Feminist action on the individual level

Introduction

One of the weaknesses of traditional community action has been its failure to deal adequately with *individual* need and to respond appropriately to particular personal conditions. Arguing that structural arrangements have a direct bearing on personal experiences, feminists have addressed this problem by linking the personal with the structural, and theorising individual predicament as a reflection of a specific constellation of social relations. In this chapter I consider feminist ways of working that tap into these dynamics such as consciousness raising, advocacy and counselling.

As individuals, women have a very personal experience of oppression, albeit one given meaning by engaging with social situations and structures. Feminists have developed theories for practice to reduce individual women's suffering and to eliminate collective hardship. Feminist therapy, counselling and work in feminist health collectives have been crucial in developing feminist responses to individual women while locating their emotional distress within structural constraints that impact on personal lives.

This chapter examines feminist action on the personal level. It focuses on the uses feminists have made of consciousness raising in individual work and small groups to highlight connections between the plight of individual women and their social subordination (Bayes and Howell, 1981; Bondi and Burman, 2001). Feminist therapy, counselling and feminist self-help health groups are major developments drawing on feminists' work with individuals in consciousness-raising groups. Besides building women's sense of confidence in challenging professions that are bastions of male privilege, these activities have provided women with community resources that they have created and control. These prefigure the egalitarian social relations that feminists strive to attain and offer concrete examples of how feminists connect an individual woman's position to the social forces within which her life is elaborated. This chapter provides guidelines for setting up feminist consciousness raising, self-help groups and advocacy groups.

Feminist approaches to the emotional well-being of women

Women's emotional well-being is a significant component of women's lives. Feminist work with individual women in counselling and therapy sessions responds to a woman's needs, especially the emotional problems she encounters. Interventions to repair emotional damage in women's existence engage women in making connections between their personal predicament and the social context within which they live. Working with women on the personal level has revealed the social origins of women's poor emotional lives, embedded as they are in adhering to feminine stereotypes (Baker Miller, 1976; Bayes and Howell, 1981; Chaplin, 1988; Atkinson and Hackett, 1995). Individual work has exposed the price that women pay in meeting community demands associated with adhering to the tenets of traditional femininity: pervasive feelings of powerlessness, psychological damage and emotional sacrifices (Bayes and Howell, 1981). Depression, frustrated hopes and ambitions, lack of worth, feelings of uselessness and drug misuse feature in women's responses to the circumscribed lives they lead (Rowe, 1983), and accept as natural and immutable.

Poverty, bad housing, unremitting childcare and arduous elder care take their toll on women's emotional welfare (Brown and Harris, 1978; Bayes and Howell, 1981), and are central in constructing women's experience of lack of emotional fulfilment and powerlessness (Bondi and Burman, 2001). The flashes of joy women experience in their relationships with children and others occur within a context of constant anxieties about their own and their children's physical and emotional well-being. Feminists have rejected analyses that pathologise women who respond to their situation with mental illness, drug misuse, alcohol misuse or excessive smoking, and point instead to the material and emotional deprivation that women manage daily. Offering women support in building a positive sense of self, highlighting connections between low self-esteem and the roles women adopt, gaining resources for women and examining the nature of women's relationships with women, children and men are important dimensions of feminist work at the individual level. Feminist approaches to emotional work have lessened the stigma attached to seeking therapeutic advice.

In therapeutic relationships fostered through feminist therapy, women are encouraged to examine the social causes of personal suffering and to consider how these might have contributed to their feelings of worthlessness and self-denigration. Women's explorations of their psychological development draw on experiences they share with other women and their feminist therapist (Bayes and Howell, 1981; Eichenbaum and Orbach, 1982; Lorde, 1984). Feminist therapists base their empathy on understanding women's situation and their own experiences of oppression as women. This lays the groundwork for relating to a woman in less remote, impersonal and hierarchical ways than is the case in traditional therapeutic relationships that rely on professional distance being maintained in client–worker relationships and that privilege expert knowledge despite its claimed client-centredness (see Rogers, 1961).

Feminists challenge prevailing definitions of professionalism and redefine it in more egalitarian directions by deprivileging expertise and valuing women's own views and understandings to reduce professional distance and to help women acquire expert knowledge. A feminist therapist listens to a woman's account of her position and works with her to make sense of its contradictory elements and overcome her dissatisfaction with her performance (Marchant and Wearing, 1986; Chaplin, 1988; McLeod, 1994). Feminist therapy enables women to grow in confidence and to make their own decisions.

The development of a helping relationship between the woman and therapist cannot be assumed. It needs to be worked at. There may be forms of oppression other than gender affecting the therapeutic relationship for feminist therapists to confront, for example, racism. White therapists need to examine very carefully the extent to which they can empathise with black women whose experience of sexism differs substantially from theirs. Black feminist therapists working with black women also have to work hard to overcome the abyss which racism and other social divisions that intersect and interact with 'race' place between them, for example, class and sexual orientation (Lorde, 1984).

Feminist therapy is not underpinned by notions imbued with the subordination of women as is therapy following Freudian understandings (Dominelli and McLeod, 1989). This enables women to develop a healthy respect and liking for other women and makes it easier for women to relate to other women without the competition, envy and jealousy characterising woman-to-woman relationships in society more generally. It can also lay the basis for women looking to other women for emotional fulfilment in both loving and working relationships. Thus, women begin to move away from dependency on men for validation of their existence and place in society and to replace it with a sense of independence and self-reliance which seeks support from others without feeling that the world is caving in if support or approval is denied.

According to Eichenbaum and Orbach (1982), feminist therapy enables women to feel worthy and deserving of attention and confirms their entitlement to receiving love, care and affection for themselves in the process. This contrasts sharply with traditional expectations of women as givers of love, care and affection. Fostering women's strengths and self-belief is a vital part of healing processes promoted by feminist therapists (Bass and Davis, 1988). Women who have worked through problems in feminist therapy have claimed that it reduces their sense of powerlessness (Ernst and Maquire, 1987; McLeod, 1987, 1994), and enables them to reject the victim role. Women have found that the work they do in feminist therapy sessions is directly relevant to their everyday lives. This makes it easier to incorporate lessons learnt and skills acquired into routine activities (McLeod, 1987, 1994; Heenan, 1988). In turn, this has made women feel more in control of their domestic and waged working lives.

While therapies founded on Freudian premises highlight the father–daughter or male–female relationship as the fundamental one in personality formation (Freud, 1977), feminist therapy focuses on developing women's understanding of their relationships with significant women (McLeod, 1987, 1994). The crucial one in this respect is the mother–daughter relationship which forms the centrepiece of object relations theory (Chodorow, 1978; Eichenbaum and Orbach, 1982; Ernst and Maquire, 1987; Hollway, 1989). This approach shifts professionals' understanding of women's condition and psychological development away from male supremacy and onto women's subjectivity, that is, capacity to act as subjects and to exercise agency.

Feminist therapy may have focused too exclusively on mother–daughter relationships in reacting against their neglect in Freudian psychology, and ignored crucial others in women's lives. Black women have experiences of important bonding taking place with a range of extended family members, including grandmothers and aunts, rather than developing exclusive relationships with mothers (Wilson, 1977b; Bryan et al, 1985). Prevailing object relations theories may only be valid for certain groups of white women who were raised in nuclear families in which mothers cared for children. Sensitivity to the impact of racism on black women's lives has made feminists question the universal applicability of analyses based on object relations theory. The Eichenbaum and Orbach (1982) approach to mother–daughter relationships also carries the danger of unwittingly contributing to blaming mothers for failing to socialise their daughters into leading independent lives.

Eichenbaum and Orbach's (1982) position leaves out crucial questions which a feminist analysis has to address if it is going to eliminate gender oppression. These include those linked to the nature of relationships between men and women. What kind of socialisation process is appropriate for the development of egalitarian relations between men and women, whether they are relating to them as intimate partners or colleagues at work? What role would men play in childrearing? That is, how do we, as feminists, challenge current definitions of fathering as primarily the biological act of impregnating women and the economic duty of providing for the material welfare of unwaged mothers and their children in order to redefine fatherhood and ensure it supports fathering relationships that nurture the emotional well-being of children, women and men according to egalitarian precepts (Dominelli, 2002a)?

Feminists also have to interrogate women's role in socialising male children in anti-sexist ways in mother–son relationships and waged work with children, be it in schools, social and community services, health services, the media or other public arena (Cannan and Warren, 1997). To what extent do women pass on sexist stereotypes to their sons, boy pupils or male clients because they have internalised the values and norms of a society celebrating male supremacy? How do men and women raise boys so that they work for rather than undermine women's liberation alongside their own? Asking these questions is not to blame women for being unable to operate outside the patriarchal contexts in which their lives are conducted. It is necessary to put forward these queries if we are to understand the complexity of the task feminists are undertaking to enable them to realise the non-oppressive social relations that will transcend patriarchy. It is also needed to prevent gains in one arena from being blocked by lack of progress in others intricately connected to it (Phillips, 1993).

These questions must be asked if feminist therapy is not to slip into supporting women and strengthening their self-esteem by disparaging the needs of children and men for emotional fulfilment. Tending to these concerns is crucial because children and men have spoken out against their own abuse and humiliation even when it has been perpetrated by other men. Kindlon et al (1999) have argued the importance of helping boys become 'emotionally literate' to assure movement away from destructive macho-type masculinity. Feminists have proposed nurturing masculinities, men's equal involvement in caring work and housework and power sharing in the public arena (Phillips, 1993; Dominelli, 1991, 2002a).

Similar points have been made in relation to undoing the emotional trauma of children sexually abused by adult carers (Bass and Davis, 1988). Complex healing processes are required by First Nations children and adults in Canada to repair the damage inflicted on their person, social structures and cultures by abusive experiences in residential schools (Fournier and Crey, 1998). The growing literature on the sexual abuse of children signifies the horrific subordination of their emotional well-being to that of men (Nelson, 1982; Ward, 1984; Dominelli, 1989; Armstrong, 1988). While girls are their major victims, boys are also sexually abused by adult men (Gartner, 1999). Women can only ignore men's exploitation of children at the expense of their commitment to egalitarian relationships among all members of society. Men's lack of social fulfilment is also coming to light as a result of feminist work that has encouraged men to challenge dominant notions of masculinity (Festau, 1975; Tolson, 1977; AHC, 1983; Bowl, 1985; Hearn, 1987; Connell, 1995). Feminists also focus on women's abuse and exploitation of children (Pizzey, 1997; Saradjian, 1996). Adults have power over children and adultist relations contribute to the abuse of children by men and women (Dominelli, 1989, 2002a). Understanding power as multidimensional is central to pinpointing sources of power that women can access.

I (see Dominelli, 1989, 2002a, 2004a) have termed the abuse of children by men and women *adultism* to focus on the power dynamics that both genders hold over children and young people. This expands our understanding of these issues by moving the discourse beyond sexism which focuses on relationships between adult men and women. The children's rights movement (Franklin, 1995; Moosa–Mitha, 2003) has also promoted the idea that children's interests are different from men's and women's and that children's dependency on adults is no excuse for their exploitation.

The emotional sphere is one in which feminists have uncovered a multilayered tissue of violence that absorbs the psychic energies of children, women and men to seriously impoverish their emotional lives. Women scholars have also begun to uncover the routine violence that is exercised over children by both men and women in the name of disciplining and socialising them into their roles in life (Miller, 1983).

Black men and women are finding their right to emotional fulfilment threatened by: racist immigration laws that deny them access to their families (Plummer, 1978; Gordon and Newnham, 1985; McGhee,

2005); poor job prospects; bad housing; and forms of racism that block access to the material conditions necessary for ensuring emotional growth (Davis, 1989). Racist practices permeate every aspect of their lives to the detriment of their psychological development. Internalised racism takes its toll by undermining black people's sense of identity, pride in their historical achievements and resistance to racism (Coard, 1971; Comer and Pussaint, 1975; Gilroy, 1987; Chakraborti and Garland, 2004). Black women have found that racism has destroyed extended family networks, increased their isolation in society, denied them a voice in its affairs (Wilson, 1993) and distorted the close relationships that they hoped to establish with other black women (Lorde, 1984).

Male perpetrated violence is an inescapable fact of women's lives in the home, factory, office and on the streets (Kelly, 1988). Most attacks on women, black and white, are committed by white men (Davis, 1989). White men's responsibility in both reproducing oppressive and damaging relations and eradicating them is deflected by playing on racist stereotypes and focusing attention on black men (Bryan et al, 1985; Davis, 1989). The world sits poised on an arsenal of nuclear weapons which can be set off at any time, but the militarisation of the earth proceeds apace (Cook and Kirk, 1983; Escobar, 1998), as does environmental degradation (Shiva, 2003). A sense of powerlessness in increasingly violent societies is exacerbated by the interminable war on terrorism following the World Trade Centre attack in 2001. Growing fears about the safety of children and families have added to the emotional pressures women face. This reality has led feminists to redefine violence, not only as physical damage, but also as a climate of terror created by men without using physical weapons, and to argue that invisible psychological damage is as pernicious as visible wounds and bruises.

Constant fear of male attack has penetrated the consciousness of all women whether or not they have been raped, physically beaten and/ or humiliated by men because all women have to take precautions to minimise the likelihood of actual assault (Brownmiller, 1976). Having to presume that an attack will happen unless women take active steps to prevent it has placed responsibility for men's behaviour on women, and operated as an effective form of patriarchal social control, including in armed conflict where men rape women to humiliate their enemies (MacKinnon, 1993). It also enables society to use the courts and legal process to blame women when violence occurs (Brownmiller, 1976; SWAF, 1980; Kelly, 1988). Men's absolution from responsibility for their violence and the burden of guilt women carry for failed self-protection when unable to stop their attackers was exemplified in a Canadian court case when a judge gave a male child molester a suspended sentence because he was 'provoked by a sexually aggressive three year old [girl] child'! (*The Vancouver Sun*, 1989). Strega (2004) attributes this trend to discourses that legitimate men as having rights, and women only responsibilities.

Women have felt compelled to reassess their views about violence – its inevitability as something natural; their powerlessness in stemming its pervasiveness; and its distortion of personal and public lives. In America, the feminist peace movement has challenged social priorities that allow 60 cents out of every income-tax dollar to be appropriated by the Pentagon (Davis, 1989), a figure substantially augmented by President Bush's 'war on terror' (*Washington Post*, 2005), while children suffer from malnutrition, women are homeless on the streets and men and women endanger their health producing and using armaments while having limited access to health insurance. American feminists have linked increased defence expenditures under Reagan to the devastation of state welfare services like Aid to Families with Dependent Children (AFDC), Medicaid, Medicare and education (Davis, 1989). Further reductions under Clinton via the 1996 Personal Responsibility and Work Opportunity Reconciliation Act and Temporary Assistance for Needy Families (TANF), which replaced AFDC, has made this situation worse (Zucchino, 1997). After 9/11, George W. Bush continued this pattern by appropriating funds for his 'war on terror', including wars in Afghanistan and Iraq. These monies have reached $350.6 billion, while welfare expenditures have been savagely cut (*Washington Post*, 2005).

The feminist peace movement has highlighted the extent to which community life could be enhanced if defence resources were channelled into welfare expenditure. The USA could develop a national comprehensive healthcare service, fund a guaranteed income for all poor Americans or finance basic health supplies for millions of children in the Third World/low income countries. In England, the feminist peace movement has made similar connections by exposing the deleterious effects the fear of nuclear war has had on individual women and children's emotional well-being, and the waste of public resources entailed in a strategy of escalating nuclear weaponry (Cook and Kirk, 1983) as countries that do not have these seek them, for example, North Korea.

Advocacy: a basis for individual and collective action

Feminists have used advocacy to improve the plight of women individually and collectively as part of their strategy of initiating social change. According to Doress and Siegal (1987) advocacy comes in four forms:

- *Personal advocacy:* under this form of advocacy, an individual woman takes action to defend her particular rights, for example, a woman wishing to lodge an unfair dismissal claim under the Sex Discrimination Act against her employer who sacks her for becoming pregnant. Although this action is aimed at securing justice for one individual, the defence of her rights deters the infringement of other women's rights. As such, personal advocacy supports social change.

- *Interpersonal advocacy:* this form of advocacy occurs when one woman supports another who has been unfairly treated to obtain justice.

- *Cooperative group advocacy:* cooperative group advocacy involves a group of women supporting each other in dealing with problems they encounter as a group. For example, a group of older women wanting to discuss the effects of ageism with a group of younger women formed a workshop for this purpose, with each older woman bringing a younger woman to it. During the workshop, each woman talked about the kind of older woman she wanted to be. Sharing anxieties about getting old, being a burden if others have to care for them in ill health and material hardship in old age enables women to contribute to each other's understanding of their own fears and puts these into context alongside similar ones being expressed by others in the group. The insights gained have enabled women to create solidarity with each other and to use their new-found strength in promoting their interests as older women (Doress and Siegal, 1987).

- *Organisational and legislative advocacy:* in this form of advocacy links are developed between groups of women with particular interests and the broader women's movement. This style of advocacy has featured in older women's contribution to feminist social action. Older women have struggled to get governments to recognise that policies for older people, especially those on pensions and social security benefits, have a differential impact on men and women.

They have convinced younger feminists to take their issues seriously (Doress and Siegal, 1987). These efforts are beginning to bear fruit as, together, older women's organisations and the feminist movement press for legislative and other changes to enhance the quality of older women's lives (Browne, 1995). Such developments are more advanced in the US than in the UK (see Doress and Siegal, 1987) where the 1984 Retirement Equity Act has been passed and mandatory retirement has been abolished as a result of such alliances. Current struggles over pensions in the UK may have a similar impact (Bourke, 2005).

The needs of older black women have been seriously neglected (Norman, 1985). It remains a pressing issue for feminist community action to promote equality for black women. By organising support for older women and demanding organisational and legislative changes, younger women safeguard their future interests when they become 'older' women. And it enables women to challenge youthism, or the celebration of young people at the expense of older ones (Dominelli, 2004b).

Organising tips

Advocating for change

Advocacy of whatever type combines an element of self-help with the attempt to achieve social change. It is an important tool in the task of eradicating gender oppression. The following offer some guidelines which may assist in the process:

- Choosing the issue to be tackled.
- Talking the problem through with other women. The problem is likely to be shared by others. Consider how you can turn your problem into an issue that others unconnected to it can support.
- Defining your plan of action:
  - if legislative changes are required, make sure you understand the relevant policies, pieces of legislation and parliamentary agenda; and how to lobby Members of Parliament (MPs) and organise parliamentary support for your proposal.
  - know what resources are available.
- Taking action and evaluating progress.

Feminist social action on health issues: women in the community challenging health professionals

Women have taken a leading role in health campaigns. Constituting the bulk of the workforce in the health service, women are primarily located in the lowest rungs of the labour hierarchy (Doyal, 1983, 1985), a feature that has not altered since the inception of the National Health Service (NHS) (DTI, 2005). Feminist critiques of health services for women reveal that they are inadequate and substantially under-resourced. Women's facilities and women workers have borne the brunt of public expenditure cuts in the NHS. Under these circumstances, it is not surprising that women are active participants in defending community health provisions.

The feminist health movement is largely a network of diverse health groups ministering to women's specific emotional and physical health needs. The feminist health movement has combined concern with women's emotional well-being with an equal interest in their physical welfare (Ruzek, 1978; Doyal, 1985; Bondi and Burman, 2001) and campaigned on identified health issues. This is in keeping with the feminist view that one aspect of women's lives interconnects with every other one and accounts for the complexity in which women's oppression is embedded.

Gender is a key element in women's analyses and actions on health issues tackled through feminist health groups. These tend to be small and have a strong consciousness-raising dimension that enables women to explore the political facets of healthcare at individual and societal levels. Besides consciousness-raising features, health groups provide women with opportunities to learn about their bodies and to pass specialist knowledge on to each other. As part of a network, one health group can refer women to other groups that provide a specialist service in a particular sphere of healthcare. Characteristically, their work enables women to:

- share experiences, knowledge and feelings
- learn from each other
- work on practical matters relating to health, for example, self-examinations
- ask questions of themselves, other women and professionals
- support one another
- create alternative resources and services for women
- acquire confidence in tackling health issues, including how to resist authoritarian doctor–patient relationships

- demand more appropriate healthcare services
- change the nature of service delivery in the formal health system
- foster egalitarian relationships between women, regardless of their roles as providers or users of healthcare services
- work collectively with other women
- focus on preventative care
- integrate women's emotional and physical well-being.

Women's attempts to challenge the power of the medical profession and to make their broader definition of healthcare a reality through self-help initiatives have produced the women's health movement. This has picked up on issues related to women's own and their children's ill health, and developed alternative forms of healthcare which have given women command of both their bodies and their treatment (Ruzek, 1978, 1986; Doyal, 1979, 1985). The feminist health movement has drawn on women's traditional skills in this area. Healthcare was once defined as 'women's work', but the rise of state and market provisions have converted health into a commodity controlled by men (Cochrane et al, 1982; Eisenstein, 1984), a feature that has been exacerbated through scientific developments in the area of reproductive technologies (Steinberg, 1997). Power relationships in the British NHS exemplify male–female roles that presume that male experts know everything while discounting female workers' and patients' practical knowledge (Cochrane et al, 1982; Barnes and Maple, 1992).

Feminists have argued that the right to health ought to be a universally recognised human right rather than a commodity sold to those who can pay the highest price (Davis, 1989). A broader definition of health – the pursuit of health in body, mind and spirit – has featured strongly in women's struggle for economic, social and political justice (Lorde, 1984; Davis, 1989). Feminists have defined health as well-being which can be achieved only in a dynamic relationship with a positive and balanced environment (Cochrane et al, 1982). This includes physical surroundings, political, economic and social structures. Aboriginal women have added spirituality to this concern (Thomas and Green, 2006). In short, health issues are embedded in the totality of how life is organised and our role within it elaborated.

Women's health groups have drawn on community techniques during their formation and development. Word-of-mouth, doorknocking notices placed strategically in places frequented by women, have brought small numbers of women together to examine a variety of health issues. These have included childbirth, skin complaints, thrush, breast cancer, menopause, ageing, tranquilliser abuse, mental health, safety in the home and children's health. Proceeding from their own experience of the subject, such groups have raised women's consciousness about the social organisation and medicalisation of health. These groups often meet in women's homes, schools or community halls with few resources other than those they provide themselves. Occasionally, they receive public funding to attract speakers or to provide specialist resources. The Well-Women Clinics (WWCs) in the UK exemplify services that have relied on public funding. Reliance on state financing has often imposed restrictions on how groups function and premises on which they base their action. This can disadvantage groups seeking feminist approaches to health issues, distorting their commitment to egalitarian practices in the process (Finch, 1982), but it can assist in mainstreaming their concerns as has happened with WWCs (Foster, 1989).

Women's health groups are also fluid in composition and the subject matter they handle. A 'core' of women may remain in a group for some time; others enter and leave the group frequently, without unduly disrupting group processes. The group's capacity to accept turnover in membership is facilitated by sharing personal experiences, a relaxed atmosphere, a lack of hierarchical group organisation and understanding the pressures that women negotiate to attend such meetings. As a result, groups:

> ... sometimes shrink in numbers, but this is not accompanied by the frustrated bafflement it occasions in many community groups. Members know more about why people have left. They also understand more about how to bring in new people and help them settle in. Thus, the group remains open. (Cochrane et al, 1982, p 125)

The openness of groups and commitment to egalitarian relationships has attracted women who do not normally participate in such gatherings. This can be crucial in attracting a broad range of women, including those from minority ethnic groups. Having women-only groups facilitates women's participation in their activities (SWAT, 1982). Although men who work at home caring for children and retired men have joined some women's health groups without seeking to dominate group dynamics, women have preferred to promote women-only ones (Cochrane et al, 1982). Meanwhile, men partners find it difficult to accept that being part of a women's health group can enhance women's well-being to the extent that they go home feeling 'happy and relaxed' (Cochrane et al, 1982).

Women's health groups have stimulated relationships between women and enabled them to contribute to each other's emotional growth. They have fostered women's confidence in their ability and capacity to ask questions of professionals about the healthcare services that they offer and demanded that whether provided by the state or the market health resources be used to further women's well-being rather than merely respond to symptoms doctors seek to cure via intrusive technology-based interventions (Ruzek, 1978; Cochrane et al, 1982; Doyal, 1985; Steinberg, 1997). Developing preventative services that keep people healthy has been a major outcome of the feminist health movement (Ruzek, 1978; Doyal, 1985; Foster, 1989).

Women's involvement in health groups has had repercussions in other aspects of their lives. Personal relationships and their attendant sexism have come under scrutiny, enabling women to draw connections between these and lack of psychological well-being. Depression within heterosexual relationships and the toll of unremitting childcare on women's emotional health, have both been related to unequal socially structured and unsatisfactory family relationships, for these poorly serve the emotional needs of children, women and men. Group members have gained confidence in tackling these problems more imaginatively in their personal lives, finding that they may have to break off certain relationships in the process and demand more sensitive collective caring facilities for children and older people. Feminist action begun in the area of emotional health has highlighted connections between this and other aspects of women's lives, particularly those linked to caring for others, and thereby exposed the seamless web woven by gender oppression.

The relationships between community workers and group members in feminist health groups follow non-hierarchical principles of organisation. Tasks are shared between women, often on a rotating basis, so that all women have the opportunity to learn new skills. This includes answering the telephone, chairing meetings, writing leaflets, speaking to the media, learning medical terms and details about their bodies, compiling websites on women's health issues and self-treating to some extent. If the process of imparting skills to one another is successful, feminist community workers find that they become redundant to the group as it becomes capable of functioning without them (Cochrane et al, 1982; Dominelli, 1982).

Unconscious bids for leadership and hanging on to roles when other women have gained these skills can mar the establishment of egalitarian relationships (Cochrane et al, 1982). A commitment to continual critical analysis, self-appraisal and listening to women's accounts of group experiences are essential in avoiding false equality traps, countering inegalitarianism and maintaining women's willingness to remain in a group. Some women's health groups resist identifying themselves with the women's movement even though they may be founded on feminist principles, operate on feminist lines and call on the services of feminist community workers for fear of being labelled militant, lesbian and aggressive (Cochrane et al, 1982). Third wave feminists also feel the label is redundant (Baumgardner and Richards, 2000), although the continuing gaps between women's and men's status in society suggest that much ground has to be covered to realise the ambitions of second wave feminism.

The unsympathetic portrayal of feminist action in the media and inadvertent exclusion of certain groups of women, particularly working-class and black women, by white middle-class feminists have exacerbated this reaction. This indicates that feminists have a major educational task to perform to further society's understanding of their activities, and to develop responses that address the differences that structure gender oppression in the lives of diverse groups of women. Handling differences on the basis of equality and using women's different starting points to develop a common strategy in eliminating sexism is a relatively new experience for women. But the process of working for unity among women in ways that do not establish hierarchies whereby one type of oppression subsumes another has begun (Dominelli and McLeod, 1989). This is often rooted in everyday routines, for example, forming childminding circles that transform women's outlook on life through the social interactions, discussions and experiences they share with others.

Health issues enable women to explore the profound link between the personal and political spheres. This is often hidden, with health and illness individualised and trivialised in the process because the traditional handling of health issues in capitalist countries has not attached importance to the social factors producing ill health among various groups in society. The relationship between structural and personal factors became the focus of mass health campaigns in China immediately after the Revolution and in creating the *barefoot doctor* system (Horn, 1969; Sidel and Sidel, 1982) to address women's health needs (Andors, 1983). In Britain, the Black Reports (Townsend et al, 1988, 2002) exposed class as a key variable in health outcomes, while Ahmad (1993) revealed the significance of 'race'.

Black women have been particularly active in making links between individual poor health and poverty. In America, the absence of a national healthcare scheme has left them personally vulnerable for many cannot afford hospital health insurance to procure healthcare. Those who have purchased it have had white administrators handling their reception into hospitals disbelieving their claims about cover and refusing admission, thereby causing untold suffering and sometimes even death (Davis, 1989). Clinton's failure to develop publicly funded healthcare is a huge setback for poor Americans (Stanley, 1998). In Britain, working-class women suffer from an 'illness-promoting environment', but middle-class women feature prominently in developing feminist self-help alternatives (Cochrane et al, 1982).

Struggles over health matters continue, including its funding as a public resource available to all in need. Working-class women have played a key role in defending the NHS from public expenditure cuts by mounting campaigns in the community and workplace to protect public provisions. Women workers, especially nurses in the NHS, have fought to improve services as well as gain recognition of the value of their work through decent pay and conditions (Joyce et al, 1987). UNISON now strongly advocates on these two points. The growth of market-oriented initiatives in health provisions such as user fees for some services, GP fundholders, foundation hospitals, the decline in the number of NHS dentists and other New Labour proposals to increase the role of private providers in healthcare have undermined the idea of a national service free at the point of need.

Organising tips

Forming consciousness-raising groups

- Key features:
    - Woman-centredness
      meeting with other women;
      listening to other women;
      sharing experiences, knowledge and skills with other women;
      developing women's capacities and empowering them to take action.
    - Small-sized groups.
    - Redefining social problems from a feminist women-centred perspective that builds on individual women's experiences.
    - Providing women with support in confronting problems that face them individually and collectively.
    - Promoting women's confidence and strengths as women.
    - Endorsing egalitarian relations and group dynamics.

- Developing feminist politics and a collective approach to problem solving.
- *Organising a consciousness-raising group*
  - Finding women to join the group
    approaching women in their homes, places where they congregate, through personal contacts and networking, leafletting, posting signs, placing adverts in local papers and forming women's caucuses in unions or other professional associations;
    meeting in places accessible to women including disabled women;
    encouraging men to facilitate women's participation in groups by providing supportive assistance such as childminding.
- *Running a consciousness-raising meeting*
  - Timing meetings at times when women can attend easily.
  - Providing support services that facilitate attendance, for example, crèches, accessible rooms, refreshments that meet vegetarian and religious needs.
  - Deciding degree of structure and leadership needed for the meeting. Completely unstructured meetings often create their own structures as informal hierarchies distort group dynamics (Dreifus, 1973). Leadership roles should be considered in advance. Rotation among group members reduces the problem of hierarchy.
  - Focusing on women-determined agendas
    having women decide the issues they wish to discuss ensures that they consider matters they deem important and increases participation.
  - Establishing egalitarian group processes
    sensitivity to privileges, differential access to resources, inequalities between women and finding ways of addressing these (Barker, 1986);
    sensitivity to differences based on social divisions like class, 'race', age and sexual orientation (hooks, 1984; Lorde, 1984);
    sensitivity to other women's difficulties in expressing themselves and supporting them to overcome these (Dreifus, 1973);
    sharing skills and knowledge;
    having open discussions;
    not blaming women for their oppression.
  - Formulating a plan of action
    linking personal experience to how society structures social relations;
    focusing on concrete experiences;
    using women's anger constructively;
    redefining personal problems as social issues;
    focusing on action that can solve social problems on a collective basis.

Challenging medical expertise

Feminists' challenges to the medical profession through the health movement have been considerable. They have questioned the patriarchal doctor–patient relationship, skewing medical services towards curative care that treats symptoms, promotion of high technology hospital care that leaves patients feeling powerless, distortion of health services by the interests of multinational drug companies seeking profits, abuse of women's bodies, particularly those of black women, for experimental purposes and eugenicist population control and restriction of medical knowledge in the hands of the 'professionals' (Bryan et al, 1985; Sidel, 1986; Steinberg, 1997).

Childbirth, gynaecological examinations and now the new reproductive technologies have been key sites in the battle raging between feminists and the medical profession over the best healthcare for women. The responses of the medical establishment to these challenges have not been encouraging. In the USA, doctors have sued feminists for illegally practising medicine by encouraging women to conduct their own gynaecological examinations (Ruzek, 1978). A massive defence of this practice by feminist groups across the US ensured that the courts accepted the feminist case. Feminist therapists promoting self-help in healing women suffering the effects of sexual abuse have also faced lawsuits for their position (Bass and Davis, 1988).

In Britain, a senior hospital obstetrician, Wendy Savage, was dismissed in 1985 for incompetence after her male colleagues objected to her attempts to give women a greater say in the birth process (Savage and Leighton, 1986). By organising direct action including mass protests, conferences and a defence fund, feminists played a key role in demanding her reinstatement and defending her right to practice in ways that gave women control over their bodies. These examples depict the vulnerability of feminists who question traditional medical practice and the importance of having a supportive mass movement that can underpin individual women's initiatives and launch their defence. These illustrations also reveal the intensely political nature of feminist intervention in the health arena.

Since the late 1970s, some struggles over health issues have been very protracted although widely supported. This has led to the formation of campaigns around health issues at work as well as the individual level. In England, campaigns have included preventing the closure of the Hounslow Hospital, averting the closure of the Elisabeth Garrett Anderson Hospital, one of three women-only hospitals in the country at the time, terminating the use of private pay-beds in NHS hospitals, exposing the inordinate use of drugs to treat depression among women and asserting women's right to control their own fertility and healthcare associated with that (Rosenthal, 1983; Steinberg, 1997). These issues are not sites of one-off struggles; they are constantly contested. Sadly, by 2005, closures of women's facilities continue while private care flourishes.

Community activists can take comfort from the organisational achievements of these campaigns. Individuals who have never before taken part in direct action have done so for the first time to defend their perception of an essential part of the welfare state. For instance, the Hounslow and Elisabeth Garrett Anderson Hospital campaigns laid the groundwork for a broad-based commitment to save these facilities. Professional workers and manual workers combined forces to oppose government policy by occupying buildings, demonstrating, petitioning the then area health authority, writing petitions and lobbying MPs. They also secured financial and material resources to look after patients left under their care, despite intense coercion by employers and management. Trade unionists have rallied in support of their activities, despite Thatcherite legislation curbing the extent of industrial action that trade unionists can undertake by abolishing 'sympathy' strikes and 'political' campaigning. This has curtailed the extent to which broad support can be procured, a legal position that New Labour has subsequently retained.

Health campaigns have also acted as springboards for national offensives defending services. The Fightback Campaign, organised nationally and locally against Thatcherite public expenditure cuts, exemplifies one of these. Besides promoting direct action, the Fightback Campaign undertook consciousness-raising endeavours through the production of a newspaper, films and speakers who could be hired by community groups fighting local battles. A major weakness of the Fightback Campaign was that although it drew heavily on feminist ideals and practice in the women's health movement and literature, women were excluded from the higher reaches of the campaign. This state of affairs can be attributed in part to the inputs of a male-dominated trade union movement and Left political parties. These campaigns stimulated discussion about the type of health services people really wanted; how health rather than sickness could become a top priority; and how service users could influence its decision-making processes. It embedded awareness of alternatives to existing provisions that have survived the campaign.

Operating throughout the country, the Fightback Campaign and women's health movement raised political questions about the health agenda. These challenged the existing medical hierarchy dominated by male professionals at the apex of a medical care pyramid that was predicated on the subordination of women staff and patients (Doyal, 1979), concerns that remain. During the 2001 and 2005 General Elections, a doctor, Richard Taylor, stood in defence of the NHS and was successfully elected on both occasions, despite sustained opposition to his position from New Labour.

Feminists have questioned the relevance of high technology medicine for the majority of people's illnesses, and the usefulness of a service concentrating on illness rather than health (Ruzek, 1978; Doyal, 1983). Feminists have demanded that users are actively involved in making decisions about the ways in which services are organised, provided and financed. Through such participation, feminists hope that a democratic health service, responsible to people's needs and emphasising prevention rather than cure, can be developed. This dream remains.

Struggles over health issues have provided useful lessons on organisational problems that must be overcome for a successful outcome to these campaigns. Achievements to date have been mixed. The health service was cut savagely under the Tories (Iliffe, 1985), and included using private pay-beds and closing NHS services. Many facilities were retained as a result of local action undertaken by women. The struggle to maintain NHS services goes on, although the terrain being fought over has shifted under New Labour. More government funding has been released for the NHS, but the market is playing a larger role in service provision under the Private Finance Initiative (PFI) and guise of giving consumers more choice. Public–private partnerships (PPPs) and quasi-markets are being encouraged by Blair. At the same time, user fees have been imposed on once free services and are rising, for example, prescription drugs, eye tests, chiropodist services and dental care.

Disability action: insights from the Terri Schiavo Campaign

The voices of disabled people, including those of disabled women, continue to have little space in the medical profession. The new technologies that successfully prolong life have become central to debates about the place of disabled people in society. Medical leaps in tackling age-old diseases catch public attention. In these, technical advances that promise cures attract support. These are often framed in disabled terms, for example, abortion is possible if the foetus is severely deformed. Testing to avoid disabled children being born is routine and continues under the new reproductive technologies, including in vitro fertilisation (IVF). Disabled adults have their right to decision making removed if medics decide that they are incapable of making these decisions themselves (Barnes, 2003). It is usually assigned to the nearest kin ostensibly to protect the interests of the person concerned. But is this guarantee sufficient? Terri Schiavo's case recently raised this dilemma in the US, attracting attention throughout the world. Its resolution shows that who decides what services are accessed by disabled people can be complex.

Answering this question in Terri's situation involved lengthy costly litigation between her parents and erstwhile husband because Terri had been in a coma for 15 years. Her spouse supported switching off her life support machines on the grounds that this is what Terri would have wanted. Her parents opposed his view. In the end, the ethical and legal questions were determined by courts that supported the husband, despite campaigns to maintain Terri's life through mechanical means. Campaigns in her favour led the American Congress to agree with Terri's parents. The Disability Convention used the Internet to lobby on Terri's behalf and argued that medical responses reflected a disablist society's values and norms. Their campaign ultimately failed. Terri's husband was given the right to represent her interests and her life support machine was switched off. But is this what Terri would have wanted? We cannot know, although Terri's smiling face from her hospital bed suggested that she enjoyed whatever elements of life she knew and understood.

Interestingly, in the conflict between Terri's parents and her spouse, no one raised the question of whether he could occupy that role. Although married to Terri, he had a long-standing relationship with another woman and had children with her. Would Terri have refused him the right to decide what happened to her if she knew that this was the case? Terri, if she had known, might have wanted a divorce from him for these actions long before he could take decisions on her behalf. Had this been the case, he would not have been her husband and would not have held the power to make decisions about ending her life. But this point was not raised in the debates that hit the public arena, maybe because Terri's parents were Catholics and would not have wanted the marriage terminated. Gender dynamics were neglected in this situation. Additionally, the question arises of the extent to which an able-bodied male-dominated health profession colluded with an able-bodied man to decide what happened to a disabled woman. Was this another example of the health technologies granting men further control over women's bodies, as Steinberg (1997) suggests?

Organising tips

Organising groups

The formation of an active, viable group is an essential element in any campaign. It is vital that community activists give considerable thought to the formation of their group and the processes and dynamics on which it operates. Empowering women should be a key concern. The following points are important considerations that require decisions to be made by those forming the group:

- *Objectives*
  Clarity of purpose
  - Why is the group being set up?
  - What is the group expected to do?
  - Are the issue(s) to be tackled understood?
- *Group membership*
  - Who will join the group?
  - How can women be encouraged to join?
  - Are people in the group they think they joined?
  - Is there agreement on the group's aims?
  - Is the group's size compatible with its aims and objectives?
- *Group name*
  What will the name be?
  - depends on group aims and membership;
  - can be difficult to work out;
  - should be 'catchy' and memorable.
- *Problem definition*
  - What problem is the group addressing?
  - Who has defined it as a problem?
  - How has the group redefined the problem?
  - Who shares the group's redefinition of the problem?
- *Powers of the group*
  - What powers does the group have?
  - What is the group's purpose – show, advisory or independent action?
- *Decision making*
  - Is everyone involved in the decision-making processes?
  - Will there be elections to select an executive committee?
  - Are members of the executive committee accountable to the group? How?
  - Are the terms of the executive committee fixed?
  - Are positions on the executive committee rotated?

- *Commitments expected of group members*
  - Time.
  - Money (fees/dues to be included).
  - Practical involvement in fund-raising, publicity and organising activities: involving people in practical ways in the group's work is crucial in maintaining group morale and sustaining the life of the group. Activities should be meaningful to the individual concerned and limited to those that they commit themselves to personally. Groups should not coerce people into contributing beyond their willingness to do so (Cook and Kirk, 1983).
- *Group process*
  - Progress may be slow. The group will 'gel' as individuals become comfortable with and trust each other.
  - Be clear about the purpose of each meeting.
  - Try to secure an early 'success' in the group's activities to maintain morale (this may be a subsidiary issue that can be dealt with quickly).
  - Decide priorities in the work and note that these may change over time.
  - Have the right atmosphere in the group: be serious, but have fun too.
  - Promote egalitarian relationships.
  - Involve all members in the activities of the group.
  - Try to obtain information for the group that is as accurate as possible.
  - Develop the group's 'fact bank' and keep records up to date.
  - Know who the group is trying to identify and influence (decision makers).
  - Decide at what points the group draws other groups into its activities and extends its demands.
- *Resources*
  - What resources does the group have?
  - Which resources are internal to the group?
    include individual skills that cover research, campaigning, organising, writing/making posters, publicity, fund-raising and analysis (for action and understanding society).
  - Which resources are external to the group?
    include premises, personnel and material resources, facilities, equipment and funds. Know what resources the group has already.
  - What additional resources does the group need to procure?
    publicly provided resources – premises, funds and publicity – can come from agencies, local authorities, social services departments and central government;

privately provided resources – premises, funds and publicity – can be obtained from charities, trusts, companies and voluntary organisations;

material resources include buildings, stationery, printing and duplicating facilities, films/videos, telephones, computers, office furniture and furnishings;

personnel: people are needed to write publicity and distribute it, to hold meetings, organise people and campaigns.

- How will the group get these resources?
- How will the group obtain support from the public?

• *Action*
  - Whose attention is the group trying to attract?
  - Which decisions is the group trying to change?
  - What needs to be done?
  - When should it be done?
  - How should it be done?
  - Who should do it?
  - Learn from the group's experience.

• *Evaluation*
  - Monitor the group's progress and evaluate it. Ideally, this should be an ongoing process, but it should be more than an instrumental technique that focuses on quantifiable outcomes taking into account interpretative approaches that examine power relationships, community competences and self-learning (Murtagh, 2001).

Conclusion

Feminist action on the individual front is an important supplement to collective activities because it allows women to respond to their emotional needs. Tackling health issues has enabled feminist community activists to challenge medical expertise and insist that its knowledge should become freely available to redress the balance between professionals and the people they serve. The objectives of empowering women to look after their physical and mental health and shift interventions to the preventative domain have been important dimensions in these interventions. The 'personal is political' is meaningless unless interventions are experienced as personally liberating as well as improving group well-being. Feminist therapy and counselling have made valued contributions to their realisation.

SEVEN

Feminist action in the workplace

Introduction

Tackling inequality in the workplace has been a sphere for feminist action aimed at encouraging social and economic developments for women in both waged labour and unpaid caring work. Feminist social action has revealed the monotony and drudgery that characterises housework (Oakley, 1974); exposed the damage to women's emotional development and careers caused by the sexual division of labour in domestic (Gavron, 1966) and waged employment (Armstrong, 1984; Coyle, 1989); indicated the pervasiveness of sexual harassment in workplaces (Benn and Sedley, 1982); and identified the compulsion for men to persist in emotionally and physically numbing work to provide for their families (Dominelli, 1986b).

Feminist action in this arena has revealed the connections and contradictions between a woman's experience of herself as a nurturer in the community and as an employee in the workplace. In pursuing their quest for social justice for women, feminists have organised within equal opportunities initiatives in both male-dominated and women-only groups to promote egalitarian relations in waged work (Kettle, 1998), political parties, autonomous feminist groups and trade union movements.

In this chapter I examine feminist action in creating a working environment more conducive to women workers and consider the patchy nature of feminist achievements on this front. In doing so, I highlight the importance of dealing with equal pay, sexual harassment and promotion prospects, issues that continue to resonate with equality in the workplace. I also look at the relationship between waged work and unpaid domestic labour and its impact on the lives of men and women in the home, including the division of domestic caring work with children and elder dependants. Using case materials, I examine how feminists have organised around these issues to improve women's position as carers within the home and as employees in the workplace. This includes the emotional work that sustains family relations. I also consider how a backlash has undermined feminist gains on employment rights despite legitimating discourses on the erroneously termed 'work–family balance' (WEU, 2003) because this terminology perpetuates the view that domestic labour is not work.

Additionally, I explore client–worker relationships and draw parallels between the position of women workers and that of the individuals they serve, and reflect on using a feminist perspective to tackle the tensions between the care and control sides of their work. I show that when nurturing roles are taken into account, the needs of women practitioners have some coterminality with users'. This convergence can provide the basis for an empathy resting on shared experiences between women. But it should not be used to mask differences between them or to presume a similar experience of gender oppression. I also consider organisational changes that improve women's position in social work and community work.

Women's lot: unpaid domestic work and low-paid waged labour

Society's definition of masculinity and femininity are intricately connected to notions of work and what legitimately constitutes work. Paid work, especially its better paid and prestigious elements, belongs to men. Unpaid work in the home is generally a woman's lot. This idea pervades the social division of labour and the educational system in preparing people for social roles and the organisation of the family (Belotti, 1975). Change in this outlook is slow, as the Equal Opportunities Commission in Britain found out in the recently released reports, *Then and Now: Thirty years of the Sex Discrimination Act* (2006) and *Sex and Power: Who runs Britain 2006?* Feminist scholars have expended considerable energy in exploring the position of women in the labour market and found that familialist ideology continues to structure employers' expectations about women employees. Women whose social position is defined by their place in the family and/or community are deemed temporary incumbents of the waged workplace and expected to leave if they marry or have children. Men are tied to the workplace to meet their responsibility of providing financial support for their families. Waged work for men furnishes a career; for women, it contributes 'pin money' (Coyle, 1989), a view that remains salient today as men's careers are valued more than women's. The US Census Bureau found that women still earn only 75.5 cents for every 100 cents earned by men and in 2003, real wages for women fell and their poverty rose. Even in the boardroom women are being paid 16% less than men. The British trade union Amicus deemed the UK position 'disgraceful' and launched a major campaign against the gender pay gap in 2005 (see www.amicustheunion.org).

Waged employment ignores several aspects of reality that are crucial to women's well-being. Women in the UK, the US and Canada earn on average around two thirds of the equivalent male wage (Armstrong, 1984; Sidel, 1986; Segal, 1987). Although less in some occupations, the 'gender pay gap' persists today (Status of Women, 2001; Census Bureau, 2005; ONS, 2004). To begin with, women's lives are constructed around having one foot at home, in the community, and the other in the workplace, but the single-earner, two-parent family is no longer the major family form (Eichler, 1983; Sidel, 1986; Segal, 1987). Dual-earner couples are necessary for a family to obtain a decent standard of living. Neither a man nor a woman working alone can earn a sufficiently high salary to provide for a family (Sidel, 1986; Segal, 1987). For single-parent families headed by women, poverty is a major obstacle to acquiring a decent standard of living (Davis, 1989; Razavi, 2000) because, even when women work, they earn less than men. Women work part time to meet family responsibilities and are located primarily in the low-waged service and retail sectors of the economy. This reduces their earnings capacities and ability to acquire credits for a sufficient pension in old age. This results in the 'feminisation of poverty' through the life cycle.

Feminists in the UK and America have campaigned around women's unequal position in the workplace and demanded equal pay for equal work. In Britain, the Equal Pay Act was passed in 1970 following feminist social action on the issue. It became effective in 1975 and created an even stricter segregation of labour than existed previously as employers sought to evade its provisions by defining more jobs as 'women-only' ones. As a result of these tactics, women's wages, which had peaked at 73% of male wages following the implementation of the Equal Pay Act, declined to 67% by the late 1980s (Segal, 1987). In America, the Equal Economic Opportunities Act passed in 1964 was followed by a period of affirmative action. Nonetheless, the position of waged women remains one of lower pay than men and their exclusion from the higher-income echelons of the labour hierarchy continues, with black men and women earning less (CEA, 1998).

But the waged labour market covers only a fraction of the work women undertake. Women's domestic work in the home, although unpaid, makes a substantial contribution to the economy (Status of Women, 2001). The United Nations (UN), responding to grassroots women's organisations and 20 years of organising, values women's unpaid work at $11 trillion annually worldwide. Its Platform for Action following the 1995 World Conference on Women in Beijing asked all governments to collect these figures in satellite accounts to the Gross

Domestic Product (GDP). Few governments do so and despite feminist endeavours in raising awareness of it, domestic work remains publicly invisible. Canada is one exception, however. In 1970, Statistics Canada estimated domestic work at about 41% of GDP. At the turn of the 21st century, Statistics Canada claimed that women's unpaid contribution to the nation's economy equalled that of the manufacturing sector (Status of Women, 2001).

Feminists sought to value domestic labour by demanding 'wages for housework' (Dalla Costa and James, 1972). The Wages for Housework Campaign did not reach its objective, but redefined public understandings of unpaid work. One problem was that the call for 'wages for housework' was not supported by the feminist movement as a whole. Socialist feminists rejected this specific demand while accepting the social importance of domestic labour women performed on the grounds that payment would lock women firmly into houseworker roles. They preferred housework to be socialised and shared equally between men and women. The Wages for Housework Campaign continues with supporters throughout the globe, for example, International Wages for Housework Campaign and Black Women for Wages for Housework.

State initiatives in socialising housework in capitalist states have been limited, affecting primarily nursery provisions for stigmatised families, and hardly merits being classified as such. China undertook a massive socialisation of housework, particularly in the areas of childcare, cooking and doing laundry during the Great Leap Forward (Andors, 1983; Dominelli, 1991). This was not a huge success, as a sexist division of labour prevailed in socialised enterprises. Women performed the bulk of socialised housework but domestic labour was not recognised as socially useful and did not earn workpoints (Andors, 1983). Women earned fewer workpoints than men for other work while also doing the housework and community work. So, 'women's work' continued to be undervalued whether socialised or not. These events suggest that 'men's work' like 'women's work' has to be included in an equation that redefines work and transforms the division of labour to subvert sexist divisions of labour and women's general servicing of life.

Feminist initiatives in the workplace have demonstrated a close connection between waged and unwaged work and shown how one feeds into the other and vice versa. The work women do in the waged labour market draws on skills women learn by working in the home. Assuming these are acquired 'naturally', employers make few provisions for training women, thus reducing training costs for waged women. Like housework, women's waged work is devalued and poorly paid.

Women tend to be in subordinate positions while men hold positions commanding authority, power and resources (Munro, 2001). Housework has a large element of drudgery (Oakley, 1974), and women's waged work can be tedious, repetitive and monotonous. Inequality at work has made many women prefer to work in the home rather than outside it. For black and working-class women, conditions of paid labour are so awful that many would rather give up their jobs and stay at home if they could afford to exercise this option (hooks, 1984; Davis, 1989). Waged work for these women may be physically hazardous because women handle dangerous substances or close work which strains their eyesight and back by being rooted to one spot in uncomfortable positions for lengthy periods. Health hazards in the workplace can be extreme in establishments in Third World/low income countries where multinational companies have not taken women's health seriously (Wichterich, 2000).

Feminists have campaigned around health issues in the workplace, transcending traditional approaches to 'health and safety' at work. These have focused on wearing protective clothing and restricting access to certain types of work. Feminists have preferred to prioritise preventative healthcare that enables people to keep their health, for example, breast and cervical screening for women. Such gains may be contradictory for they may intensify pressures to keep women working longer and ignore women's emotional and mental health needs when they are expected to perform a double shift every day – in waged labour and unpaid domestic work.

Women face additional hazards in waged work that do not confront their male colleagues, for example, sexual harassment from male workers. Women face physical, psychological and emotional attacks that can destabilise their sense of well-being. Feminists have focused on both verbal and physical abuse, demonstrating that sexual harassment creates an atmosphere that intimidates women and prevents them from developing their full potential in waged work (Benn and Sedley, 1982). Feminist action in the workplace has tackled this issue and made eliminating sexual harassment and racial harassment an integral part of equal opportunities policies aimed at encouraging women to enter the paid workforce, particularly in male-dominated occupations. Feminist action on these fronts has, however, been fraught with difficulties (Munro, 2001). Men have resisted acknowledging its presence and refused to accept responsibility for perpetuating and condoning it. This has meant few men have taken active steps to eradicate it (Munro, 2001).

Feminist initiatives against sexual harassment revealed that the problem has to be confronted at a number of points, beginning with the socialisation of girls, their expectations at school and training for the world of work. For feminist efforts on this front to be effective, sexual harassment has to become an issue taken seriously by men. They have to accept responsibility for obnoxious behaviour and take determined steps to end it. Men need training to make them aware of sexist power dynamics and to learn how their own behaviour unwittingly perpetuates sexist stereotypes.

Meanwhile, feminists have organised women's support groups and caucuses to make sexual harassment an issue in the trade union movement and to convince employers to adopt policies that make it a disciplinary offence. Unions like the AUT, NALGO and NUPE, before they merged into their successor UNISON, have responded to feminist concerns by highlighting this problem among members. These have exposed the prevalence of sexual harassment in women's working lives, the reluctance of men to admit it, fears that inhibit women from bringing forward complaints and difficulties encountered in making sexual harassment a serious workplace issue.

Shifting trade union membership and employers' attitudes on this matter have been problematic because this involves men in rethinking their attitudes and changing their behaviour in a direction that condemns earlier behavioural patterns. Men have to learn that comments, actions and structures that they had previously accepted as 'normal' have trivialised and degraded women and are socially reprehensible. While agreeing there was a problem, women workers have been sceptical about the extent to which feminists could successfully challenge such 'natural' male behaviour and introduce new codes of conduct in workplace relations until they see evidence of men taking the issue seriously. Their responses indicate the significance of feminist ways of working in encouraging women to consider social issues from their own personal position and experience if they are to work through them in their own time.

Not all forms of oppression are gender-based. Focusing on men's abuse of women at work has exposed bullying at work for both genders. Men may be responsible for the majority of sexual harassment incidents, but women can also be culprits. Women are capable of abusing managerial power and of bullying both men and women in waged work (Ishmael and Alemoru, 1999). This shows the significance of not essentialising gender or seeing it as biologically determined, but focusing on power relations as multidimensional.

Making connections between domestic work and waged labour

Feminist struggles to secure equal opportunities for women in the workplace have encompassed demands for publicly supported childcare (NCC, 1985) and elder care (Doress and Siegal, 1987). They have worked through their trade unions, joined ad hoc equal opportunities committees, formed workplace-based support groups and networked with other feminists to introduce equal opportunities policies and practices in waged work. Sustained feminist and black people's activities on workplace inequalities have compelled public sector unions like NALGO (now UNISON) to establish an Equal Rights Working Party to examine the rights of women, lesbian women, gay men and black people in local government employment. This came about as a result of these groups organising in autonomous groups within NALGO itself, for example, the Black Members Group. UNISON has continued with these investigations.

Feminists have highlighted the connection between women's work in the home and their access to waged work. They have argued that housework, particularly childcare, should be socialised to free women's time for other activities. Campaigns aimed at improving childcare provisions have featured strongly in feminist social action. This has included campaigns to defend public nursery provisions threatened with closure through public expenditure cuts, for example, Save the Wheatley Street Nursery[1]; to end racist practices in day care centres, for example, Hackney; and to improve nursery and childcare provisions nationally, for example, the National Childcare Campaign (NCC).

Women affected by the proposed closure of Wheatley Street Nursery formed the Parent's Action Group (PAG) to oppose it. At first, PAG organised petitions, lobbied councillors to alter the council's decisions and produced a document that spelt out their reasons for opposing the nursery's closure. Meanwhile, PAG continued meeting with parties relevant to the dispute. Its members collectively drew up a series of contingency plans, including occupying the building. The right of individual women to determine their own contribution to the struggle was maintained in that no woman in the group was compelled to undertake action to which she personally did not feel committed. PAG sought support for their position among professionals, trade unionists, local government employees and parents in the community.

These preparations paid off when the building housing the nursery had to be occupied to prevent closure. Trade unionists in NUPE endorsed the occupation straightaway. But, under orders from the council, senior NALGO officials who had not been involved with PAG members locked the building, switched off the electricity and turned off the gas while women were occupying the premises. These actions demonstrate the importance of acquiring support for a campaign at all levels of the trade union movement before crisis point is reached.

During the occupation of the building, PAG prepared publicity for the campaign and organised public meetings to present its case and to secure further support for the occupation. PAG arranged meetings with the local authority officials responsible for the decision to close the nursery and demanded that they reverse it. PAG organised marches to the council buildings. As they wound through the streets, people sang protest songs PAG members had written. Keeping members actively participating in PAG's activities was one way of keeping up morale and commitment. Their tactics paid off. The occupation succeeded and Wheatley Street Nursery was saved.

Struggles around day care for the under-fives have a substantial history behind them, and the majority are local. Women organise in response to a need – the loss of places, absence of provisions and desire to provide children with anti-sexist and anti-racist environments. Working together, in non-hierarchical ways in such campaigns, women have shared their skills, expertise and fears. Some struggles may be protracted, especially if the local authority being challenged is the one threatening closure of existing facilities. Its response may move women to occupy buildings and undertake all manner of other activities prior to reaching this position as occurred in 'Save the Wheatley Street Nursery'. This included lobbying local councillors, obtaining media and community support for their cause and working through the unions.

Women in unionised workplaces have sought union support for their causes. One form of supportive action undertaken by unions has been facilitating women's access to buildings they intend to occupy (NCC, 1984). Unions can furnish useful information and advice on practicalities that need to be followed, provide legal counsel and negotiate policy changes with employers. Collaborative relationships help create links between women in the community and workers, male and female, in the workplace. Women occupying buildings disrupt family life to a certain extent – meals will no longer appear on the table, and housework will not get done. This makes the connection between women having a public role and a private one readily apparent (Cook and Kirk, 1983). Women also draw the community more closely into their action (Gallagher, 1977) by relying on informal networks among women to secure political and practical forms of support, thus drawing on and creating social capital. Women not directly involved in these actions sign petitions, attend demonstrations and supply those occupying the building with food, drink and bedding. Some women help members of the family left at home.

Campaigns around childcare issues have been an important aspect of community action. Many have involved women in fairly extensive ways. These campaigns increase in number when nurseries become casualties of reduced public expenditures. Scattered throughout the country, childcare campaigns have been fragmented, each replicating organising efforts elsewhere and placing those involved in the position of learning lessons on strategies and tactics on their own instead of drawing inspiration from other women's struggles (NCC, 1985). Fragmentation prevents women from supporting one another in moments of acute struggle or demoralisation. However, women would meet at various conferences and discussion seminars and spontaneously begin to contact women in other campaigns. Women substantiated these links later through mutual support at demonstrations.

Contacts of this nature culminated in the launch of the NCC in July 1980 (NCC, 1985). Its formation made campaigning experiences available to women wishing to protect whatever local childcare provisions were threatened. NCC members were not prepared to let the NCC rest at the level of defending inadequate provisions. They raised questions about childcare more generally, highlighting women's role in society, their responsibilities vis-à-vis children and the oppression they experienced because they had dual roles in both waged work and domestic labour. This issue retains its currency. The NCC's endeavours have borne some fruit in gaining New Labour's support for the objective of making high-quality childcare the norm.

Participants handled many of the problems encountered by specific nursery campaigns imaginatively, for example, overcoming differences in women's preparedness to undertake 'militant' action by enabling individual women to participate only in those actions in which they felt able to, and coping with the legal aspects of confrontation between community groups and the authorities and broadening their base of support. The Wheatley Street Nursery Campaign was a case in point.

A declining birth rate and a lower number of young school leavers who are reaching the waged labour market in 2004 have caused employers fearing a labour shortage in the near future to rethink their attitudes, policies and provisions regarding women employees (Benyon, 1989). The dwindling supply of young workers coupled with the UK's restrictive position on immigration, means that women looking after children and older people in the home form the largest sources of untapped labour that employers can access. Employers can meet growing workforce demands by attracting women workers, responding to their needs and incorporating them into their firms.

Recognising that they will have to deal with the problem of childcare if they want to encourage women into the workforce, private employers are becoming more receptive to feminist demands for adequate childcare provisions, at least for waged working women. In late 1989, larger private companies such as the Midland Bank (now HSBC) provided workplace crèches and nurseries so that their employees could be assured of high-quality care. Such employers have made these provisions available not because they endorse feminist positions, but because they are aware that such provisions will attract women employees (see Allenspach, 1975). Others have followed suit and New Labour is committed to ensuring that childcare places cover all children from poor families. Sure Start, a major national initiative for children up to four years old, seeks to overcome parental disadvantage through childcare and educational opportunities.

Public sector trade unions supported feminist demands for nurseries, crèches, flexible working hours and job sharing. But, unless discrimination against waged women workers is tackled directly, these measures can be used to exploit women's labour. Their exploitation can be exacerbated if the resultant increase in productivity is not recognised in the form of pay increases for women, better career prospects for women including those working part time, men's equal involvement in childcare work and the creation of egalitarian working relations. In other words, working relations will have to be restructured in keeping with feminist objectives in the workplace and home by abolishing the distinction between 'women's work' and 'men's work' in both locations. The failure of New Labour to subscribe to all the provisions of the European Social Chapter does not augur well in this regard.

Challenging the definition of caring as 'women's work' is not limited to childcare. Elder care also needs to be moved out of the female ghetto. Care of older people is already taxing the energies of more women than childcare (Higgins, 1989), and more men and young people are becoming carers (Twigg and Atkin, 1994; Fisher, 1997). Given the demographic make-up of the British population, elder care is likely to rise. The 2001 Census identified over 11 million people over pensionable age in the UK. This is expected to reach 15.2 million by 2031. One in five lives in poverty. Most are women. Carers' demands for recognition of their carework and promulgation of policies that respond to their needs have drawn extensively on women organising to pursue carers' interests (OWL, 1986). The National Association of Carers (now Carers UK) is one of these groups. Through carers' endeavours, the Carer's Allowance (formerly the Invalid Care Allowance) is paid to informal carers in recognition of the work of caring for others, if they do 35 or more hours per week. A study conducted in 2002 by Carers UK found that carers contribute £1 billion per year to supporting communities (Carers UK, 2002).

Elder care cannot be left as an isolated task that women perform in the privacy of their home or in low-paid ghettos in private sector residential or nursing homes. Men must become more engaged in these activities and see the merit of working in egalitarian directions that do not infantilise older people. Intergenerational divisions that split people into young and old who do not interact have to cease. This can be done successfully as black people have indicated by creating community-based provisions for elders that address ageism and racism (ASRA, 1981).

Feminist initiatives in the workplace have been partially successful. They have raised the public profile of women's inequality at work, opened more sectors of the economy to women workers, helped employers and workers become aware of more blatant forms of discrimination against waged working women and encouraged employers to monitor recruitment practices, interviewing procedures and promotion opportunities for gender bias (Coyle, 1989). These moves have not produced the intended results. Women recruited to workplaces traditionally dominated by men often leave shortly after joining because they encounter extensive hostility from male colleagues. They are subjected to sexist jokes, sexist innuendo and sabotage as men fight to keep women 'in their place' (Benyon, 1989).

This picture contrasts sharply with men entering traditionally female occupations, for example, office work, teaching, nursing and social work. Men are supported by women colleagues and made to feel comfortable. Their superiors consider them promotion material and they quickly advance to the managerial and higher echelons (Howe, 1986; SSEC, 1986; Benyon, 1989). Women continue to fight the 'glass ceiling' that blocks their advancement up the managerial ladder (DTI, 2005). It seems that equal opportunities policies that focus only on limited aspects of the dynamics leading to gender discrimination at work advance men's interests more readily than they promote equality for women.

Women workers and women clients: shared interests

Feminist community workers have sought to form egalitarian relationships between themselves and the women with whom they work. In redefining relationships between them, feminist community workers have recognised that women in the community face triple workloads – waged work, unwaged housework and unpaid caring work including voluntary work – and refused to lock them into these categories. Feminist community workers have supported women making their plight known and raised public consciousness through campaigns, street theatre and audio-visual productions – films and videos, community newspapers, leaflets, posters and websites – alongside lobbying for changes in the law.

At the local level, feminist community workers have involved men in assuming tasks normally deemed 'women's work' in their strategy of breaking down the division of labour in community groups, for example, getting men to mind children in a group's crèche. Feminists have attempted to convince men that they should do housework, mind the children or care for older relatives to free women wishing to join community groups and undertake supportive roles rather than dominating community groups (Curno et al, 1982). Encouraging men to support women's involvement in community action can release women participants, community workers and activists from domestic commitments that eat into their time for doing other things.

While acknowledging that they wield power by virtue of their skills as practitioners, feminist community workers have tried to reduce it by imparting their knowledge to women they work with and to focus their attention on facilitating women's ability to make their own decisions about the group's orientation and sponsorship activities. Also, they have tried to place women in community groups on a more egalitarian footing with them by highlighting areas of shared experiences as women where their interests might converge. This has been particularly evident in the redefinition of work so that it includes both waged and unwaged work and assigns significance to both while recognising interdependence between the two.

Feminist community workers and women in community groups can empathise with the need to establish childcare facilities that suit all their needs and work together as equals to develop these in practice. Demanding facilities that meet the requirements of both groups of women enables them to support each other in arguing for childcare that is available around the clock. Provisions of this nature would open up waged employment opportunities for women and make it easier for them to choose the lifestyles they find most rewarding. Both sets of women are concerned to provide the best care possible for their children. Thus, they can sit down together to discuss what facilities will provide children with intellectual stimulation, emotional fulfilment, physical care and bodily growth. They can pool resources to develop provisions that accord equal importance to meeting the needs of women waged workers, women working at home and children. These have to incorporate diversity and respond to conflicts raised by working together. In fighting for good quality childcare, all groups have to meet the needs of black women and children and disabled women and children.

Developing relationships of equality between women community workers and women activists is crucial if feminist community workers are not going to fall into the trap of enforcing domesticity on women in the community and arguing that the needs of waged women have priority over those of unwaged women. If they get caught up in relations of domination and subordination, feminist community workers will promote oppressive and controlling forms of community work, reinforce women's domestic role as their lot and ignore their choices and opportunities for alternative lifestyles.

Caring for older people: work undertaken in the home

Older people constitute a large proportion of the British population. Two major problems facing older people today are material poverty including inadequate pensions and social isolation (Walker and Hennessy, 2004). Many older people are unable to heat their homes adequately or to keep them in good repair. Thus, older people die unnecessarily of hypothermia each year and cannot adapt their homes to meet age-related physical needs, for example, accessible bathrooms, bedrooms and central heating.

The debilitating effects of poverty during old age are most likely to be experienced by women. They survive men by six years, constitute the largest proportion of the older age group and have the lowest incomes (Phillipson, 1998). In 1979, Peter Townsend discovered that older women were likely to have half the income of older men at their disposal (Townsend, 1979). By 2003, 21% of older women living on their own compared to 17% of older men experienced poverty (ONS, 2004). Women are over-represented among this group because they have not gained pension credits when undertaking domestic work nor accumulated enough of these through waged employment careers that were badly paid and often interrupted.

The social isolation of older people cannot automatically be attributed to increased frailty generated by declining physical health due to old age (Doress and Siegal, 1987). Rather, it has to be understood in terms of ageism or discrimination against older people on the basis of age and devaluation of their contributions to society as carers of others and retired waged workers. In British society, people without a productive role in both waged and unwaged work arenas lose their place in society (Phillipson, 1982, 1998). This loss of status and roles causes individuals to experience declining confidence, lowered self-esteem and feelings of uselessness and irrelevance. These emotions are major threads running through the lives of older people living on low incomes (Walker and Hennessy, 2004). Older people can feel overwhelmed and disempowered by the mere fact of their existence. These sentiments are particularly oppressive for older women whose experience of ageing is more problematic than men's because they have lost social significance as beings with a purpose and been denied their sexuality. Even when they contribute to society through volunteer work and caring for grandchildren, their endeavours are not reflected in public accounts. Women's experiences of ageism differ because they face ageism at a younger age, live out old age in poverty, are stigmatised to a greater degree and endure more isolation than men (Doress and Siegal, 1987).

Ultimately, to eliminate ageism, the basis on which society is organised must be changed in accordance with feminist principles. In these, people secure dignity and purpose by virtue of being alive and not by the productive role they occupy in society (Dominelli, 1991). In the interim, older women have reacted against the treatment being meted out to them and organised as carers and pensioners, for example, Grey Panthers (Kuhn, 1991). Older women have protested against closures in residential homes and council taxes that have risen more than their pensions. One woman, a retired social worker, went to prison for her stance (Court, 2005). Older women have highlighted the interdependence between generations (Doress and Siegel, 1987) and sought to bring groups of women together to share problems, develop understanding and offer support to one another across age and other barriers.

The working relations of women caring for adult dependants in the home are indicative of women's subordinate position in society. Unpaid carers working from home are unsupported and isolated. The burden of caring for dependent adults falls largely on women who can be caring for children and/or older parents and holding waged employment at the same time (Bonny, 1984; Walker and Hennessy, 2004). Women compelled to give up paid work and an independent life of their own can find this predicament extremely distressing. Within families, single women are often expected to volunteer care so that their married sisters can be spared. This places them in the unenviable position of having their welfare subordinated to siblings who are servicing men. The pitting of a single woman's welfare against her married sister's is an unequal one for the social balance is heavily tipped against the single woman. It also damages her emotional well-being and distorts her relationships with her sisters if she harbours resentment at being landed with the task. Her brothers are not called on to make similar sacrifices and the injustice of the situation is evident.

While the position of unpaid carers in the home is appalling, the state is increasing demands for women's labour by closing institutional provisions as part of formal community care. Ageism, combined with low incomes, have left older people unprotected and had a major impact in limiting welfare provisions for older women. These closures have been exacerbated under the privatisation of these services as profit-making opportunities dwindled (Batty, 2002). Poverty in old age, the product of low incomes in women's waged work and none for their unwaged labour during their employment active years, make it virtually impossible for women, especially working-class and black women, to buy private pensions to ease the hardships of old age. They are reliant on miserly state provisions that even with 40 years' worth of contributions reached a maximum of £79.60 per week as state pension in 2005, and support obtained from family and friends (Stack, 1975). These are extended through self-help initiatives, for example, the Older Women's Network (OWN), a national grassroots movement in Australia that is supported and run by older women.

Current age demographics mean that older women will often be cared for by other women either 'in the community', through poorly supported kin, or neighbourhood care or public or commercial nursing homes. The majority will be cared for at home while around 5% will be in institutional care (Johnson and Falkingham, 1992). Women constitute 71% of the workforce providing personal care in both state and market provisions. The appalling lack of publicly funded support to carers of older people has prompted feminists to develop supportive networks and demand payment for carers (Bonny, 1984). These are a source of support to individual caregivers and challenge society's neglect of older people and its ageist practices in both home-based and institutional care. This individualised and fragmented approach does little to enhance social solidarity between generations and among older people. In the UK, Carers UK links local carers' support groups and presses for legislative changes to improve services for carers, those they care for and their families.

Organising around old age

Organising around old age has been undertaken by both carers and older people. They have formed feminist campaigns and networks, for example, America's Grey Panthers, started by Maggie Kuhn, and the Older Women's League (Doress and Siegal, 1987). In the UK, Carers UK and other organisations have unravelled ageist stereotypes by:

- challenging ageism and society's definition of old age, especially its enforced dependency, symbolised in compulsory retirement ages;
- redefining 'the elderly' as older people or elders, recognising their experience and wisdom, challenging ageist assumptions of their position and capacities;
- highlighting the connection between women's low incomes in old age and their broader financial status, low wages in waged work, married women's enforced economic dependency on men and/or interrupted working careers to care for others, including children, aged relatives and husbands;
- breaking down barriers between different age groups and challenging the division of people into young and old;
- demonstrating the strengths of older women and building up their sense of pride and confidence;
- identifying the specific health needs of older women in non-ageist terms, for example, breast screening for women regardless of age and testing for osteoporosis; and
- giving older women their voices.

Areas that have been identified as problematic by older people themselves include:

- ageist definitions of their position;
- their feelings of isolation and powerlessness;
- remaining independent and in their own homes;
- dependency on relatives, adult children or neighbours for social contact;
- low incomes and/or low pensions;

- poor public transportation, difficult to manage buses and expensive taxis;
- bad housing;
- lack of good housing; accommodation fails to meet current needs, regarding size and facilities, especially for those with physical disabilities;
- inadequate domiciliary services, home help, meals-on-wheels, gardeners;
- a complicated social services system and poor interaction with healthcare;
- lack of centres and open spaces which are easily accessed by older people;
- an unobtrusive monitoring service to check on their safety;
- the high price of fuel and other necessities of life;
- the absence of a service to prepare people for an active post-retirement life;
- inadequate and expensive communications systems; and
- the expense and poor availability of aids and adaptations.

The Grey Panthers and Older Women's League in the US organise older women and connect local support groups. Feminists have established carers' support groups to question society's neglect of women caring for older people (Bonny, 1984) and to challenge the ageist oppression of people. Their concerns straddle the needs of carers and those being cared for. More recently, feminists have begun to root the right to 'care about' and 'care for' people in the rights of citizenship (Knijn and Ungerson, 1997).

Carers' support groups provide a supportive environment for carers to discuss their problems openly, sharing their experiences with others and frustrations in giving care to dependent adults, including disabled adult children. By sharing and exploring concerns, carers discover that they are not alone in facing problems that make their task unenviable. Consciousness raising is an important dimension in carers' support groups. It not only develops women's understanding of the relationship between their personal situation as unsupported carers who have to sacrifice their own wishes and the requirement or need to provide care because society has neglected the needs of the 'cared for', but it enables women to comprehend the nature of the resources available and initiate the development of appropriate services for carers and those they care for. There is a debate about the best forms of care for older people – institutional or family-based care – that is consistent with feminist principles (see Dominelli, 1982; Finch, 1984).

The position is a tricky one to resolve because to be consistent with feminist principles, neither the interests of the carer nor the person they are caring for can be subordinated by the other. Institutional care may be appropriate for some people provided that both caring and working relations in such institutions follow feminist theory and practice. This requires institutions that are run along egalitarian lines; engage careworkers and people being cared for in decision-making processes; ensure residents lead as independent a life as is compatible with their mental and physical capacities and right to control their destiny; and live a full life in which all their human and civil rights are respected including the right to invite long-term visitors to 'their home', have privacy and undertake sexual activity. Carers' support groups enable members to share knowledge of available resources, to hire specialist speakers, to learn about health problems in old age and to organise social and fund-raising events.

Community workers in the UK have paid scant attention to the needs of older people and until recently seldom worked directly with them. This is changing because older people are organising themselves. The British Pensioners and Trade Unions Action Association (BPTUAA) has been extremely active in organising older people locally and nationally. It operates as a mixed organisation catering for the needs of older men and women. Older people in BPTUAA have held conferences, drawn up a manifesto of demands and organised demonstrations against government policy on low pensions and high fuel charges that burden them. Pensioners have opposed home closures and council tax and risked going to jail (Mulholland, 2005).

BPTUAA's demands, as expressed in their declaration of intent, are wide-ranging and cover most aspects of need affecting pensioners. Besides demanding independence, dignity and security as full members of society, they cover incomes, housing, personal social services, fuel allowances, healthcare, education, recreational facilities, inflation-linked pensions, tax-free Christmas bonuses, retention of pensions if they work after retirement and a death grant. Feminist community activists can support older people through such organisations in a servicing role as facilitators of processes in which older people make demands and control the show.

BPTUAA's activities can be criticised for lacking radical demands that challenge institutionalised ageism in society as American feminists have done. Its impact in organising older people and raising British pensioners' consciousness of their rights and entitlements cannot be minimised. Nor can its influence on the trade union movement be ignored. It has made trade unions recognise that older people are part of the working class with interests that are an integral part of their concerns and responsibilities. Its newspaper, the *British Pensioner*, improved communications among pensioners and informed others which areas of life are most problematic for them.

'We're all in it together': Women Against Pit Closures

Feminist community activists have consistently argued that workplace relations and domestic arrangements are intricately linked. The protracted British miners' strike of 1984–85 provided an example of community action that linked community issues with workplace ones and involved alliances covering a wide cross-section of the population locally and nationally. Women Against Pit Closures initially defended mining communities threatened with decimation if the pits closed[2]. Women refused to remain on the sidelines in a subordinate role to men. Protecting their communities meant women had to leave the communities and convince others to support their cause. Women travelled the length and breadth of Britain, giving talks, appearing on television and performing their own sketches of the situation. In the course of their struggle, women developed both gender and class consciousness.

The domestic division of labour that held miners' wives responsible for housework initially acted as a drag on their involvement. To free women's time for undertaking public activities of this nature, domestic arrangements had to be changed. Domestic relations were challenged, and men used to going home to their wives' cooked meals, began cooking for them. In some communities, domestic tasks like cooking and childcare, were 'socialised' or undertaken by groups of women working together to enable individual mining communities to stretch limited financial resources and to survive the lengthy conflict. Women retained responsibility for these 'collective' welfare services, but, while working in them, women talked to each other about their experiences and developed a sense of solidarity and awareness of their position as *working-class women*. The classist and gendered nature of society became very visible to them. As did the repressive might of a state that spent millions policing their communities but would not finance better healthcare or welfare services.

Acquiring these social insights prompted women to ask questions about society's organisation and for whose benefit things were as they were. Their greater awareness drew women closer together and enabled those from mining communities to form alliances with different groups of women – academics, lesbian, black and white women. These groups of women supported women from mining communities in their struggles in practical ways – financially and by organising and signing petitions.

The Women Against Pit Closures and the National Union of Mineworkers (NUM) were unable to prevent the closure of many mines, but their experiences of organising profoundly changed relationships between men and women in mining communities and raised questions about the kind of life people wanted to lead (Lewycka, 1986; McCrindle and Rowbotham, 1986). They realised that both men and women needed to fight for their communities and that events at work had serious repercussions for home life and affected women, children and men. This led Women Against Pit Closures to request associate membership in the NUM so that they could influence its policies. The NUM rejected this proposal as many men felt threatened by the power that feminists could potentially acquire if women joined the union in this capacity.

Feminist prefigurative forms

Besides feminist action aimed at changing existing provisions, feminists have created a variety of autonomous ventures that endorse feminist principles and practices in the workplace. These prefigure the non-oppressive social relations feminists aim to establish in society as a whole. Their efforts have covered a range of autonomous initiatives in the community and included restructured traditional workplaces, for example, the Lee Jeans Cooperative; commercial unwaged cooperatives like food cooperatives on council housing estates; commercial waged enterprises and cooperatives such as the *Spare Rib* Collective; feminist services located within the public sector such as the Well-Women Clinics (WWCs) within the NHS; voluntary organisations which include carers' support groups, rape crisis centres, incest survivor lines; women's refuges; women's resource centres; and women's therapy centres.

These initiatives enable women to challenge definitions of work, workplaces and working relations. Getting women to undertake collective action is a major thrust. Women working in these have begun to reduce hierarchical relations in all their manifestations by tackling a variety of social divisions including class, 'race', gender, disability and sexual orientation, to lessen differentials in pay, status and skills, to eliminate divisions between managers and workers, to blur distinctions in work processes between workers and users, to involve waged workers and consumers in an agency's decision-making processes, to acknowledge interconnections between the demands of home life and waged working life and to give women's interests a high profile in their activities.

The British WWCs are illustrative of feminist prefigurative working relations (Deacon, 1983; Doyal, 1983; Foster, 1989). These represent feminist workplaces carved out within the interstices of paid and unpaid self-help work in which service providers undertake to relate to service users collectively and democratically and to address directly those points at which their interests are at variance. Feminists have formed WWCs outside and inside the NHS, depending on the extent of local support or hostility generated when putting forward proposals to provide women-centred and controlled spaces in healthcare. Eschewing the passive patient role and its emphasis on curative medicine, WWCs provide healthcare that is more responsive to women's needs. They were founded on the belief that women have a right to participate actively in healthcare and have fostered preventative approaches to it.

WWCs' teams were composed of doctors, nurses and volunteers seeking to work together in less hierarchical ways. This enabled WWC workers to learn medical, organisational and interpersonal skills from each other. Their efforts were not always successful as users responded to volunteers' advice with less alacrity than a doctor's, thereby devaluing volunteers' experience and status (Foster, 1989). Besides promoting more equitable relationships, WWCs maximised the use of available resources and offered alternative working relations to the problematic ones encountered by feminists working individually within NHS hospital settings. Working on their own, they may become isolated and extremely vulnerable, as Wendy Savage discovered when trying to empower midwives (Savage and Leighton, 1986).

By adopting a holistic approach to medical care, WWCs gave women sufficient time to talk through their concerns so that both their physical and emotional states were considered in treatment. Professionals worked with each woman as a complete person whose interdependent parts made up the whole individual. Listening was also important in validating women's own definitions of their health needs. Preventative strategies and listening strategies freed WWCs from relying largely on drugs and surgery in dealing with women's health problems. Moving away from drugs facilitated processes whereby women could play active roles in treatment programmes. Workers in WWCs were expected to be sensitive and caring and to show their own vulnerabilities and emotions throughout their interaction with women seeking help. By these means, WWCs challenged neutral, uninvolved professionalism in traditional approaches and began the task of redefining professional roles. Working in this way carried dangers for practitioners if they did not take care of themselves. They could become totally exhausted. Foster (1989) reported the story of a WWC that closed down after two years because of worker 'burnout'.

WWCs aimed to dissolve social divisions and reach women who did not normally use medical facilities. However, inadequate resources impeded progress on this front. The numbers of working-class and black women using these facilities were few. WWCs sought to tackle this problem by seeking urban aid funding (Foster, 1989), but this was limited and precarious. Outstanding grants could be withdrawn suddenly and unilaterally. Funding was dependent on women acquiring the support of both local and central states. Receiving approval could be difficult for projects deemed to have 'political aims'. Additionally, workers appointed through urban aid programmes were marginalised as they did not enter the career structures of mainstream health services. The employment of black women under such terms affirmed institutionalised racism. WWCs were marginal provisions, whether inside the NHS as supplements to mainstream provisions or outside it. Marginalisation limited the potential of WWCs to control employment policy and practice in the wider NHS, but they contributed to eradicating racism and ensured that black women accessed promotions in it.

WWCs often operated on a shoestring, for example, the first WWC to open in Manchester provided one clinic session per week. Others had restricted hours, further limiting their accessibility to women. WWCs located within GPs' surgeries did not receive state funding for services other than cervical smears given to women over 35 once every three to five years (Foster, 1989). By 1987, 100 area health authorities had WWCs (Foster, 1989, p 345). The name was misused by some authorities that included family planning clinics in this classification simply because they were staffed by women. These did not practice according to feminist principles (Foster, 1989). WWCs have persisted and are also found in other countries, for example, the US and Australia.

WWCs have strengths and weaknesses shaped by being self-help initiatives carved from a dominant medical model antagonistic to their existence. Their provisions are accessible because they are located in the communities they are intended to serve. Practitioners within them exercise a degree of autonomy in running their affairs. But their size means that workers' time and energies are consumed by keeping the WWC going (Foster, 1989). This leaves little space for further developmental or outreach work. Limited resources also resulted in only small numbers of women receiving the services that WWCs provide. Waiting lists for feminist health provisions like mainstream ones can be lengthy (McLeod, 1987). The growth of WWCs is hindered by their being unable to act as referral centres to other NHS services and by being abused by unsupportive NHS doctors who pass 'difficult' patients on to them (Foster, 1989). WWCs have a limited impact on the dominant mode of service delivery and labour organisation in the NHS, and are unlikely to threaten established medical interests.

On the positive side, WWCs offered women services not otherwise available, increased choice in the community and provided women with treatments they could enthuse over (Foster, 1989). Their significance was local, including giving women more choices about where to go for medical attention. They stand as examples of good medical practice that did not rely on the glorification of high technology medicine which disempowered and alienated female patients (Doyal, 1985). Despite such innovations, disempowering women through the medicalisation of their bodies has proceeded apace through technological inventions that impact on women's reproductive rights, for example, in vitro fertilisation (Steinberg, 1997).

Feminist self-help provisions sought to make the market responsive to women's needs. Feminists in the US have discovered the contrary holds in practice. Medical service providers, especially large healthcare corporations, have cynically used the information gathered through feminist ventures to advance high technology medicine and drug-oriented therapies for women, for example, progesterone therapy in treating Pre-Menstrual Syndrome. These have attracted healthy women to facilities promoting fulfilling lives while catering for higher-income women (Dreifus, 1973; Ruzek, 1986; Worcester and Whatley, 1988). Cosmetic surgery to undo the physical ravages of old age has become the latest fad and reinforces ageism and youthism (Dominelli, 2004b).

The British scenario depends largely on how far the Conservative dismantling of the NHS continues under New Labour, or whether user-oriented democratic reforms occur. Developments like the Foundation Hospitals being promoted by New Labour are not encouraging as alternatives to Conservative patterns of health provision. If opposition to Tory dismemberment of the NHS succeeds and New Labour's market-oriented initiatives are blocked, change in keeping with democratic reforms that favour patients can be realised. These could take the form of curbing doctors' powers, making them salaried state employees instead of independent contractors and giving consumers a greater voice in the NHS' power structures and administration (Iliffe, 1985). Simply turning consultants into state workers will not guarantee user empowerment. Despite opposition to Foundation Hospitals from trade unionists and Members of Parliament (MPs), there have been no such moves and users' powers have not been enhanced.

Employment in state welfare can make workers less rather than more sensitive and produce more bureaucratic, remote and alienating provisions (Maynard and Bosanquet, 1986), as has happened under New Labour's health reforms. The division of labour still has women dominating frontline positions. Developments in the NHS under the aegis of New Labour governments have intensified the unravelling of the NHS as a socialist institution begun under Thatcherism. Quasi-markets and fund-holding have turned doctors and dentists into contractors running small-scale enterprises. Endorsed as modernising public services, increasing user advice and making professionals more accountable to consumers, people's experiences of these provisions are the opposite. User fees, long waiting lists and inaccessible or absent services undermine their experiences of the NHS as a caring, publicly funded institution that responds to their needs whether as users or as carers.

In the final analysis, change conducive to people's welfare will only take place if the ruling elite facilitates user-determined change. Changes giving women equality will not endure if they are not underwritten by the infusion of feminist principles in theory and practice at both central and local state levels and in society more generally. The present welfare state stands as witness to how far removed from users' expectations of being placed in the centre of service provision they are (Croft and Beresford, 1989).

Conclusion

The workplace has been an important site of feminist struggle in ensuring women's equality at work. Their initiatives include eradicating sexual harassment, promoting equal opportunities, demanding a career structure for women and creating alternative services for them. With these innovations, feminist initiatives have been partially incorporated into mainstream services. Gender, the position of women, a redefinition of professionalism and user control of their care are on the change agenda without underwriting the major gains that feminists sought. Women have had less success in transforming domestic labour as an activity occupying both men and women. Discussions to redress the 'work–family' balance have done little to change this.

Notes

[1] I have retained the 'Save the Wheatley Street Nursery' in this current edition because it holds rich lessons for women organising around the closure of day care services, a matter that continues to trouble women in the present day.

[2] The example of women organising in the miners' strike remains because it is a historically significant piece of women's history in collective action that transformed personal relationships in the home as well as the workplace and broader community. Thus, it has important insights for women organising today.

EIGHT

Feminist political action

Introduction

The political domain and machinery of government have provided the terrain for feminist social action. Despite gaining the right to vote early in the 20th century in the UK, government structures have proved resistant to demands for equality and full representation, and few women are found in the top echelons of government. This deplorable situation has ensured that the political arena has been subjected to feminist social action. More women are now being elected to the British House of Commons and one woman – Margaret Thatcher – has actually acquired the status of Prime Minister, without women being fully represented in Parliament. The Blair landslide of 1997 brought more women than ever into the corridors of Westminster, but only 18% of Members of Parliament (MPs) and 28% of councillors in local authorities were women (Norris, 2000). Nordic countries lead in having women as a substantial proportion of parliamentarians, including in its upper reaches as heads of state.

Feminist intervention in the political sphere has been guided by the realisation that 'the personal is political' (Dreifus, 1973), 'the political is personal' (Ungerson, 1987) and 'sisterhood is universal'[1] (Adamson et al, 1988). These have led to a redefinition of 'politics' to expand its horizons and to focus on power relations in interpersonal relations and governance structures (UNDP, 2002). Feminist activities target barriers to women's participation ranging from the timing of meetings and way they are run to selection processes and attitudes to women politicians. Hence, feminists reject definitions of politics that focus only on electoral processes that exclude women.

Feminists seek to eliminate the separation of politics into the public realm of electoral politics which people influence by casting their vote, and all other decisions which profoundly affect people's lives but which are made on their behalf by elected representatives (Dominelli and Jonsdottir, 1988). Feminist understandings of political processes transcend definitions of politics that are concerned primarily with the party political arena. Participation in political processes cannot be limited to casting a vote once in four or five years. This definition couples the abrogation of one's responsibilities as a citizen to a remote and rarely accountable, usually male, elected representative with actions that mystify the gendered nature of power in social interactions. Feminists have argued for power-sharing endeavours that empower women and combine personal responsibility with collective accountability.

Feminists have engaged in the political processes of government and placed feminist social action on its agenda. This activity is political because it aims to dissolve power relations that establish hierarchies between people and transform society at all levels – political, economic, social, cultural and (inter)personal. Meeting these objectives entails changing social relations between men and women, between adults and children, and between women, men and children and both local and central states.

During the 1980s, feminist political action in the UK centred on the activities of women's committees sponsored by the local state, particularly in London (Campbell et al, 1986; Whitlock, 1987; Tobin, 1990). The central state's refusal to fund feminist activities exposed their vulnerability even when endorsed by the population at large. In Nordic Iceland, feminist political parties were established to intervene directly in the electoral process (Dominelli and Jonsdottir, 1988). Neither of these paths to power led to feminist principles and practice becoming diffused throughout political life at either local or central state levels. But women have become significant players in the Icelandic government. However, their developmental project indicates that there is scant opportunity for the transformation of social relations in the political arena in accordance with feminist objectives without feminist action at all levels, including the integration of feminist action vis-à-vis the state with other feminist initiatives in the community and alliances with others.

Many of the provisions that feminists have demanded require substantial inputs from public funds and changes in the social distribution and use of power and resources. In this chapter I identify the lessons to be learnt from unsuccessful examples of feminist political action and argue for feminist political action that permeates both local and central state structures. I use case materials to examine feminist initiatives in the political arena and consider some of the reasons for their limited impact to date.

Feminism and municipal socialism

Feminist political action has taken place through a variety of forms, ranging from the formation of a Women's Party concerned with getting women the vote, as in the US at the turn of the 20th century (Irwin, 1971), to women's sections in existing major political parties and a feminist party attempting to challenge patriarchal representative democracy, as Kwenna Frambothid did in Iceland in the 1980s (Dominelli and Jonsdottir, 1988). British feminists have worked to secure change through existing political parties, the labour movement and Emily's List.[2]

British innovations in the 1980s occurred in Labour-controlled local authorities practicing a 'municipal socialism' that sought to eliminate 'race' and gender oppression in establishing genuine socialist praxis (Livingstone, 1987). These local authorities were located primarily in larger cities like Leeds, Sheffield, Birmingham and Bradford. Some defunct metropolitan counties and the Greater London Council (GLC) established Women's Committees or Women's Equal Opportunities Officers to promote women's welfare, or appointed leading feminists as staff, for example, Hilary Wainwright in the GLC's Women's Unit, Valerie Amos in Camden Borough Council's Women's Committee and Lee Comer in the Bradford Women's Committee.

The Women's Committee Support Unit of the GLC, Camden Council's Women's Unit, Birmingham Council's Women's Unit, Sheffield's Equal Opportunities Officer for Women and Leeds' Equal Opportunities Officer for Women provided major examples of feminist ventures within the local state. As feminist councillors had played key roles in promoting the development of Women's Units, these were included in their portfolios. Women workers in them made furthering the interests of women as workers and service users their main objectives. These initiatives recognised that women faced specific problems that men did not and have given priority to addressing them by establishing links with women in the community. Women normally excluded from local authority provisions were given particular attention – lesbians, disabled women, older women and black women. Reaching women in novel ways and involving them in a local authority's decision-making processes constituted major elements of their agenda. Units could draw on existing feminist networks to facilitate their reaching women usually ignored by locally elected representatives.

Working groups were one strategy adopted by feminists to link councillors and women in the community. These working groups held open meetings through which local women residents could participate in moving local state power downwards and outwards. The establishment of community forums was another venue through which this purpose was facilitated. In Camden, the Women's Unit created women's forums through which women residents met directly with women councillors.

These arrangements were flawed, however. The working groups and forums lacked power in that they could only make recommendations to the full council if women councillors accepted often controversial and radical demands. Local women were disadvantaged in having to rely on personalities to convey their wishes, thereby subverting feminist commitments to participative democracy. They were also unable to challenge either political priorities or the hierarchical nature of the political decision-making process which itself marginalised women, as the woman councillor heading the Women's Unit in Birmingham discovered when she was sacked for allegedly jeopardising Labour's electoral prospects by promoting women's equality (Whitlock, 1987).

Women's Unit activities were poorly funded, for example, in 1984 the GLC allocated £500,000 for *all* the city-wide initiatives launched by its Women's Unit. This funding was vulnerable. Authorised under Section 137 of the 1972 Local Government Act, its continuation depended on the willingness of central government to countenance it. The anti-feminist and anti-socialist sentiments of the Thatcher government ultimately in charge of the funds were echoed at the local level by its supporters who condemned the use of Section 137 monies for feminist, anti-racist or socialist purposes.

These Units' success in reaching groups formerly disenfranchised in local authority provisions contributed to their undoing. The radical nature of some demands women in the community made of Women's Units, for example, the provision of hostels and refuges for prostitutes working in the Kings Cross area of London and transport for lesbian women, were used by the popular press and Conservative opposition to accuse Labour of being under the control of the 'Loony Left', and mishandling public money by serving the interests of 'unworthy and unrepresentative' groups such as lesbians, gay men and prostitutes. Their views found resonance in the media (*News on Sunday*, 1987, p 13) and among progressive politicians who feared the loss of electoral power.

These initiatives began under a woman Prime Minister, but Margaret Thatcher had little sympathy for feminist causes and felt that individual merit (or lack of it) rather than structural inequalities accounted for women's place in society. Women lost a number of significant welfare gains during her period in power, for example, the elimination of universal maternity benefits. The abolition of the metropolitan and

GLC levels of government by the Thatcher administration, and, with these, key sites for feminist projects, indicates the importance of having a feminist political presence in the national state, and brings home the vulnerability of feminist initiatives that are located in the margins of local state activity. The marginalising of feminist political action subordinates women's work to electoral vicissitudes. Labour authorities retaining electoral popularity continued to support women's initiatives, for example, Leeds and Manchester. Others that had their electoral buoyancy punctured by negative publicity quickly panicked into scapegoating feminists and Left activists. This occurred in Birmingham where its Women's Committee was axed when Labour's share of the vote declined during the 1987 local elections (Whitlock, 1987). Attacks on feminist initiatives during moments of electoral adversity have seriously damaged feminist gains on equal opportunities policies, childcare programmes, women's safety, women's health and research projects on women's needs (Armstrong and Connelly, 1997).

Homophobic, racist and sexist opposition to these ventures ensured that many activities sponsored by the GLC's Women's Unit ceased when its abolition terminated funding. The prevalence of such sentiments in public bodies charged with promoting the welfare of *all* residents in their locality highlights how much more work feminists have to undertake if their theory and practice is to infuse local and central government structures. It also demonstrates how feminist gains have to be underwritten at all levels of society if they are to be protected from attack. This includes the trade union movement, community groups, political parties and the local and central state.

Unelected bodies such as the House of Lords and High Court also reinforce gendered social relations. They are dominated by men and their decisions often endorse anti-feminist stances, for example, the Court of Appeal striking down all-women lists that aimed to increase women's representation in Parliament. Emily's List, begun in the US in 1985 and copied later in the UK, contributed to these gains. Yet the Blair government, with the largest proportion of women MPs ever, failed to include women in the cabinet in substantial numbers. Nor were independent minded women in those ranks highly valued as Mo Mowlam, Secretary of State for Northern Ireland, and Harriet Harmon, Secretary of State for Health, discovered during the first Blair administration (Langdon, 2000). Even the reshuffle after the 2005 election retained Gordon Brown, Charles Clarke and Jack Straw in the top three posts of Chancellor, Home Secretary and Foreign Secretary respectively.

An autonomous feminist political organisation: lessons from Iceland

Feminists in Iceland sought to influence the electoral process in dramatic ways. They established a feminist political party, Kwenna Frambothid (KF), in November 1981. Entering the arena as a new force guided by feminist principles, theories and practice, KF women organised themselves according to egalitarian precepts. Each woman in the party had a role in promoting its potential among the electorate. Their party programme was developed collectively. Women supported each other in learning how to handle the media by role-playing their parts with each other and sharing their skills and experiences so that they could learn from one another. Their endeavours paid off, and they gained a sizeable share of the vote under a system of proportional representation in the 1982 local elections, and successfully elected feminist councillors in Reykjavik and Akureyri, Iceland's two largest cities.

KF councillors maintained links with the feminist movement beyond the local state by networking and holding open meetings to enable women in the community to have direct access to them. This extended their store of social capital and kept women connected. It enabled them to develop an understanding of the issues that worried women in the community, to facilitate feminist research, to support the creation of specific resources for women, such as a women's resources centre, a women's newspaper and a refuge, and to attract working-class women members (Dominelli and Jonsdottir, 1988).

The formation of the Organisation of Women in the Labour Market (SKV) was one of KF's major initiatives aimed at recruiting working-class women and creating an organisation for tackling inequality in the workplace. KF also supported women in direct action as they attempted to raise public consciousness about the plight of women. The format adopted in raising consciousness was often highly imaginative. For example, KF women protested women's low wages by staging a public demonstration in Reykjavik's supermarkets. Selecting the ingredients for rice pudding which a male government minister had promoted as being nutritious and within the financial reach of all Icelanders, the women who demonstrated offered to pay 60% of the price of the goods since women earned that proportion of men's wages.

Some of the perplexed women cashiers accepted the amounts tendered, others called their male managers. When KF women refused to leave and started singing protest songs and dancing in the supermarkets, the managers called the police(men). The police watched the women's performance helplessly and sought to tread a fine line between maintaining law and order and allowing a peaceful protest. The women protesters left the premises of their own accord once they had made their point. Their protest made interesting copy in the newspapers.

The KF women's organisational daring also came to the fore when they responded to a sexist challenge inadvertently pronounced by Reykjavik's mayor at a 'beauty contest'. He commented that if KF women had such beauties, they could more readily ensure women's equality in the council chambers. KF women arranged to bring their 'beauty contest' into Reykjavik Council's deliberations. Assuming titles of virtues men wish women to hold, for example, 'Miss Patience', the KF women entered the meeting room wearing the sashes of 'beauty queens'. The one KF councillor who participated in the proceedings (the other refused) read out a statement from the group and tabled their previously agreed comments on each agenda item. The group then sat down and did not speak for the rest of the meeting. The media, alerted to the action, had a field day, to the chagrin of the mayor (Dominelli and Jonsdottir, 1988).

For a brief period, KF women's commitment, the newness of the venture and the enthusiasm of women participants worked, giving Icelandic women a sense of power in the electoral arena, and reduced hierarchies between the elected representatives and women residents. The hierarchical council structures within which the feminist councillors had to operate quickly sapped KF's organisational initiatives and distorted the processes and group dynamics that the KF councillors had established to promote interaction with the women electorate.

Collective deliberations on KF councillors' responses to the many items on their lengthy council agendas consumed most of their time and energies. While consistent with feminist ideals of ensuring representation, this method of working destroyed both the process in and spontaneity of the meetings that councillors held with constituents. Responding to council issues consumed all the available time and prevented women from raising other issues that worried them. Demoralisation and disillusionment set in, creating divisions among the women (Dominelli and Jonsdottir, 1988). The failure of KF to tackle key impediments to women's full involvement in political activities contributed to their disenchantment. KF lacked a position on the role of men in the organisation and was unable to address inequalities arising from women's responsibilities in the home as well as waged work. And by responding to issues on an ad hoc basis, KF did not offer women a vision of the future.

Eventually, KF women's inability to agree on their approach to electoral politics caused a split between feminist women and woman-centred women. In 1983, the latter went on to form Kwenna Listin (KL) while KF folded. The basis of their disagreement was critical to feminist strategies in the electoral arena. KF women who refused to join KL felt that their experience of the electoral process warranted their removing themselves from it to serve women's interests more effectively through autonomous organising outside state political processes. KL women felt that the modest gains they had made in improving women's welfare, raising women's issues for debate and extending women's involvement in traditional parties, demanded their continued participation in electoral structures. They felt there had been a shift leftwards as the other major political parties adopted women candidates and gave women's issues a higher profile to stem erosion in support from progressive factions of the electorate. KL women stood for the 1983 and 1987 national elections and won 3 and 6 seats respectively (Dominelli and Jonsdottir, 1988). KF and KL increased the number of women in government from 5% in 1981 to 30% by 1995.

Tensions continued about what constituted feminist action in the political arena, who defined it and how it was carried out. KL later regrouped as the Women's Alliance (Samtö kum kvennalista), but split in 1997. The Women's Alliance had some success in promoting feminist concerns for the environment, equality and social justice, a fair and prosperous economy and independent political movement. The Women's Alliance joined a Left–Green Movement in 1999 that brought it together with social democrats and conservationists to promote Left politics in a neoliberal global context.

The Icelandic experience suggests that the formation of a feminist political party alone cannot transform the electoral process and orient it in feminist directions. Rather, its existence in isolation from a feminist presence at all levels of society is likely to dissipate feminist energies and lead to the fractures that occurred in Iceland (Dominelli and McLeod, 1989). The price feminists may have to pay for becoming involved in the electoral process in the short term can negate feminist egalitarian principles as happened when collective processes in meetings between KF councillors and women were usurped by having to respond to bureaucratically derived agendas.

Feminist political action outside electoral politics

Existing political institutions have proven poor vehicles for promoting feminist aims and objectives. British feminists have attempted to transcend the limitations involved in these by developing forums that unite different groupings in progressive 'fragments of the Left', as these became known (Rowbotham et al, 1980). The first of these was the 'Beyond the Fragments Conference' in 1980. Socialists disillusioned with the Labour Party have followed this with other organisational forms, for example, the newspaper *Red Pepper*, left-leaning political parties and conferences. These have failed to 'unite the fragments' in effective opposition to Thatcherism or later Blairism.

Other feminist initiatives have focused on changing their personal politics and have given rise to 'identity politics' which enable women to change particular forms of oppression affecting them personally (Adams, 1989). The danger of this strategy is that it will fragment feminist initiatives even further and ignore the broader sources of oppression emanating from social divisions other than gender, for example, 'race', class and disability (hooks, 1984; Morris, 1991). Feminists need to affirm diversity within unity by finding commonalities among women whose experiences of oppression are dissimilar. As bell hooks (1984, p 58) explains:

> … our different experiences often meant that we had different needs, that there was no one strategy or formula for the development of political consciousness. By mapping out various strategies, we affirmed our diversity while working towards solidarity.

Feminists have undertaken a range of women-only initiatives that challenge the lack of provisions capable of meeting women's specific needs and seek to eliminate the destructive consumerist orientation of late capitalist society. The women's peace movement illustrates these. It has uncovered connections between the squandering of social resources on armaments while children around the world die of hunger; the massive profits made by multinational companies dealing in weapons; the failure of these corporations to pay taxes; the destruction of non-military jobs to provide resources for the defence industry; the usurping of welfare monies to feed the war machine (Davis, 1989); and the environmental degradation caused in pursuit of peace through war, for example, in Iraq in 1991 and 2003 and in Afghanistan. The destruction wrought through these conflicts is but a larger, more public version of the atrocities that occurred in Rwanda, the former Yugoslavia and Sudan. Feminists have redefined the concept of defence by arguing for non-violent solutions to social conflict. To illustrate these, I turn to examine the implications for feminist community action of the Greenham Common Women's Peace Movement of the 1980s. Its lessons remain resonant today and the organisational techniques it followed remain inspirational.

The contribution of the Greenham Common Women to feminist political action

The Women's Peace Camp at Greenham Common near Newbury, England, unlike its mixed counterparts, the Campaign for Nuclear Disarmament (CND) and European Nuclear Disarmament Campaign (END) and its local derivatives like the Leamington European Nuclear Disarmament Campaign (LEND), is a women-only endeavour based on feminist principles. Its feminist stance has separated Greenham Common from other initiatives that women have mounted for peace, for example, Olga Maitland's Families for Peace. Maitland's group supported the multilateral disarmament position advocated by the British government.

Greenham embodies a different kind of politics that links people's welfare, concern for the environment, world peace and local forms of organisation in empowering those whose normal experience is one of powerlessness. Its commitment to change is total, demanding the radical alteration of intimate personal relations and more remote social ones articulated through representative democracies. Greenham Women's organising potential depended on the creative use of the limited resources that people brought when confronting a powerful state backed by multinational finance. This form of organisation draws strength from its capacity to facilitate individual contributions to the collective effort according to their own personal assessment of it (Dominelli, 1986c) rather than subjecting individual endeavours to negative evaluations by others.

The principle of allowing women to make their own decisions about their personal contributions to collective activities enabled Greenham Women to maintain loyalty to the group, interact with each other on a more egalitarian basis and be absolved from feeling guilty for not conforming to group expectations. These organisational advantages were fashioned by Greenham Women's commitment to feminist principles of practice. Unlike traditional groups which rely on group coercion that compels individuals to commit themselves beyond their personal capacity and engender guilt if they fail to respond in prescribed ways, Greenham Women's responsibility to the group was discharged by each individual woman admitting where her personal limits lay (Cook and Kirk, 1983). This approach ensured that women committed themselves to action that they would carry out and that others could value and count on.

The Greenham Common Women's Peace Movement was created spontaneously by a group of women who had not previously participated in political protests. Women formed the Camp after marching from Cardiff to Greenham in August 1981 to protest the siting of cruise missiles in Britain. Their major motivation was the nightmarish one of seeing powerful military figures over whom they had no control threaten to plunge the world into a nuclear holocaust, thereby holding theirs and others' lives to ransom and destroying the planet (Cook and Kirk, 1983). Fear for the future fired their determination to resist the escalation of nuclear weaponry by community-based political action and by demanding British unilateral nuclear disarmament. These women organised without community workers. Belying assumed powerlessness as women, Greenham Women and their supporters, particularly the inner core of activists living in 'benders' (tents constructed of plastic sheets) at the Camp, undertook mass actions that brought bridging capital into play. By expanding bridging capital through mobilisation and interactions among women – friends, relatives and supporters – they demonstrated that women have power that can be exercised in novel ways.

The Greenham Women created a peace camp that ultimately became a women-only one capable of surviving continuous harassment, threats of eviction, imprisonment and state violence. Greenham Women formed a women-only camp after considerable discussion among themselves. Not all the women were adherents of feminist theory and practice, but their experience of a mixed camp with both men and women during a brief period at the beginning of their venture prompted the women to exclude men from the Camp. During their short sojourn at Greenham, men supporters established patriarchal forms of organisation. These included hierarchical relationships among participants, the control of knowledge and organisational skills by a small clique and men occupying the key decision-making roles, taking aggressive stances that endorsed violence towards and the sexual harassment of women (Cook and Kirk, 1983). Believing that these behaviours replicated the system that was causing the problems they wanted to solve, the women asked the men to leave.

Greenham Women eschewed patriarchal forms of organising and

resisted women's exclusion from the public arena. They held machismo responsible for pushing the world to the brink of nuclear war and rejected all it stood for. Maintaining that only women could deconstruct male forms of organisation, they set up a women-only Camp and developed new ways of structuring social relations among themselves. Their attitudes have been criticised as essentialist and alienating men. The presence of feminists at Greenham meant that there was an ideology that countered patriarchy, and offered women an alternative world view (Feminism and Non-Violence Study Group, 1983) and provided a constituency outside the Base in the Women's Liberation Movement from which Greenham Women could draw support during a lengthy dispute. Despite earlier imprisonment for action at Greenham, several veterans went to protest environmental degradation at Fylingdale in 2001 (Barwick, 2001) and 2005.

Greenham Women's decision to have a women-only Camp enabled them to increase their contact with other women and discover how women could work collaboratively with one another. Working together enabled women to focus on eroding the social divisions that existed among them, especially those concerning class, 'race', age, disability and sexual orientation. It enabled them to confront familial ideology and constraints placed on women's ability to participate in public activities and events. Greenham provided another arena for highlighting the link between women's place in the home and lack of involvement in public life. Greenham Women experienced the pain of leaving their families, especially their children. But they discovered that they, their children and partners could cope. Their menfolk were compelled to accept 'women's work' as their own, and, in undertaking childcare and housework, challenge their own stereotypes and attitudes (Cook and Kirk, 1983) about gender roles and the division of labour attendant on it.

Some men feared the power of women symbolised by the Greenham Women. They felt threatened by their exclusion from the Camp and related activities because they had not previously experienced being unilaterally deprived of power by women. Heterosexual women, who were still in the process of working out their position, felt undermined by the charges of lesbianism which formed part of the media's smear campaign, lamenting the demise of family ties caused by women's presence at the Camp. The media's stance played on and compounded women's feelings of guilt at 'abandoning' children and partners. The schism among Greenham's supporters inside and outside the Base made it easier for the media to condemn Greenham Women for doing their own thing, even if this included ultimately nurturing the world by preventing its destruction through nuclear war.

Collective, egalitarian relations became the Greenham Women's hallmark as they struggled against state harassment and physical deprivation. Working cooperatively enabled women to assert their power both individually and collectively. Individual women were encouraged to reach their own decisions about their involvement in Greenham activities and not be coerced by group cohesion and dynamics into adopting decisions others made on their behalf. Participative democracy created the ethos in which they worked, lived and played. They were assertive and confident without being aggressive. Non-violence was their counter to violence (Feminist and Non-Violence Study Group, 1983). Women outside the Base came to their defence spreading their stories, providing material and emotional support and participating in the mass activities that sprung from Greenham.

Greenham Women were unclear about their long-term strategy but they knew that they had to redefine politics and grasp the initiative from the state that had set the parameters around the nuclear debate. They focused sharply and simply on the lethal potential of cruise missiles. This they hoped would reach the hearts and minds of people typically uninvolved in politics and rouse them in a process of self-discovery to consciousness of the threat hanging over them, and convince them of their power to challenge the state's construction of the issue and decision to locate cruise missiles in the UK.

The Greenham Women furthered their objective of supplanting the state's position by contrasting the destructive anti-life potential of nuclear weapons with the celebration of everyday life. They persistently refused to vacate their Camp and made it their home against all odds for 20 years. They called for mass action bringing together public displays of fragments of ordinary existence pregnant with meaning to validate everyday reality for the individuals involved. They celebrated items that embodied the principles of daily life in practice. Photographs of loved ones and other memorabilia formed symbols of protest adorning the perimeter fence at Greenham. The symbolic juxtaposition of daily joy and life with the slaughter of war achieved prominence during mass actions. The encircling of the Base by 30,000 women and their individual statements in December 1982 proved an extremely powerful demonstration of the fusion between society's political decision-making processes and their impact on people's personal lives and everyday routines.

Having women individually develop their own spaces and statements increased their sense of participation and confidence in this mass project. Acting in accordance with the principles of women personally determining their contribution to the struggle also ensured that the definition of the situation was one that each woman had created rather than one determined by others and imposed on them. Each woman's statement was a personalised comment embedded in her own beliefs. Conducting their action on these premises enabled women to share their personal consciousness and fears with others. It was also a way of maximising the impact of the limited resources available to the group. The actions at Greenham revealed that a non-violent, collective show of strength and quiet determination was possible and could be influential. These popularised Greenham Women's vision of a peaceful world and contrasted sharply with the aggressive man-made one the state was peddling (Cook and Kirk, 1983).

Greenham Women followed feminist principles and processes in their actions. Small group discussions and workshops were the main forums that Greenham Women used to consider their activities, to take decisions about their exact nature and identify their individual contributions to it. Following principles of feminist non-violence, women discussed and examined the law, the possibility of their arrest and precautions they could take to ensure their physical and emotional safety (Cook and Kirk, 1983).

Networking was an important means through which Greenham Women acquired influence that went beyond the numbers living at the Camp and surpassed national boundaries. This enabled them to receive financial and moral support from women in other countries and encouraged the creation of women-only peace camps elsewhere, for example, Iceland and Italy. Networking is an important means through which community work can transcend parochial boundaries and augment resources in non-competitive ways. More recently, the World March of Women has extended feminist forms of organisations globally, bridging countries in the North and South and forming extensive networks including with the World Social Forum to promote peace and demilitarisation in a troubled world (Prigoff, 2000).

The powerful nature of their working methodology was evident in all Greenham Women's activities. The 'die-in' at the Stock Exchange on 7 June 1982, where women lay down on a major road in the City to disrupt traffic, provides one illustration of its expression in practice (Kirk and Cook, 1983). In the 'die-in', Greenham Women demonstrated how easily women can release their creativity and make political statements through the artefacts of everyday life. Small self-selected decentralised groups planned the 'die-in' and facilitated the processes through which individuals proceeded to develop their personal contribution to a collective undertaking. The working principles enshrined in the relationships fostered within these groups promoted a form of organisation that empowered rather than deskilled women. Individual women were supported when they voiced their fears about being run over, being verbally abused or imprisoned for being in conflict with the law. No woman was coerced by others to take on more than she personally felt able to handle. Nor was she made to feel guilty for drawing boundaries around the extent of her involvement and sticking to feeling comfortable with her contribution. As indicated above, these principles also underpinned Greenham Women's mass actions.

Greenham Women's challenge to the state's definitions of the cruise missile problem quickly generated enormous support for and mobilised large numbers of people – men and women – in favour of unilateral nuclear disarmament, a position formally adopted by the Labour Party and put before the electorate in the 1985 General Election. Labour failed to achieve electoral victory, but its programme was endorsed by one third of those voting, indicating that a significant proportion of the British populace endorsed this stance. Greenham Women's influence spread to the broader peace movement, especially CND and END, and inspired organisations concerned with other issues, for example, the 'March for Jobs Campaign', and captured the imagination of sundry individuals.

Those moved by the Greenham Women's actions implemented many of their ideas and practices in their own organisations. The mixed peace movement became more aware of gender oppression and adopted many of the methods used by the Greenham Women in its own activities (Dominelli, 1986c). The impact of Greenham was especially evident in the 1983 Easter demonstrations. Linking personal experiences and non-violent direct action to political decisions made by a small caucus of politicians in government were to feature prominently in these.

Organisations like CND promoted the work of Greenham Women by asking them to speak to members and impart lessons gained from their way of organising. Besides helping women to engage in further consciousness raising, this sharing of their views with others enabled Greenham Women to obtain both moral and material support for their cause. Many women from these other organisations joined in the major protests that took place at Greenham.

Growing public support for Greenham Women and the penetration of their ideas and methods to other organisations made the state fear the powers that could be unleashed by them. The state launched a concerted counter-offensive that encouraged women to form hierarchically structured 'peace groups' endorsing the North Atlantic Treaty Organisation (NATO) decisions, for example, Olga Maitland's Families for Peace. These groupings were unable to attract either mass public sympathy or large numbers of women.

The state also initiated a massive media campaign disparaging Greenham Women and belittling their concerns. It placed a powerful and articulate government minister, Michael Heseltine, the then Minister of Defence, in charge of its media onslaught and propaganda against them. The state also intensified the harassment of Greenham Women, although they had already undergone frequent evictions from their Camp and destruction of their 'benders'. State harassment was intensified as legal processes swung into action against them. In some instances, local by-laws were changed to deal with their presence. Legal intimidation of Greenham Women also included their being denied voting rights in local elections and access to social security benefits.

The physical security of the Base was strengthened in recognition of the damage that could be caused by a few committed women acting without offensive weapons. Barbed wire was placed around the perimeter fence and policing assumed a higher profile. Vast sums of public money were invested in these measures as the state redefined the issue of Greenham as a matter of 'law and order'. Evidence emerged suggesting that 'ray guns' had been used to repel the women camping at the gates (Beasley, 1986). Thus, 'Star Wars' became a reality for the women at Greenham.

The state's responses ultimately signalled the weaknesses of the Greenham Women's approach, despite its replication in peace camps in Australia, Iceland, Italy and the US. Relying almost exclusively on resources generated among themselves and their supporters, Greenham Women failed to shift the existing balance of power between themselves and the state. But they needed to achieve this if they were to successfully reverse state policy. Like other feminist initiatives in the political arena, Greenham demonstrates the importance of having a feminist presence in both local and central state structures, the trade union movement and society more generally for its achievements to be sustained over lengthy periods of time, especially if under sustained attack by a state and media whose actions they are trying to subvert.

Another weakness of the Greenham Women's approach stemmed from their analysis of patriarchy. Identifying *men's* construction of the social order as the problem held the danger of seeing 'men' as the enemy rather than patriarchal and militarised social relations. And by ignoring some men's contributions to the struggle for peace, it allows other men to continue reinforcing oppressive relations. Some feminists, for example, black feminists like Angela Davis (1989) and bell hooks (1984), argued that men, especially working-class men, have a crucial role to play in the peace movement because the war movement is advanced by capitalist social relations that oppress working-class men and women. This is highly relevant to black men who are over-represented in the lower ranks of the army, often choosing it as career because they lack other options. The question of the nature of the relationship between men and feminist social action remains problematic and has yet to be addressed adequately.

The polarisation of values into negative ones held by men and positive ones embraced by women simply inverts the existing hegemonic dyad of gender oppression and runs the risk of endorsing biological determinism. It also ignores the merging of people's value systems in reality and the roles women play in reinforcing patriarchal relations when conforming to dominant ideological norms, as Olga Maitland's group demonstrated. Both men and women support capitalist patriarchal relations and it is these which men and women have to eradicate to create egalitarian relationships between them. The feminist message that the 'personal is political' and the 'political is personal' has to be unpacked more fully if both women and men are to engage in creating a new egalitarian world order that values and celebrates diversity and individuals and links personal action to institutional change.

The impact of the Greenham Women's Peace Movement on traditional community action

Networking with individuals and progressive fragments were crucial to spreading the word about developments at Greenham Common, and created solidarity from transient forms of bridging capital that touched people's lives. Widespread public exposure in the media, the involvement of thousands of women community activists in Greenham Common activities and the talks that Greenham Women have had with community groups have meant that the ideas and forms of organisation initiated by a nucleus of women at Greenham Common have filtered through to large numbers of people active in more traditional types of community work. Greenham Women's contributions have highlighted the development of a new strand of community action that has questioned traditional forms of community organisation. Particularly relevant in this context are: the hierarchical nature of accepted relationships between the organisers and the organised; community workers' expectations about group dynamics; and traditional concepts of locality-based organising. Additionally, Greenham Women challenged state power and transcended local boundaries to reach out globally to other women who shared their desire for lasting peace.

By compelling community workers to re-examine traditional positions, Greenham Women became a catalyst for changing the nature of community work to promote more egalitarian organisational and less stigmatising forms of participation. These acknowledge individual contributions to collective ends from their own standpoint and recognise their expertise and knowledge of life events. Revitalising methods of organising has been noticeable in community work among women who supported Greenham events, for example, the Coventry Women's Health Network (CWHN, 1985).

Community workers can pick up on experiences of empowerment that flow from feminist work in small groups like those fostered at Greenham. Most people feel uninvolved in key decisions affecting community life. These include school closures, factory relocations, road-building programmes, destruction of the local environment and absence of leisure facilities. People redefine their aspirations for communities by wresting initiative from the state and powerful others who problematise their existence and deny their right to act for themselves in creating the social and physical environment best suited to fulfilling existences. Redefining their lives requires people to raise their individual consciousness and to make explicit connections between macro-level political processes and the microcosms within which they lead personal lives.

Community work allegedly embarks on such processes. However, it usually does this within the parameters of traditional thought that do not challenge established knowledge and modes of action. Foremost among these are the separation of an issue from its holistic social context, the subordination of social criteria to economic ones in political decision-making processes and devaluing of non-expert knowledge. Bureaucratic procedures are used to manipulate discussions and hinder free flowing creativity (see Alinksy, 1971). The conduct of a public meeting considering the demolition of housing for road construction can illustrate this restrictive methodology in traditional community work. People attending it can feel frustrated and angry if they have been treated as passive participants and their concerns have not been prominent in the proceedings. This is because there has been no fusion between the political and the personal and no connection between remote political decision making and people's daily lives. Aggressive posturing rather than a true confrontation of the issues has taken place (Dominelli, 1986c).

Other features of Greenham Women's approach to community action include:

- creating women-only spaces to empower women;
- challenging gender stereotypes by ensuring that men do not grab all the powerful decision-making positions such as being chairperson; highlighting women's capacity to take and play key roles in making decisions; having men undertake nurturing tasks such as making the tea and minding the children; and freeing women's energies to assume other responsibilities; and
- altering worker–group interaction by endorsing collective group dynamics that eliminate hierarchical relationships between community workers and group members and provide individuals with the space to reach their own decisions.

Working along Greenham Women's lines makes community workers more accountable to community groups. Community workers maintain organisational expertise and play a role in initiating ideas, but do so as group members and participate in implementing action on the same basis as everyone else. Community workers boost group morale and refuel group commitment to the task at hand. They endorse collective working, sharing skills and developing participatory mechanisms. In forming groups consistent with feminist practice, community workers encourage people to use their own skills and assume personal responsibility for the decisions each takes as a group member. Ensuring a group's survival as a collective democratic entity marks the task of a community worker as different from that of other activists.

Moreover, community workers can facilitate the liberation of thought by enabling people to become involved in consciousness-raising exercises that help them redefine their personal realities in social terms. In these, people can give expression to affective responses and emotions, thereby connecting external decision making with personal experiences of its impact on their lives.

Community workers can contribute to eliminating the sexist domestic division of labour. Confronting the constraints that familial ideology places on women enables community workers to play an active role in overcoming barriers to the participation of women in protest actions. They can also encourage men to assume nurturing roles and childcare duties. Facilitating such activities allows community workers to tackle social divisions that inhibit collective community responses and move people into forming non-oppressive relationships. And they would be resisting the subordination of welfare needs to economic exigencies.

Community workers will encounter state hostility if they organise challenges to state power or hegemony of the dominant ideology. Preparing for negative state responses to their endeavours requires community workers to build extensive networks with overwhelming public support locally, nationally and internationally. They have to mobilise both public and personal resources in favour of their cause. Community activists can confront the state through non-violent action but must develop extensive support bases and alliances before taking action and as it unfolds. They can endorse collective ways of working but these may be problematic. Consciousness raising is a powerful medium. Yet its impact on community work will be limited if groups do not acquire the resources and widespread support they need to translate awareness into action promoting transformational social change. Only by securing these can community workers avoid losing gains however circumscribed, as exemplified by the Greenham Women's Peace Movement (Dominelli, 1986c).

Ecofeminism and redefining economic and environmental issues

Some of these themes have been picked up in feminist environmental campaigns. Ecofeminism, a political ideology located in 'new' social movements concerned with ecological diversity, shows that industrialisation destroys interdependence and promotes economic growth as if it occurs without social and physical contexts. Ecofeminist Vandana Shiva's work on environmental campaigns against transnational corporations that have usurped farmers' right to harvest and plant their own seeds in India illustrates the connections between people's daily lives, knowledge, identity, autonomy, livelihoods, the environment and loss of basic human rights (Shiva, 1993, 2003). Diverse Women for Diversity is a global movement defending 'food rights and biological cultural diversity' (Shiva, 2003). It seeks to undermine economistic development, promote women's strengths and extend limited resources by a locally rooted holistic activism that cares for the earth when producing food. It deems decentralised production, nurturing the environment and localism capable of protecting biodiversity and defying globalisation to stay the appropriation of local knowledge and genetic resources. In short, these movements question traditional definitions of production and reproduction (Leff, 1995; Shiva, 2003; Reisch, 2004).

Arundhati Roy, another ecofeminist, has raised similar concerns in the campaign against the construction of the Sardar Sarovan Dam. Begun as a struggle against the damming of the Narmada river valley in India, it grew into an anti-dam movement that challenged the Indian political system, American corporatism and transnational companies seeking profit-making opportunities in industrialising countries (Roy, 1999). Pseudo-scientific claims that newly created jobs outweighed the ensuing environmental destruction and homelessness were challenged by grassroots mobilisation that included big names like Roy (1999). She was subsequently taken to court and ended up in the Supreme Court of India in 2002 over her actions in defence of this environment and its peoples, especially the Dalits (formerly the Untouchables). These actions show that ecofeminism has been important in turning the community as a marginal site into an emerging centre of critique, innovation and alternative visioning of the world. It challenges neoliberal tenets, favours local production and supports bio-cultural diversity (Escobar, 1998). Ecofeminists use the World Wide Web (WWW) to get support for and publicise their causes, create transnational practices that link virtual and place-based modes of activism, and promote a cyber-cultural politics that defends place. These movements pit economic rationality against an alternative, ecological rationality rooted in identity (Escobar, 1998).

Organising tips

To work in non-oppressive ways consider the following critical questions:

- What are the implications of particular actions for women, other oppressed peoples and the environment?
- How do these differ from those of the group being worked with? Why?
- How are marginalised groups supported through daily activities?

Conclusion

Feminist social action in the political arena has challenged both electoral politics and traditional ways of working within community groups. These activities aim to include women more fully in this sphere and create more collaborative ways of involving individuals in collective action. And they seek to deprivilege economic rationality in determining the development of the social and physical environments that are necessary in sustaining life. These threads have been picked up by the women's environmental and peace movements to challenge global corporatist destruction of the balance between the earth and the people who rely on its resources.

Notes

[1] The 'sisterhood is universal' slogan captured women's commitment to eradicating gender oppression early in the Women's Liberation Movement. Its view of *sameness* in women's experiences of oppression has been rejected to acknowledge and value women's differences and to work towards a unity that celebrates diversity and to improve women's specific positions in practical ways.

[2] Emily's List stands for 'Early Money is Like Yeast'. It raises money to increase Democratic women's representation in American federal elections and was launched in 1993 by Labour women in the UK.

NINE

Conclusions: changing communities and women's roles within them

Women's lives are grounded in the communities in which they reside and people they relate to. The boundaries between communities of interest, identity and location are often blurred for them. Matters of environmental degradation and other quality of life issues are of central concern and they engage in activities that defend personal and communal spaces through direct action. Women play important, if unacknowledged, roles in communities, their endeavours being taken for granted or ignored. I end this book by arguing that women's work in communities becomes visible, celebrated and valued.

Organising women in the community

Patriarchal relations prevailing in society have been reflected in community work. Women are significant participants in community action defending humanitarian, caring values in the community and maintaining the standards of living of working-class peoples and other marginalised groups, but their contributions are consistently underrated. Only occasionally does the community work literature recognise this reality and emphasise women's involvement in general community issues (Mayo, 1977; Curno et al, 1982; Dominelli, 1990; Lowndes, 2000). It is almost as if women were invisible, operating only in supporting roles behind the scenes. Historically, community action by women has been crucial in advancing community causes. Housing struggles over rent controls, for example, Glasgow in 1915 (Mayo, 1977; Ginsburg, 1979) and continued contributions to a community's store of social capital through associational activities to improve people's well-being indicate this (Lowndes, 2000).

The Women's Liberation Movement and women's increasing consciousness of their position as subordinate members of society has led to organising with other women over issues of major concern to their welfare – military violence, physical and sexual assaults on women in intimate relationships and elsewhere, women's poor emotional well-being and pitiable quality of life in late capitalist society. Supporting women through the traumas associated with these experiences has preoccupied the Women's Peace Movement, the National Women's Aid Federation, Women's Rape Crisis Centres, feminist therapists and ecofeminists. By undertaking gender-specific action, women have exposed the material hardship and emotional suffering that permeates their lives. They have exposed constraints on women's ability to organise and care for themselves imposed by family responsibilities they continue to carry, limited financial independence exacerbated by precarious positions in the waged labour market and unwaged married women's dependence on men for financial security. These constraints receive legitimacy in the marriage contract; state legislation, including those concerning social security, taxation and pensions that aggregate 'family' resources without recognising their unequal distribution within families; and limited opportunities and facilities accessed by waged and unwaged women.

Community activists intending to organise with women need to understand these structural constraints and facilitate women's handling of them in practice and take practical steps that nurture their willingness to meet others and organise over common issues. Community workers should be prepared to dissolve the distinction between professionals and ordinary group members by undertaking role reversals which have them as professionals servicing lay people, for example, community workers preparing the tea while women meet and men mind children. Community workers should aim to become redundant by ensuring that a group quickly assumes responsibility for making decisions and acquires the knowledge and skills needed to conduct its business.

When organising with women in the community, it is not enough to organise them in small groups, although this is essential for women to understand personal experiences, strengthen their demands, develop their confidence and raise consciousness about the positions of women in society. Making connections between the social organisation of reality and personal experiences acquires political significance and facilitates crucial challenges to gender oppression. This can become widespread if women form alliances with others outside small, women-only groups. These can cover trade unionists, politicians, professionals, men and women in voluntary organisations, neighbours and others contacted via the Internet (Burrows et al, 2005).

As the experiences of British feminists working in the local state to foster anti-racist and anti-sexist initiatives and American feminists' lengthy struggle over reproductive rights reveal, limited feminist gains have to be underpinned by broader support to withstand determined anti-feminist opposition (Adamson et al, 1988). This has to encompass the central state which must be permeated by a feminist political presence if it is to underwrite social change at all levels of society. When forming alliances with others to maximise the group's strengths and increase its numerical standing, a feminist group has to ensure that it is not incorporated by their allies (Bishop, 1994). Otherwise, it will lose its own political thrust and independent impact and find its commitment to egalitarian processes of interaction and relationships subverted.

Organising with women in the community is not easy, given that women are isolated from one another in the workplace and when performing their domestic tasks at home. Feminists have shown that these obstacles are not impossible to overcome. Women's involvement in local community issues, homeworkers' campaigns (Hopkins, 1982), housing campaigns (Mayo, 1977), campaigns around issues concerning single-parent families (Mayo, 1977), older women's campaigns (Doress and Siegal, 1987), health campaigns (Ruzek, 1978; Doyal, 1983), nuclear disarmament (Cook and Kirk, 1983), workplace issues such as sexual harassment (Benn and Sedely, 1982) and equal pay (WEU, 2003) and environmental campaigns (Shiva, 2003) provide testimonials to women's organising abilities and supportive actions. Women will come together to fight for their interests if the forms of organising used are those which pick up on their needs as **women** *organising*. Women's resilience in struggle has been evident in women workers' industrial action and community initiatives. Some of the most protracted battles on the wage labour front in recent times have been mounted and sustained by women, for example, Mansfield Hosiery, Imperial Typewriters, Grunwick, Chix, Lee Jeans, Kigass and Gateway Gourmet.

Community workers organising with women have to walk a tightrope. They must ensure that their activities do not ghettoise organising with women and relegate it to second place in the wider community work movement. Preventing this from occurring is crucial if organising with women is not to be subsumed by male prerogative and to act as an extension of male community workers' preserve. The welfare needs of women community workers and demands for equal pay have to be addressed. Safeguarding women's interests entails considering their waged work and domestic commitments, ensuring equality of opportunity and recognising their specific contributions to organising. Many of the rights women demand in both waged working and domestic life, for example, the right to an independent income, a violence-free existence and personal well-being, are as relevant to children and men as to women. Hence, alliances to secure these for all people are possible. It is not an either/or situation that produces only winners and losers. All can win by working together in egalitarian ways.

Feminist community action has advanced the welfare of children, women and men. But its achievements have suffered reverses, and its goal of eliminating gender oppression remains distant. The progress made has maintained women's morale and encouraged the continued struggle for their rights, a humanity-oriented world and social justice. It has also affirmed women's conviction that there is nothing 'natural' about their subordinate position and that the fatalistic outlook that follows from this is inimical to their interests. Women can and do act to promote their visions of the world and work to make these a reality. Moreover, the intersection between gender oppression and other forms of oppression, for example, racism, ageism, disablism and classism, have to be tackled specifically. Gender equality will not magically feature on the world's agenda if the issue is not tackled directly.

Feminist community action and the future

Feminist community action appears to have increased relevancy to people caught in a web of declining welfare services, rising joblessness and diminished civil and human rights as cost-conscious governments seek to repress people's resistance to oppressive social relations through both 'hard' and 'soft' forms of social control and to claw back earlier feminist gains, for example, women's reproductive rights in the USA, and women's employment protection and social benefits in the UK. Women are organising in the community, albeit on a self-help basis, to promote their interests. The principles that feminists use in guiding these activities are relevant to all community workers irrespective of the gender of group members because they aim to eliminate hierarchy and relations of dominance in individual and group interactions throughout society.

Feminist theory and practice: guiding principles

Good quality general training for community workers is provided by groups like the Federation for Community Development Learning, the Community Development Foundation and others using the National Occupational Standards for the profession. Those linked to social justice, sustainable communities and reflective practice, overlap with feminist concerns (Ledwith, 2001). But there is no magic tool kit that can be labelled 'Feminist Practice – Ready for Use'. Feminist practice is about forming relationships that will bring out the best in people through collaborative egalitarian ways of working and initiating social change that eliminates inequalities especially those impacting on women. Its principles can be used in judging social interactions and providing guidance for working in empowering ways. These are:

- developing an individual's full potential;
- eliminating gender oppression;
- transforming social relations in egalitarian directions;
- fostering the well-being of all women in society regardless of social status, including class, 'race', sexual orientation, age, physical or mental capacities;
- acknowledging the political nature of all social relations;
- acknowledging the political nature of knowledge;
- promoting egalitarian relations between men and women, adults and children;
- increasing women's control over their lives;
- having a right to welfare;
- making caring a collective responsibility undertaken by both men and women;
- acknowledging interconnectedness between the public and private spheres;
- ensuring that work, whether in the home or workplace, gives women choices about what they are doing, how they are doing it and why they are doing it;
- democratising institutional decision-making processes;
- shifting public priorities and resources in favour of meeting human needs;
- highlighting the connections between social policy and economic policy, and ensuring that social policy is not subordinated to economic exigencies; and
- promoting egalitarian social relations and human rights among and between people, whether they are men, women or children.

In practical terms these principles have led feminists to demand:

- recognition of the social causes of unbalanced emotional development and individual hardship;
- egalitarianism in all social interactions;
- not pathologising individuals for their plight;
- support for individual and collective actions from public institutions and organisations;

- elimination of all forms of sexism in social institutions, social policy, cultural values, social norms and individual behaviour;
- elimination of all forms of oppression;
- publicly guaranteed freedom from violence and coercion for all individuals;
- a publicly guaranteed minimum income for all individuals;
- women's rights to an independent income;
- a non-oppressive redefinition of masculinity and femininity;
- a familial ideology that ensures egalitarian relations in families;
- recognition of diversity in 'family' forms;
- recognition of parenting as a social activity involving men and women in bringing up children in a socially supportive environment;
- transformed working relations to ensure equality of status, pay and humane conditions of work for all workers;
- the eradication of the hierarchical division of labour;
- state support in developing personal, familial and community relationships;
- goods and services that foster women's creative potential and talents;
- social planning that reflects social needs and involves workers and service users in formulating services;
- prioritising the prevention of avoidable material and emotional distress in planning social services and healthcare systems; and
- a professionalism that reflects the interests of the users of the service.

Feminists have sought to incorporate these demands in their own practice at both the strategic and tactical levels. These have resulted in:

- creating prefigurative forms of the social relations they envisage for the future in their current practice; and
- forming alliances with others to eliminate social injustice.

Although feminist community action falls short of achieving feminists' ultimate goal of transforming society and redistributing power and resources in egalitarian directions, feminist action has had two immediate beneficial effects. One is that feminist activities are likely to safeguard the present position of women and to provide women, and to some extent children and men, with improvements to their emotional well-being and material circumstances in the hostile climate currently created by neoconservatives and neoliberal globalisation. In the face of a serious deterioration in the standards of living of women, black people and working-class people, defending past gains is a worthy endeavour although care needs to be taken to ensure that this defensive stance does not become a substitute for the goal of transforming social relations.

The second effect is the positive influence that struggling for progress has had on women's consciousness and, consequently, that of children and men. This includes:

- the exposure of current myths of equality that disguise society's unequal distribution of resources and degradation of marginalised groups like women, black people and sections of the working class in a capitalist social system; and
- the feeling of power and confidence achieved by powerless groups who challenge their ascribed position in society by acting collectively.

At the level of the community, therefore, women and other marginalised groups are organising against their oppression with some degree of success in demanding changes in existing provision for them and creating services previously missing. Figure 9.1 below indicates the complex and interactive levels in which women act.

The state seems to be withdrawing support for community action, particularly its more challenging versions, in favour of community organisation and community care models of community work, although even these are inadequately financed for the tasks given them (Hoatson, 2001). These restrictions have not totally protected the state from the impact of community action, including feminist community action. Social workers, as state employees, are forming alliances with community groups in endeavouring to provide users with appropriate services. Welfare workers' idealistic fervour and commitment to helping people aptly lend energy to forming alliances that facilitate processes whereby powerless people organise to take control of their lives.

Feminist community action is riddled with contradictions at whatever level it is operating. But because it heralds the dawning of non-oppressive working relations, feminist community action is a sphere of activity of significance to all those intent on promoting people's welfare. Traditional community workers need to take note of its potential and to make its theory and practice their own.

Figure 9.1: Holistic interactional model for community action

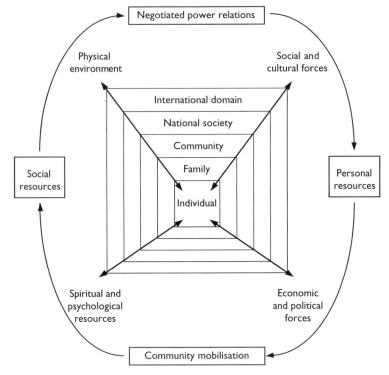

Source: Dominelli (2005, p 712)

References

Abercrombie, N., Hill, S. and Turner, C. (1994) *The Penguin Dictionary of Sociology*, Harmondsworth: Penguin.

Adams, A.L. (1989) 'There's No Place Like Home: On the Place of Identity Politics', *Feminist Review*, no 31, Spring, pp 22-34.

Adamson, N., Briskin, L. and McPhail, M. (1988) *Organising for Change: The Contemporary Women's Movement in Canada*, Oxford: Oxford University Press.

AHC (Achilles Heel Collective) (1983) *Achilles Heel Special Issue on Masculinity*, no 5, London: ACH.

Ahmad, W. (1993) *'Race' and Health in Contemporary Britain*, Buckingham: Open University Press.

Aldred, C. (1981) *Women at Work*, London: Pan.

Alinksy, S. (1969) *Reveille for Radicals*, New York, NY: Vintage Books.

Alinksy, S. (1971) *Rules for Radicals*, New York, NY: Random House.

Allenspach, H. (1978) *Flexible Working Hours*, Geneva: ILO.

Amos, A. and Parmar, P. (1984) 'Challenging Imperial Feminism', *Feminist Review*, no 17, pp 3-17.

Anastacio, J., Gidley, B., Hart, L., Keith, M., Mayo, M. and Kowarzik, U. (2000) *Reflecting Realities: Participants' Perspectives on Integrated Communities and Sustainable Development*, Bristol/York: The Policy Press/Joseph Rowntree Foundation.

Andors, P. (1983) *The Unfinished Liberation of Chinese Women: 1949-1980*, Brighton: Wheatsheaf Books.

Armstrong, J. (1977) 'Analysis of the Inner Area Partnership Scheme Applications', Paper for the Leicester Community Work Unit Management Meeting, Leicester: CWTU.

Amstrong, J. (1988) 'Toward a Plan for Capacity Building in the UK', in A. Twelvetrees (ed) *Community Economic Development: Rhetoric or Reality?*, London: Economic Community Development.

Armstrong, P. (1984) *Labour Pains: Women's Work in Crisis*, Toronto: Women's Press.

Armstrong, P. and Connelly, M.P. (eds) (1997) *Feminism, Political Economy and the State: Contested Terrain*, Toronto: Canadian Scholars Press.

Arshad, R. (1995) *Anti-Racist Community Work: A Radical Approach*, Edinburgh: Moray House.

Asante, M. (1987) *The Africentric Idea*, Philadelphia, PA: Temple University Press.

Ashurst, P. and Hall, Z. (1989) *Understanding Women in Distress*, London: Tavistock/Routledge.

ASRA (Asian Sheltered Residential Accommodation) (1981) *Asian Sheltered Residential Accommodation*, London: ASRA.

Atkinson, D.R. and Hackett, G. (1995) *Counselling Diverse Populations*, Madison, IL: Brown and Benchmark.

Babacan, H. and Gopalkrishnan, N. (2001) 'Community Work Partnerships in a Global Context', *Community Development Journal*, vol 36, no 1, pp 3-17.

Bailey, R. and Brake, M. (eds) (1975) *Radical Social Work*, London: Routledge and Kegan Paul.

Baker Miller, J. (1976) *Toward a New Psychology of Women*, Boston, MD: Beacon Press.

Balbo, L. (1987) 'Crazy Quilts: Rethinking the Welfare State Debate from a Woman's Point of View', in A. Showstack-Sassoon (ed) *Women and the Welfare State: The Shifting Boundaries of Public and Private*, London: Hutchinson.

Baldwin, S. (1985) *The Cost of Caring*, London: Routledge and Kegan Paul.

Banks, O. (1981) *Faces of Feminism*, London: Martin Robinson.

Barclay, P.M. (1982) *Social Workers: Their Roles and Tasks, The Barclay Report*, London: Bedford Square Press.

Bari, J. (1994) *Timber Wars*, San Francisco, CA: Common Courage Press (see also www.judibari.org and www.earthfirstjournal.org, accessed 11 June 2005).

Barker, H. (1986) 'Recapturing Sisterhood: A Critical Look at "Process" in Feminist Organisations and Community Action', *Critical Social Policy*, vol 16, Summer, pp 80-90.

Barlett, D.L. and Steele, J.B. (1998) 'Corporate Welfare: Special Report', *Time*, 9 November.

Barnes, C. (2003) 'Rehabilitation for Disabled Children: A Sick Joke?', *Scandinavian Journal of Disability Research*, vol 5, no 1, pp 7-24.

Barnes, M. (1999) *Building a Deliberative Democracy*, London: IPRR.

Barnes, M. and Maple, N. (1992) *Women and Mental Health*, Birmingham: Venture Press.

Barnes, M. and Prior, D. (2000) *Private Lives as Public Policy*, Birmingham: Venture.

Barrett, M. and McIntosh, M. (1985) 'Ethnocentrism and Socialist Feminist Theory', *Feminist Review*, vol 20, pp 23-47.

Barwick, S. (2001) 'Greenham Women Face Jail over Radar Protests', *The Telegraph*, 3 May.

Bass, E. and Davis, L. (1988) *Courage to Heal Workbook: A Guide for Women Survivors of Child Sexual Abuse*, New York, NY: Perennial Library and Harper and Row.

Batten, T. (1967) *The Non-Directive Approach in Group and Community Work*, Oxford: Oxford University Press.

Batty, D. (2002) 'Funding Halves Places', *The Guardian*, 23 October.

Bauman, Z. (2000) 'Issues of Law and Order', *British Journal of Criminology*, 40, pp 205-221.

Baumgardner, J. and Richards, A. (2000) *Manifesta: Young Women, Feminism and the Future*, New York, NY: Farrar, Straus and Giroux.

Bayes, M. and Howell, E. (eds) (1981) *Women and Mental Health*, New York, NY: Basic Books.

Beasley, K. (1986) 'Who's Zapping Who?', *Spare Rib*, no 166, May, pp 10-11.

Begum, N. (1992) 'Disabled Women and the Feminist Agenda', *Feminist Review*, vol 40, Spring, pp 71-84.

Belenky, M.F., Clinchy, M.B., Goldberger, N.R. and Tarule, M.J. (1997) *Women's Ways of Knowing: The Development of Self, Voice and Mind*, New York, NY: Basic Books.

Bell, C. and Newby, H. (1971) *Community Studies*, London: Allen and Unwin.

Bell, S. (1988) *When Salem Came to the Boro*, London: Pan Books.

Belotti, E. (1975) *Little Girls*, London: Writers and Readers Publishing Co-operative.

Benyon, M. (1989) *Report on Gender and the Education System Study Day*, Coventry: Warwick University Senate Sex Equality Committee.

Benn, M. and Sedley, A. (1982) *Sexual Harassment at Work*, London: National Council for Civil Liberties.

Berger, P. and Luckmann, T. (1967) *The Social Construction of Reality*, New York, NY: Doubleday.

Bernstein, E., Wallerstein, N., Braithwaite, R., Guttierez, L., Labonte, R. and Zimmerman, M. (1994) 'Empowerment Forum: A Dialogue Between Guest Editorial Board Members', *Health Education Quarterly*, 21, pp 281-94.

Bhatti-Sinclair, K. (1994) 'Asian Women and Domestic Violence from Male Partners', in C. Lupton and T. Gillespie (eds) *Working with Violence*, London: BASW/Macmillan.

Bhavani, K.K. (1993) 'Taking Racism and the Editing of Women's Studies', in D. Richardson and V. Robinson (eds) *Introduction to Women's Studies*, London: Macmillan.

Biddle, L. and Biddle, W. (1965) *The Community Development Process: The Rediscovery of Local Initiative*, New York, NY: Holt, Reinhart and Winston.

Binney, V., Harkell, G. and Nixon, J. (1981) *Leaving Violent Men: A Study of Refuges and Housing for Battered Women*, London: Women's Aid Federation.

Bishop, A. (1994) *Becoming an Ally: Breaking the Cycle of Oppression*, Halifax: Fernwood Publishing.

Blagg, H. and Derricourt, N. (1982) 'Why We Need to Reconstruct a Theory of the State for Community Work', in G. Craig, N. Derricourt and M. Loney (eds) *Community Work and the State*, London: Routledge and Kegan Paul.

Blair, T. (1999) 'PM's 20 Year Target to End Poverty', *The Guardian*, 19 March.

Blair, T. (2002) 'I have Learned the Limits of Government', *Renewal*, vol 10, no 2 (www.renewal.org.uk, accessed 2 May 2003).

Blankenhorn, D. (1995) *Fatherless America*, New York, NY: Basic Books.

Bondi, L. and Burman, E. (2001) 'Women and Mental Health: A Feminist Review', *Feminist Review*, vol 68, no 1, pp 6-33.

Bonny, S. (1984) *Who Cares in Southwark?*, London: National Association of Carers and their Elderly Dependents.

Bourdieu, P. (1986) 'The Forms of Capital', in J. Richardson (ed) *The Handbook of Theory and Research for the Sociology of Education*, New York, NY: Greenwood Press.

Bourke, L. (2005) 'Women Facing Pensions Crisis', *Citywire*, 3 November.

Bowl, R. (1985) *Changing the Nature of Masculinity: A Task for Social Work*, Norwich: University of East Anglia Monographs.

Brah, A. (1996) *Cartographies of Diaspora*, London: Routledge.

Brandwein, R. (1987) 'Women and Community Organisation', in D.S. Burden and N. Gottlieb (eds) *The Woman Client: Providing Human Services in a Changing World*, London: Tavistock.

Bridges, L. (1975) 'The Ministry of Internal Security: British Urban Social Policy: 1968-1974', *Race and Class*, vol 16, no 4, pp 376-98.

Brook, E. and Davis, A. (1985) *Women, the Family and Social Work*, London: Tavistock.

Brown, G. and Harris, T. (1978) *The Social Origins of Depression*, London: Tavistock.

Browne, C. (1995) 'A Feminist Life Span Perspective on Aging', in N. Van Den Bergh (ed) *Feminist Practice in the 21st Century*, Washington, DC: NASW Press.

Brownmiller, S. (1976) *Against Our Will: Men, Women and Rape*, New York, NY: Bantam Books.

Bryan, B., Dadzie, S. and Scafe, S. (1985) *The Heart of the Race: Black Women's Lives in Britain*, London: Virago.

Burden, D.S. and Gottlieb, N. (eds) (1987) *The Woman Client: Providing Human Services in a Changing World*, London: Tavistock.

Burrows, R., Ellison, N. and Woods, B. (2005) *Neighbourhoods on the Net: The Nature and Impact of Internet-Based Neighbourhood Information Systems*, Bristol/York: The Policy Press/Joseph Rowntree Foundation.

Butler, J. (2000) 'Critically Queer', in P. Du Gay, J. Evans and P. Redman (eds) *Identity: A Reader*, London: Sage Publications.

Buynan, T. (1977) *The History and Practice of the Political Police in Britain*, London: Quartet Books.

BWHC (Boston Women's Health Collective) (1979) *Our Bodies, Ourselves*, New York, NY: Simon and Schuster.

Cahn, S. (ed) (1995) *The Affirmative Action Debate*, London: Routledge.

Calouste Gulbenkian Foundation (1968) *Community Work and Social Change: A Report for Training*, London: Longman.

Calouste Gulbenkian Foundation (1973) *Current Issues in Community Work*, London: Calouste Gulbenkian Foundation/Routledge and Kegan Paul.

Campbell, B., Coote, A. and Rowbotham, S. (1986) 'Feminism and Class Politics', *Feminist Review*, vol 23, pp 13-30.

Campbell, C. (2000) 'Social Capital and Health: Contextualising Health Promotion within Local Community Networks', in S. Baron, J. Field and T. Schuller (eds) *Social Capital: Critical Perspective*, Oxford: Oxford University Press.

Cannan, C. and Warren, C. (1997) *Social Action with Children and Families: A Community Development Approach to Children and Families*, London: Routledge.

Carby, H. (1982) 'White Woman Listen! Black Feminism and the Boundaries of Sisterhood', in Centre for Contemporary and Cultural Studies (ed) *Empire Strikes Back*, London: Hutchinson.

Carers UK (2002) *'Without Us…?' Calculating the Value of Carers' Support*, London: Carers UK.

Castles, S. and Kosack, G. (1972) 'The Function of Labour Immigration in Western European Capitalism', *New Left Review*, vol 73, May/June, pp 8-21.

CCCS (Centre for Contemporary Cultural Studies) (1982) *The Empire Strikes Back*, London: Hutchinson.

CDP (Community Development Projects) (1977a) *Gilding the Ghetto*, London: CDP.

CDP (1977b) *The Limits of the Law*, London: CDP.

CDP (1977c) *The Costs of Industrial Change*, London: CDP.

CEA (Council of Economic Advisers) (1998) *Explaining Trends in the Gender Wage Gap*, Washington, DC: CEA.

Census Bureau (2005) *Income, Earnings and Poverty: Findings from the 2004 American Community Survey*, Boston, MA: US Census Bureau.

Chakraborti, N. and Garland, J. (2004) *Rural Racism*, Cullompton: Willan Publishing.

Chaplin, J. (1988) *Feminist Counselling in Action*, London: Sage Publications.

Chapman, P., Phimister, E., Shucksmith, M., Upward, R. and Vera-Toscano, E. (1998) *Poverty and Exclusion in Rural Britain: The Dynamics of Low Income and Employment*, York: Joseph Rowntree Foundation.

Chodorow, N. (1978) *The Reproduction of Mothering*, London: University of California Press.

CIR (Commission on Industrial Relations) (1973) *Report into the Mansfield Hosiery Dispute*, London: CIR.

Clarke, A. (2004) *e-Learning Skills*, London: Palgrave.

Clarke, J. and Newman, J. (1997) *The Managerialist State*, London: Sage Publications.

Coard, B. (1971) *How West Indian Children are Made Educationally Subnormal*, London: New Beacon.

Cochrane, M., Miller, J., Tetlow, K. and Stiles, J. (1982) 'South London Community Health Projects', in A. Curno, A. Lamming, L. Leach, J. Stiles, V. Ward, A. Wright and T. Ziff (eds) *Women and Collective Action*, London: Association of Community Workers, pp 113-29.

Cockburn, C. (1977a) 'When Women Get Involved in Community Action', in M. Mayo (ed) *Women in the Community*, London: Routledge and Kegan Paul.

Cockburn, C. (1977b) *The Local State*, London: Pluto Press.

Cohen, J. (1999) 'Trust, Voluntary Association and Workable Democracy: The Contemporary American Discourses of Civil Society', in M. Warren (ed) *Democracy and Trust*, Cambridge: Cambridge University Press.

Coleman, J. (1990) *Foundations of Social Theory*, Cambridge, MA: Belknap.

Collins, P.H. (1991) *Black Feminist Thought: Knowledge, Consciousness and the Politics of Empowerment*, London: Routledge.

Comer, J.P. and Poussaint, H.P. (1975) *Black Child Care*, New York: Pocket Books.

Community Regeneration Online (2004) 'Girls Aloud' (www.newstartmag.co.uk, accessed 21 March 2005).

Connell, R.W. (1995) *Masculinities*, Cambridge: Polity Press.

Cook, A. and Kirk, G. (1983) *Greenham Women Everywhere: Dreams, Ideas and Action from the Women's Peace Movement*, London: Pluto Press.

Cooper, M. (1980) 'Normanton: Interweaving Social Work and the Community', in R. Hadley and M. McGrath (eds) *Going Local*, London: Bedford Square Press.

Court, C. (2005) 'Council Tax Rebel Sylvia, 73 Jailed', *The Independent*, 26 September.

Cowley, J., Kaye, A., Mayo, M. and Thompson, M. (1977) *Community or Class*, London: Stage One/Routledge and Kegan Paul.

Coyle, A. (1989) 'Women in Management: A Suitable Case for Treatment', *Feminist Review*, vol 31, pp 117-25.

CPS (Current Population Survey) (2002) *Labour Force Data*, New York: Labour Market Information Office of Research.

Craig, G. (1989) 'Community Work and the State', *Community Development Journal*, vol 26, no 4, pp 3-18.

Craig, G. and Mayo, M. (1995) *Community Empowerment: A Reader in Participation and Development*, London: Zed Books.

Craig, G., Derricourt, N. and Loney, M. (1982) *Community Work and the State: Towards a Radical Practice*, London: Routledge and Kegan Paul.

Craig, G., Mayo, M. and Taylor, M. (2000) 'Globalisation from Below: Lessons for Community Development', *Community Development Journal*, vol 35, no 4, pp 323-5.

Croft, S. and Beresford, P. (1989) 'User Involvement, Citizenship and Social Policy, *Critical Social Policy*, 26, pp 5-18.

CRU (Civil Renewal Unit) (2004) *Firm Foundations: The Government's Framework for Community Capacity Building*, London: Home Office Communities Group.

Curno, A., Lamming, A., Leach, L., Stiles, J., Ward, V., Wright, A. and Ziff, T. (eds) (1982) *Women in Collective Action*, London: Association of Community Workers.

Curno, P. (1978) *Political Issues in Community Work*, London: Routledge and Kegan Paul.

CWHN (Coventry Women's Health Network) (1985) *Discussions with members of the CWHN during 1984-85*, Coventry: CWHN.

CWIT (Center for Women and Information Technology) (2005) 'Women and ICT: Creating Global Transformation' (www.wtci.org/CWIT/WomenandICT_CreatingGlobalTransformation.htm, accessed 14 Feb 2006).

Dalla Costa, M. and James, S. (1972) *The Power of Women and the Subversion of Community*, Bristol: Falling Wall Press.

Daniels, A.K. (1985) 'Good Times and Good Works: The Place of Sociability in the Work of Women Volunteers', *Social Problems*, vol 32, no 3, pp 363-74.

David, M. (1999) 'Home, Work, Families and Children: New Labour, New Directions and New Dilemmas', *International Studies in Sociology of Education*, vol 9, no 2, pp 111-32.

David, M. and New, C. (1985) *For the Children's Sake: Making Childcare More Than Women's Business*, London: Penguin.

Davies, W. (1982) 'A Women's Group – A Case Study to Think About', in A. Curno, A. Lamming, L. Leach, J. Stiles, V. Ward, A. Wright and T. Ziff (eds) *Women's Collective Action*, London: Association of Community Workers.

Davis, A. (1981) *Women, Race and Class*, London: Women's Press.

Davis, A. (1989) *Women, Culture and Politics*, New York, NY: Random House.

Davis, A. (1995) 'Prison, Repression and Resistance', in J. James (ed), *Angela Y. Davis: A Reader*, Oxford: Blackwell Publishers Ltd.

Davis, R. (1988) 'Learning from Working Class Women', *Community Development Journal*, vol 23, no 2, pp 110-16.

Davis, S. and the Committee for Abortion Rights and Against Sterilisation Abuse (1988) *Women Under Attack: Victories, Backlash and the Fight for Reproductive Freedom*, Boston, MD: South End Press.

Deacon, B. (1983) *Social Policy and Socialism: The Struggle for Socialist Relations of Welfare*, London: Pluto Press.

Dearlove, J. (1974) 'The Control of Change and the Regulation of Community Action', in D. Jones and M. Mayo (eds) *Community Work One*, London: Routledge and Kegan Paul.

De Haan, A. and Maxwell, S. (eds) (1998) 'Poverty and Social Exclusion in North and South', *IDS Bulletin*, vol 29, no 1, January, pp 10-19.

Department of Employment and Productivity (1969) *In Place of Strife*, Cmnd 3888, London, HMSO.

Dhesi, A.S. (2000) 'Social Capital and Community Development', *Community Development Journal*, vol 35, no 3, pp 199-214.

Diamond, J. (2004) 'Local Regeneration Initiatives and Capacity Building: Whose "Capacity" and "Building for What"?', *Community Development Journal*, vol 39, no 2, pp 177-89.

Dinham, A. (2005) 'Empowered or Over-Powered? The Real Experiences of Local Participation in the UK's New Deal for Communities', *Community Development Journal*, vol 40, no 4, pp 301-312.

Dixon, G., Johnson, C., Leigh, S. and Turnbull, N. (1982) 'Feminist Perspectives and Practice', in G. Craig, N. Derricourt and M. Loney (eds) *Community Work and the State*, London: Routledge and Kegan Paul.

Dominelli, L. (1974) 'Autogestion in Boufarik', *Sociologia Ruralis*, vol XIV, no 4, pp 243-60.

Dominelli, L. (1982) *Community Action: Organising Marginalised Groups*, Reykjavik: Kwenna Frambothid.

Dominelli, L. (1986a) 'The Power of the Powerless: Prostitution and the Reinforcement of Submissive Femininity', *Sociological Review*, vol 34, no 1, Spring, pp 65-92.

Dominelli, L. (1986b) *Love and Wages: The Impact of Imperialism, State Intervention and Women's Domestic Labour on Workers' Control in Algeria, 1962-1972*, Norwich: Novata Press.

Dominelli, L. (1986c) *Women Organising. An Analysis of Greenham Women in Action*. Paper given at the IASSU Conference, Tokyo, 15–18 July.

Dominelli, L. (1988; 2nd edn, 1997; 3rd edn, forthcoming) *Anti-Racist Social Work*, London: Macmillan.

Dominelli, L. (1989) 'Betrayal of Trust: A Feminist Analysis of Power Relationships in Incest Abuse and its Relevance for Social Work Practice', *British Journal of Social Work*, no 19, pp 291-307.

Dominelli, L. (1990) *Women and Community Action*, Birmingham: Venture Press, 1st edition.

Dominelli, L. (1991) *Women Across Continents: Feminist Comparative Social Policy*, Hemel Hempstead: Harvester/Wheatsheaf.

Dominelli, L. (1996) 'Deprofessionalising Social Work: Equal Opportunities, Competence and Postmodernism', *British Journal of Social Work*, no 26, April, pp 153-75.

Dominelli, L. (1997) *Sociology for Social Work*, London: Macmillan.

Dominelli, L. (2000) 'Empowerment: Help or Hindrance in Professional Relationships', in D. Ford and P. Stepney (ed) *Social Work Models, Methods and Theories: A Framework for Practice*, Lyme Regis: Russell House Publishing.

Dominelli, L. (2002a) *Anti-Oppressive Social Work Theory and Practice*, London: Palgrave.

Dominelli, L. (2002b) *Feminist Social Work Theory and Practice*, London: Palgrave.

Dominelli, L. (2002c) *Gendered Relations in Social Work*, Southampton: Southampton University ASCODEV paper.

Dominelli, L. (2003) *Sure Start: A Report for Funders*, Southampton: Southampton University.

Dominelli, L. (2004a) 'Practising Social Work in a Globalising World', in T.N. Tan and A. Rowlands (eds) *Social Work Around the World III*, Berne: IFSW.

Dominelli, L. (2004b) *Social Work: Theory and Practice for a Changing Profession*, Cambridge: Polity Press.

Dominelli, L. (2005) 'Community Development Across Borders: Avoiding Dangerous Practices in a Globalizing World', *International Social Work*, vol 48, no 6, pp 702-13.

Dominelli, L. and Hoogvelt, A. (1996a) 'Globalisation and the Technocratisation of Social Work', *Critical Social Policy*, vol 16, no 2, pp 45-62.

Dominelli, L. and Hoogvelt, A. (1996b) 'Globalisation, Contract Government and the Talyorisation of Intellectual Labour', *Studies in Political Economy*, vol 49, pp 71-100.

Dominelli, L. and Jonsdottir, G. (1988) 'Feminist Political Organisation in Iceland', *Feminist Review*, no 27, pp 36-60.

Dominelli, L. and Leonard, P. (1982) *Power, Participation and Collective Intervention*. Report to Coventry Social Services. Coventry: University of Warwick.

Dominelli, L. and McLeod, E. (1989) *Feminist Social Work*, London: Macmillan.

Doress, P.B. and Siegal, D.L. (1987) *Ourselves Growing Older*, New York, NY: Simon and Schuster.

Doyal, L. (1983) 'Women's Health and the Sexual Division of Labour: A Case Study of the Women's Movement in Britain', *Critical Social Policy*, issue 7, Summer, pp 21-33.

Doyal, L. (1979) *The Political Economy of Health*. London: Pluto Press.

Doyal, L. (1985) 'Women and the National Health Services: The Carers and the Careless', in E. Lewin and V.L. Olesen (eds) *Women, Health and Healing*, London: Tavistock Publications.

Dreifus, C. (1973) *Women's Fate: Raps from a Feminist Consciousness-Raising Group*, New York, NY: Bantam Books.

Drummond, J. (2004) 'Ethics and Selfhood: Alterity and the Phenomenology of Obligation', *Philosophy Today*, 49, pp 78-87.

DTI (Department of Trade and Industry) (2005) *Report of the Trade and Industry Select Committee on Occupational Segregation*, London: DTI.

Duffy, K. (1995) *Social Exclusion and Human Dignity*, Report for the Council of Europe. Brussels: CDPS.

Dunton, J. (2005) 'Two Die as Gangs Riot in City', *Birmingham Express and Star*, 24 October.

DWP (Department for Work and Pensions) (2004) *Households Below Average Income*, London: DWP.

Edwards, M. and Gaventa, J. (eds) (2001) *Global Citizen Action*, London: Earthscan.

Eichenbaum, L. and Orbach, S. (1982) *Outside In, Inside Out*, London: Penguin.

Eichler, M. (1983) *Families in Canada*, Toronto: Gage.

Eichler, M. (1988) *Nonsexist Research Methods: A Practical Guide*, London: Allen and Unwin.

Eisenstein, H. (1984) *Contemporary Feminist Thought*, London: Allen and Unwin.

Eisenstein, Z. (1979) *Capitalist Patriarchy and the Case for Socialist Feminism*, New York: Monthly Review Press.

EOC (Equal Opportunities Commission) (2004) *Sex and Power: Who Runs Britain?*, Manchester: EOC.

Ernst, S. and Maquire, M. (eds) (1987) *Living with the Sphinx – Papers from the Women's Therapy Centre*, London: The Women's Press.

Escobar, A. (1998) 'Whose Knowledge, Whose Nature? Biodiversity, Conservation, and the Political Ecology of Social Movements', *Journal of Political Ecology*, vol 5, pp 53-83.

Etzioni, A. (1993) *The Spirit of Community: The Reinvention of American Society*, New York, NY: Simon and Schuster.

EUMC (European Monitoring Centre on Racism and Xenophobia) (2005) *Fifth Report of Session 2005-6*, Brussels: EUMC. London: TSO.

Farrah, M. (1986) *Black Elders in Leicester: A Report*, Leicester: Leicester Social Services Department.

Farrell, W. (1994) *The Myth of Male Power*, New York, NY: Fourth Estate.

Fathers 4 Justice (2005) 'The Evidence' (www.fathers-4-justice.org/evidence, accessed 24 May 2005).

FCDL (Federation for Community Development Learning) (2004) *A Summary of Good Practice Standards for Community Development Work*, Sheffield: FCDL.

Fellin, P. (2001) *The Community and the Social Worker*, Itasca, IL: F.E. Peacock Publishers, Inc.

Festau, M. (1975) *The Male Machine*, New York, NY: Delta Books.

Finch, J. (1982) 'A Women's Health Group in Mansfield', in A. Curno, A. Lamming, L. Leach, J. Stiles, V. Ward, A. Wright and T. Ziff (eds) *Women in Collective Action*, London: Routledge and Kegan Paul.

Finch, J. (1983) 'Can Skills be Shared? Pre-School Playgroups in Disadvantaged Areas', *Community Development Journal*, vol 18, no 3, pp 251-6.

Finch, J. (1984) 'Community Care: Developing Non-Sexist Alternatives', *Critical Social Policy*, Issue 9, Spring, pp 6-18.

Finch, J. and Groves, D. (1983) *A Labour of Love: Women, Work and Caring*, London: Routledge and Kegan Paul.

Fine, B. (2001) *Social Capital versus Social Theory*, London: Routledge.

Finn, D. (1985) *The Community Programme*, London: Centre for the Unemployed.

Finn, J.L. (2001) 'The Women of Villa Paula Jaraquemada: Building Community in Chile's Transition to Democracy', *Community Development Journal*, vol 36, no 3, pp 183-97.

Fisher, M. (1997) 'Man-Made Care: Community Care and Older Male Carers', *British Journal of Social Work*, vol 24, pp 659-80.

FNVSG (Feminism and Non-Violence Study Group) (1983) *Piecing it Together: Feminism and Non-Violence*, Buckleigh: FNVSG.

Foster, J. (1997) 'A Woman's Liberation', *Community Care*, 4-10 December, pp 18-19.

Foster, P. (1989) 'Improving the Doctor–Patient Relationship: A Feminist Perspective', *Journal of Social Policy*, vol 18, no 3, July, pp 337-62.

Foucault, M. (1980) *Power/Knowledge: Selected Interviews and Other Writings, 1972-77*, New York, NY: Pantheon Books.

Fournier, S. and Crey, E. (1998) *Stolen From Our Embrace: The Abduction of First Nations Children and the Restoration of Aboriginal Communities*, Vancouver: Douglas and McIntyre.

Francis, D. and Henderson, P. (1992) *Working with Rural Communities*, London: Macmillan.

Frankenburg, R. (1997) *Displacing Whiteness: Essays in Social and Cultural Criticism*, London: Duke University Press.

Frankfort, I. (1972) *Vaginal Politics*, New York, NY: Quadrangle Books.

Franklin, B. (1995) *The Handbook on Children's Rights*, London: Routledge.

Fraser, H. (2005) 'Four Different Approaches to Community Participation', *Community Development Journal*, vol 40, no 3, pp 286-300.

Frean, A. (2004) 'Being Pregnant Can Still Cost You Your Job', *Times Online*, 26 February (www.timesonline.co.uk, accessed 24 May 2005).

Fremeaux, I. (2005) 'New Labour's Appropriation of the Concept of Community: A Critique', *Community Development Journal*, vol 40, no 3, pp 265-74.

French, M. (1985) *The Power of Women*, Harmondsworth: Penguin.

Freud, S. (1977) *On Sexuality*, Pelican Freud Library, vol 7, London: Penguin.

Friedan, B. (1963) *The Feminine Mystique*, New York, NY: Bell.

Friedan, B. (1993) *Fountain of Age*, New York, NY: Basic Books.

Friedlin, J. (2002) 'Second and Third Wave Feminists Clash Over the Future', *Women's eNews* (www.womensenews.org/article.cfm, accessed 24 May 2005).

Gallagher, A. (1977) 'Women and Community Work', in M. Mayo (ed) *Women in the Community*, London: Routledge and Kegan Paul.

Gartner, R.B. (1999) *Betrayed as Boys,* New York, NY: Guildford Press.

Gaskin, K. and Davis Smith, J. (1995) *A New Civic Europe? A Study of the Extent and Role of Volunteering*, London: London Volunteer Centre.

Gathiram, N. and Hemson, D. (2002) 'Transformation of Welfare? Race, Class and Gender in the Management of Welfare Agencies in South Africa', *Community Development Journal*, vol 37, no 3, pp 209-19.

Gavron, H. (1966) *The Captive Wife*, London: Routledge and Kegan Paul.

Geddes, M. (1997) *Partnerships Against Poverty and Exclusion? Local Regeneration Strategies and Excluded Communities in the UK*, Bristol: The Policy Press.

Giddens, A. (1990) *The Consequences of Modernity*, Cambridge: Polity Press.

Giddens, A. (1998) *The Third Way: The Renewal of Social Democracy*, Cambridge: Polity Press.

Gilchrist, A. (2000) 'The Well-Connected Community: Networking to the "Edge of Chaos"', *Community Development Journal*, vol 35, no 3, July, pp 264-75.

Gilchrist, A. (2003) 'Community Development in the UK: Possibilities and Paradoxes', *Community Development Journal*, vol 38, no 1, pp 16-25.

Gilchrist, A. (2004) *The Well-Connected Community: A Networking Approach to Community Development*, Bristol: The Policy Press.

Gilligan, C. (1982) *In a Different Voice: Psychological Theory and Women's Development*, Cambridge, MA: Harvard University Press.

Gilroy, P. (1987) *There Ain't No Black in the Union Jack*, London: Hutchinson.

Ginn, J. and Arber, S. (2002) 'Gender and the Relationship between Social Capital and Health', in A. Morgan and C. Swann (eds) *Social Capital and Health: Insights from Quantitative Studies*, London: Health Development Agency.

Ginsburg, N. (1979) *Class, Capital and Social Policy*, London: Macmillan.

Gittell, M., Ortega-Bustamante, I. and Steffy, T. (1999) *Women Creating Social Capital and Social Change*, New York: City University of New York.

Glazer, N. (1988) *The Limits of Social Policy*, Cambridge, MA: Harvard University Press.

Glen, A., Henderson, P., Humm, J., Meszaros, H. and Gaffney, M. (2004) *Survey of Community Development Workers in the UK: A Report on Paid and Unpaid Community Workers*, London: CDF.

GMPLU (Greater Manchester Low Pay Unit) (2004) *The Gender Pay Gap*, Manchester: GMPLU.

Goodman, R.M. (2004) 'Collaborative Community Empowerment: An Illustration of a Six-Step Process', *Health Promotion Practice*, vol 5, no 3, pp 256-65.

Gordon, L. (1988) *Heroes of their own Lives: The Politics and History of Family Violence*, Harmondsworth: Penguin.

Gordon, P. and Newnham, A. (1985) *Passport to Benefits: Racism in Social Security*, London: CPAG and Runnymede Trust.

Goulbourne, H. (1999) *Caribbean Transnational Families*, London: Pluto Press.

Goulbourne, H. and Solomos, J. (2003) 'Families, Ethnicity and Social Capital', *Social Policy and Society*, vol 2, no 4, pp 329-38.

Graham, H. (1983) 'Caring: Labour of Love', in J. Finch and D. Groves (1983) *Labour of Love: Women, Work and Caring*, London: Routledge and Kegan Paul.

Greenwood, V. and Young, J. (1976) *Abortion in Demand*, London: Pluto Press.

Greer, G. (1993) *The Change: Women, Aging and the Menopause,* New York, NY: Ballantine Books.

Greer, P. (1994) *Transforming Central Government: The Next Steps Initiative*, Milton Keynes: Open University Press.

Grenier, P. and Wright, K. (2001) *Social Capital in Britain: A Critique of Hall's Analysis*. Paper at JHU Conference, December.

Griffiths, J. (1974) 'Carrying on in the Middle of Violent Conflict: Some Observations of Experiences in Northern Ireland', in D. Jones and M. Mayo (eds) *Community Work One*, London: Routledge and Kegan Paul.

Griffiths, R. (1988) *Community Care: Agenda for Action: The Griffiths Report*, London: HMSO.

Grimwood, C. and Popplestone, R. (1993) *Women in Management*, London: BASW/Macmillan.

Guru, S. (1987) 'An Asian Women's Refuge', in S. Ahmed, J. Cheetham and J. Small (eds) *Social Work with Black Children and their Families*, London: Batsford.

Hadley, R. and Hatch, S. (1981) *Social Welfare and the Failure of the State: Centralised Social Services and Participation*, London: Allen and Unwin.

Hadley, R. and McGrath, M. (1980) *Going Local: Neighbourhood and Social Services*, London: Bedford Square Press.

Hadley, R., Cooper, M., Dale, P. and Stacey, G. (1987) *A Community Social Worker's Handbook*, London: Tavistock.

Haidari, S.H. and Wright, S. (2001) 'Participation and Participatory Development among the Kalhor Nomads of Iran', *Community Development Journal*, vol 36, no 1, pp 53-62.

Hall, P. (1999) 'Social Capital in Britain', *British Journal of Political Science*, vol 29, pp 417-61.

Hallett, C. (1991) *Women and Social Services*, London: Sage Publications.

Halpern, M. (1963) *The Politics of Social Change in the Middle East and North Africa*, Princeton: Princeton University Press.

Hamd, H.S. and Wright, S. (2001) 'Participation and Participatory Development among the Kalhor Nomads of Iran', *Community Development Journal*, vol 36, no 1, pp 53-62.

Hanifan, L.J. (1916) 'The Rural School Community Center', *Annals of the American Academy of Political and Social Science*, vol 67, pp 130-8.

Hanifan, L.J. (1920) *The Community Center*, Boston, MD: Silver Burdett.

Hanmer, J. and Statham, D. (1988; 2nd edn, 2002) *Women and Social Work: Towards a Woman-Centered Practice*, London: Macmillan.

Harding, S. (1990) 'Feminism, Science and the Anti-Enlightenment Critiques', in L Nicholson (ed) *Feminism/Postmodernism*, London: Routledge.

Hartsock, N. (1987) 'The Feminist Standpoint: Developing the Ground for a Specifically Feminist Historical Materialism', in S Harding (ed) *Feminism and Methodology*, Bloomington, IN: Indiana University Press.

Hearn, J. (1987) *The Gender of Oppression: Men, Masculinity and the Critique of Marxism*, Brighton: Harvester Wheatsheaf.

Heenan, C. (1988) 'An Analysis of a Feminist Therapy Centre', MA thesis, Coventry: University of Warwick.

Hencke, D. (2001) 'Private Jail Makes Huge Profit', *The Guardian*, 4 July.

Henderson, P. and Salmon, H. (2001) *Social Exclusion and Community Development*, London: CDF Publications.

Henderson, P. and Thomas, D. (2002) *Skills in Neighbourhood Work* (3rd edn; 1st edn, 1982), London: Routledge.

Henderson, P., Jones, D. and Thomas, D.N. (1980) *The Boundaries of Change in Community Work*, London: Allen and Unwin.

Higgins, J. (1989) 'Caring for the Carers', *Journal of Social Administration*, vol 26, no 3, pp 382-99.

Hillman, M. (2002) 'Environmental Justice: A Crucial Link Between Environmentalism and Community Development', *Community Development Journal*, vol 37, no 4, pp 349-60.

Hinsliff, G. (2004) 'More Help for Pregnant Staff', *The Observer*, 25 July.

Hinton, W. (1966) *Fanshen*, New York: Vintage Books.

Hirst, J. (1999) 'Does the Face Fit?', *Community Care*, 7-13 October, pp 20-3.

Hoatson, L. (2001) 'Community Development Practice Surviving New Right Government: A British and Victorian Comparison', *Community Development Journal*, vol 36, no 1, pp 18-29.

Hobson, M. and Beresford, P. (2001) 'Regenerating Regeneration', *Community Development Journal*, vol 36, no 4, October, pp 312-20.

Hocking, G. (2003) 'Oxfam Great Britain and Sustainable Livelihoods in the UK', *Community Development Journal*, vol 38, no 3, pp 235-42.

Hollway, W. (1989) *Subjectivity and Method in Psychology: Gender, Meaning and Science*, London: Sage Publications.

Home Office (2003) *Building Civic Renewal*, London: Home Office.

Home Office (2004a) *Change Up: Capacity Building and Infrastructure Framework for the Voluntary and Community Sector*, London: Home Office.

Home Office (2004b) *Developing Domestic Violence Strategies: A Guide for Partnerships*, London: Home Office Violent Crime Unit.

Hood, M. and Woods, R. (1994) 'Women and Participation', in R. Gilroy and R. Woods (eds) *Housing Women*, London: Routledge.

hooks, b. (1984) *Feminist Theory: From Margins to Centre*, Boston, MD: South End Press.

hooks, b. (1990) *Yearning: Race, Gender and Cultural Politics*, Boston, MD: South End Press.

hooks, b. (2000) *Where We Stand: Class Matters*, London: Routledge.

Hoong Sin, C. (2002) 'The Limits to Government Intervention in Fostering an Ethnically Integrated Community – A Singapore Case Study', *Community Development Journal*, vol 37, no 3, pp 220-32.

Hooper, C. (1992) *Mothers Surviving Child Sexual Abuse*, London: Routledge.

Hopkins, M. (1982) 'Homeworking Campaigns: Dilemmas and Possibilities in Working with a Fragmented Community', MA dissertation, Coventry: University of Warwick.

Horn, J.S. (1969) *Away with All Pests*, New York: Monthly Review Press.

Howe, C. (1998) 'Competing Strategies in the Struggle for Public Education', in N. Naples (ed) *Community Activism and Feminist Politics: Organizing Across Race, Class and Gender*, London: Routledge.

Howe, D. (1986) 'The Segregation of Women and their Work in the Personal Social Services', *Critical Social Policy*, vol 15, pp 21-36.

Hudson-Weems, C. (1993) *African Womanism: Reclaiming Ourselves*, Troy, MI: Bedford Publishers.

Hughes, B. (1995) *Older People and Community Care: Critical Theory and Practice*, Buckingham: Open University Press.

Humphries, B. (eds) (1996) *Critical Perspectives on Empowerment*, Birmingham: Venture Press.

Hunt, M. (1990) 'The De-eroticization of Women's Liberation: Social Purity Movements and the Revolutionary Feminism of Sheila Jeffreys', *Feminist Review*, no 34, Spring, pp 23-46.

Ife, J. (1997) *Rethinking Social Work: Towards Critical Practice*, Sydney: Longman.

Ife, J. (1998) *Community Development*, Sydney: Longman.

Iliffe, S. (1985) 'The Politics of Care: The NHS under Thatcher', *Critical Social Policy*, issue 14, pp 57-72.

Ingleby, R. (1960) *The Ingleby Report on Children and Young Persons*, Cmnd 1191, London: HMSO.

Innerarity, F. (2003) *Gender Dimensions of Social Capital in the Caribbean*, Kingston: University of the West Indies Press.

Irwin, I. (1971) *The Story of the Women's Party*, New York, NY: Harcourt and Brace.

Ishmael, A. and Alemoru, B. (1999) *Harassment, Bullying and Violence at Work*, London: Industrial Society.

Jacobs, S. and Popple, K. (1994) *Community Work in the 1990s*, Nottingham: Spokesman Books.

James, S. (1992) *Gender, Equality and Citizenship*, Toronto: Canadian Scholars Press.

Janssen-Jurreit, M. (1976) *Sexism: The Male Monopoly on History and Thought*, London: Pluto.

John-Baptiste, A. (2001) 'Africentric Social Work', in L. Dominelli, W. Lorenz and H. Soydan (eds) *Beyond Racial Divides: Ethnicities in Social Work*, Aldershot: Ashgate.

Johnson, P. and Falkingham, J. (1992) *Ageing and Economic Welfare*, London: Sage Publications.

Jordan, B. (2000) *Social Work and the Third Way: Tough Love as Social Policy*, London: Sage.

Joyce, P., Corrigan, P. and Hayes, M. (1987) *Striking Out: Trade Unionism in Social Work*, London: Macmillan.

Kaseke, E. (1994) 'Social Work and Social Development in Zimbabwe'. Paper given at the IASSW Board Seminar, Sheffield University, 28 February.

Kay, A. (2000) 'Art and Community Development: The Role The Arts Have in Regenerating Communities', *Community Development Journal*, vol 35, no 4, pp 414-24.

Kelly, L. (1988) *Surviving Sexual Violence*, Cambridge: Polity Press.

Kenny, S. (2002) 'Tensions and Dilemmas in Community Development: New Discourses or New Trojans?', *Community Development Journal*, vol 37, no 4, pp 284-99.

Kettle, A. (1988) 'Women and Collective Action: The Role of the Trade Union in Academic Life' in D. Malim and S. Maslin-Prothero (eds) *Surviving the Academy: Feminist Perspectives*, London: Falmer Press.

Kindlon, D., Thompson, M. with Barker, T. (1999) *Raising Cain: Protecting the Emotional Life of Boys*, New York, NY: Ballantine Books.

Knijn, T. and Ungerson, C. (1997) 'Introduction: Care Work and Gender in Welfare Regimes', *Social Politics*, Fall, vol 4, pp 323-7.

Kramer, R. and Specht, H. (1969) *Readings in Community Organisation Practice*, New York, NY: Prentice-Hall.

Kuhn, M. (1991) *No Stone Unturned: The Life and Times of Maggie Kuhn*, New York, NY: Ballantine Books.

Kwo, E.M. (1984) 'Community Education and Community Development in Cameroon: The British Colonial Experience, 1922-1961', *Community Development Journal*, vol 19, no 4, pp 204-13.

Ladd, E.C. (1999) 'Bowling with Tocqueville: Civic Engagement and Social Capital', Bradley Lecture, American Enterprise Institute, 15 September.

Lahiri-Dutt, K. and Samanta, G. (2002) 'State Initiatives for the Empowerment of Women of Rural Communities: Experiences from Eastern India', *Community Development Journal*, vol 37, no 2, pp 137-56.

Land, H. (1976) 'Women Supporters or Supported?', in S. Allen and D. Barker (eds) *Sexual Division and Society*, London: Tavistock.

Lane, J. (2005) 'The Battles of Grunwick' (www.workersliberty.org, accessed 24 May 2005).

Langdon, J. (2000) *Mo Mowlam: The Biography*, Dublin: Real Ireland Bookstore.

La Rossa, D. (1995) 'Fatherhood and Social Change' in E. Nelson and B. Robinson (eds) *Gender in the 1990s: Images, Realities and Issues*, Toronto: Nelson Canada.

Lederer, L. (1982) *Take Back the Night: Women on Pornography*, New York, NY: Bantam Books.

Ledwith, M. (1997) *Community Development: A Critical Approach*, Bristol: BASW/Policy Press.

Ledwith, M. (2001) 'Community Work as Critical Pedagogy: Re-envisioning Freire and Gramsci', *Community Development Journal*, vol 36, no 3, pp 171-82.

Ledwith, M. and Asgill, P. (1998) 'Black and White Women Working Together: Transgressing the Boundaries of Sisterhood', in M. Lavalette, L. Penketh and C. Jones (ed) *Anti-Racism and Social Welfare*, Aldershot: Ashgate.

Leff, E. (1995) *Green Production: Toward an Environmental Rationality*, New York, NY: Guilford Press.

Leissner, A. and Joslin, J. (1974) 'Area Team Community Work: Achievement and Crisis', in D. Jones and M. Mayo (eds) *Community Work One*, London: Routledge and Kegan Paul.

Leonard, P. (ed) (1975) *The Sociology of Community Action*, Keele: University of Keele.

LEWRG (London-Edinburgh Weekend Return Group) (1979) *In and Against the State*, London: Pluto Press.

Lewycka, M. (1986) 'The Way We Were', *New Socialist*, vol 36, March.

Lister, R. (1997) *Citizenship: Feminist Perspectives*, London: Macmillan.

Livingstone, K. (1987) *If Voting Changed Anything, They'd Abolish It*, London: Collins.

Loney, M. (1983) *Community Against Government: The British Community Development Project, 1968-1978: A Study of Government Incompetence*, London: Heinemann.

Lorde, A. (1984) *Sister Outsider*, New York, NY: The Crossing Press.

Lorenz, W. (1994) *Social Work in a Changing Europe*, London: Routledge.

Lovett, T. and Percival, R. (1982) 'Politics, Conflict and Community Action in Northern Ireland', in P. Curno (eds) *Political Issues and Community Work*, London: Routledge and Kegan Paul.

Lowndes, V. (2000) 'Women and Social Capital: A Comment on Hall's "Social Capital in Britain"', *British Journal of Political Science*, vol 30, pp 533-40.

LRN (London Regeneration Network) (1999) *Capacity Building: The Way Forward*, London: LRN.

LSCC (Leeds Social Security Cuts Campaign) (1986) *The Campaign Against the Fowler Review*, Leeds: LSCC.

MacKinnon, C. (1993) *Only Words*, Cambridge, MA: Harvard University Press.

McClennen, J. (2005) 'Domestic Violence Between Same Gender Partners: Recent Findings and Future Research', *Journal of Interpersonal Violence*, vol 20, no 2, pp 149-54.

McCrindle, J. and Rowbotham, S. (1986) 'More than just a Memory', *Feminist Review*, no 23, Summer, pp 109-21.

McGhee, D. (2005) *Intolerant Britain? Hate, Citizenship and Difference*, Maidenhead: Open University Press.

McLean, C. (2002) 'Social Capital, Ethnicity and Health: Factors Shaping African-Caribbean Residents' Participation in Local Community Networks' (www.lse.ac.uk/depts/gender, accessed 8 June 2005).

McLeod, E. (1982) *Women Working: Prostitution Now*, London: Croom Helm.

McLeod, E. (1987) 'Women's Experience of Love: The Significance of Feminist Therapy', Coventry: University of Warwick.

McLeod, E. (1994) *Women's Experience of Feminist Therapy and Counselling*, Milton Keynes: Open University Press.

McNeil, S. and Rhodes, D. (eds) (1985) *Women Against Violence Against Women*, London: Onlywomen Press.

McPherson, W. (1998) *Report of the Inquiry Into the Murder of Stephen Laurence: The McPherson Report*, London: The Stationery Office.

Malek, F. (1985) *Asian Women and Mental Health or Mental Ill Health: The Myth of mental Illness*, Southwark, London: Asian Women's Aid.

Mama, A. (1989a) *Hidden Struggle: Statutory and Voluntary Responses to Violence Against Black Women in the Home*, London: Race and Housing Unit.

Mama, A. (1989b) 'Violence Against Black Women: Gender, Race and State Responses', *Feminist Review*, vol 32, summer, pp 30-48.

Marchant, H. and Wearing, B. (1986) *Gender Reclaimed*, Sydney: Hale and Iremongers.

Marris, P. and Rein, R. (1974) *Dilemmas of Social Reform*, New York, NY: Penguin.

Marsden, D. and Oakley, P. (1982) 'Radical Community Development in the Third World', in G. Craig, N. Derricourt and M. Loney (eds) *Community Work and the State*, London: Routledge and Kegan Paul.

Maynard, A. and Bosanquet, N. (1986) *Public Expenditure in the National Health Service: Recent Trends and Future Problems*, London: Institute of Health Services Management.

Mayo, M. (ed) (1977) *Women in the Community*, London: Routledge and Kegan Paul.

Mayo, M. (1982) 'Community Action Programmes in the Early Eighties', *Critical Social Policy*, vol 1, no 3, Spring, pp 25-40.

Mayo, M. (1994) *Communities and Caring: The Mixed Economy of Welfare*, London: Macmillan.

Mayo, M. (2000) *Culture, Communities, Identities: Cultural Strategies for Participation and Empowerment*, London: Palgrave.

Mies, M. and Shiva, V. (1993) *Ecofeminism*, London: Zed Books.

Millar, J. (2000) *Keeping Track of Welfare Reform*, York: Joseph Rowntree Foundation.

Miller, A. (1983) *For Your Own Good: Hidden Cruelty in Childbearing and the Roots of Violence*, New York, NY: Faber and Faber.

Millet, K. (1969) *Sexual Politics*, Garden City, NY: Doubleday.

Milner, R. and Holland, E.M. (1965) *The Milner Holland Report on London Housing*, London: HMSO.

Mizra, H. (1997) *Black, British Feminism: A Reader*, London: Routledge.

Moosa-Mitha, M. (2003) 'The Rights of Children Sex Trade Workers', PhD, Southampton: Southampton University.

Morgan, R. (1970) *Sisterhood is Powerful*, New York, NY: Vintage Books.

Morgan, R. (1984) *Sisterhood is Global*, New York, NY: Anchor Books.

Morris, J. (1991) *Pride Against Prejudice: Transforming Attitudes to Disability*, London: The Women's Press.

Morris, L. (1995) *Dangerous Classes: The Underclass and Social Citizenship*, London: Routledge.

Mowbray, M. (2005) 'Community Capacity Building or State Opportunism?', *Community Development Journal*, vol 40, no 3, pp 255-64.

Mulholland, H. (2005) 'Pensioner Faces Court over Council Tax Protest', *The Observer*, 11 March.

Mullard, C. (1973) *Black Britain*, London: George Allen and Unwin.

Mullender, A. (1997) *Rethinking Domestic Violence: The Social Work and Probation Responses*, London: Routledge.

Munro, A. (2001) 'A Feminist Trade Union Agenda? The Continued Significance of Class, Gender and Race', *Gender, Work and Organisation*, vol 8, no 4, pp 454-71.

Murphy, M. (2002) 'Social Partnership – Is It "the Only Game in Town"?', *Community Development Journal*, vol 37, no 1, pp 80-90.

Murray, C. (1990) *The Emerging British Underclass*, London: Institute of Economic Affairs.

Murtagh, B. (2001) 'The Politics and Practice of Urban Policy Evaluation', *Community Development Journal*, vol 36, no 3, pp 223-33.

Naples, N. (ed) (1998) *Community Activism and Feminist Politics: Organizing Across Race, Class and Gender*, London: Routledge.

NCC (National Childcare Campaign) (1984) *National Childcare Campaign Annual Report*, London: NCC.

NCC (1985) *National Childcare Campaign Policy Statement*, London: NCC.

Nelson, S. (1986) *Incest: Facts and Myth*, Edinburgh: Stramullion Press.

Ng, R. (1988) *The Politics of Community Services: Immigrant Women, Class and the State*, Toronto: Garamond Press.

Ng, R., Walker, G. and Muller, J. (eds) (1989) *Community Organisation and the Canadian Welfare State*, Toronto: Garamond Press.

Nicholson, L. (ed) (1990) *Feminism/Postmodernism*, New York, NY: Routledge, Chapman and Hall.

Norman, A. (1985) *Triple Jeopardy: Growing Up Old in a Second Homeland*, London: Centre for Policy on Ageing.

Norris, P. (2000) 'Gender and Contemporary British Politics', in C. Hay (ed) *British Politics Today*, Cambridge: Polity Press.

Oakley, A. (1974) *The Sociology of Housework*, London: Martin Robertson.

ODPM (Office of the Deputy Prime Minister) (2004) *Tackling Social Exclusion: Taking Stock and Looking to the Future: Emerging Findings*, London: SEU.

Ohri, A. and Manning, B. (1982) *Community Work and Racism*, London: Routledge and Kegan Paul.

Oliver, M. (1990) *The Politics of Disablement*, London: Macmillan.

ONS (Office for National Statistics) (2004) *The Annual Survey of Hours and Earnings*, London: ONS.

Orme, J. (2000) *Gender and Community Care*, London: Palgrave.

Orr, C. (1997) 'Charting the Currents of the Third Wave', *Hypatia*, vol 12, no 3, pp 9-33.

OWL (Older Women's League) (1986) *Family Caregivers – A Fact Sheet*, November.

Pahl, J. (1981) 'Patterns of Money Management within Marriage', *Journal of Social Policy*, vol 9, pp 326-39.

Parmar, P. (1986) 'Can Black and White Women Work Together', *Spare Rib*, no 168, July, p 20.

Parsons, T. (1957) *Essays in Sociological Theory*, New York, NY: Free Press.

Perlmutter, F. (1997) *From Welfare to Work: Corporate Initiatives and Welfare Reform*, Oxford: Oxford University Press.

Phillips, A. (1993) *The Trouble with Boys: Parenting Men of the Future*, London: HarperCollins.

Phillips, B. (2004) 'Re-generation Games: The Politics of Childhood in Urban Renewal', *Community Development Journal*, vol 39, no 2, April, pp 166-76.

Phillipson, C. (1982) *Capitalism and the Construction of Old Age*, London: Macmillan.

Phillipson, C. (1998) *Reconstructuring Old Age: New Agendas in Social Theory and Practice*, London: Sage Publications.

Pizzey, E. (1997) 'Working with Violent Women', (www.fathersforlife.org/pizzey/terror.htm, accessed 16 June 2005).

Plowden, L. (1967) *The Plowden Report on Children and Their Primary Schools*, Report of the Central Advisory Council on Education, London: HMSO.

Plummer, J. (1978) *Divide and Deprive*, London: Joint Council for the Welfare of Immigrants.

Popple, K. (1995) *Analyzing Community Work: Its Theory and Practice*, Milton Keynes: Open University Press.

Popple, K. and Redmond, M. (2000) 'Community Development and the Voluntary Sector in the New Millennium: The Implications of the Third Way in the UK', *Community Development Journal*, vol 35, no 4, pp 391-400.

Prigoff, A. (2000) *Economics for Social Workers: Outcomes of Economic Globalization with Strategies for Community Action*, Stamford, CT: Wadsworth Publishing.

Pringle, K. (1995) *Men, Masculinities and Social Welfare*, London: UCL Press.

Purdue, D., Razzaque, K., Hambleton, R., Stewart, M., Huxham, C. and Vangen, S. (2000) *Community Leadership in Area Regeneration*, Bristol: Joseph Rowntree Foundation/Policy Press.

Putnam, R. (1993) *Making Democracy Work: Civic traditions in modern Italy*, Princeton, NJ: Princeton University Press.

Putnam, R. (2000) *Bowling Alone: The Collapse and Revival of American Community*, New York, NY: Simon and Schuster.

Razavi, S. (2000) *Gendered Poverty and Well-Being*, Oxford: Blackwell Publishing, Inc.

Rees, S. (1991) *Achieving Power: Practice and Policy in Social Welfare*, London: Allen and Unwin.

Reisch, M. (2004) 'Community Practice Challenges in the Global Economy', in M. Weil (ed) *The Handbook of Community Practice*, London: Sage Publications.

Reitsma-Street, M. and Neysmith, S. (1999) *Restructuring Caring Labour: Discourse, State and Everyday Practice*, Oxford: Oxford University Press.

Remfry, P. (1979) 'North Tyneside Community Development Project', *Community Development Journal*, vol 14, no 3, pp 186-9.

Roberts, H. (1982) *Doing Feminist Research*, London: Routledge and Kegan Paul.

Robson, T. (2000) *The State and Community Action*, London: Pluto Press.

Rogaly, J. (1977) *Grunwick*, Harmondsworth: Penguin.

Rogaly, B. and Johnson, S. (1997) *Microfinance and Poverty Reduction*, Oxford: Blackwell Publishing Inc. and Oxfam.

Rogers, C. (1961) *Client-Centred Therapy*, London: Constable.

Rooney, B. (1987) *Resistance or Change?*, Liverpool: Liverpool University.

Rose, H. (1973) 'Up Against the Welfare State: Claimants Union', *Socialist Register*, vol 44, no 1, pp 179-207.

Rosenthal, H. (1983) 'Neighbourhood Health Projects: Some New Approaches to Health and Community Work in Parts of the United Kingdom', *Community Development Journal*, vol 18, no 4, pp 120-31.

Rothman, J. (1970) 'Three Models of Community Organisation Practice', in F. Cox, J. Erlich, J. Rothman and J. Tropman (eds) *Strategies of Community Organisation*, Itaska, Il: Peacock Publishing.

Rowbotham, S., Segal, L. and Wainwright, H. (1980) *Beyond the Fragments: Feminism in the Making of Socialism*, London: Merlin.

Rowe, D. (1983) *Depression: The Way Out of Your Prison*, London: Routledge.

Roy, A. (1999) 'Lies, Damn Lies and Statistics', *The Guardian*, 5 June.

Russell, D. (1984) *Sexual Exploitation*, London: Sage.

Russo, N.F. (1976) 'The Motherhood Mandate', *Journal of Social Issues*, vol 32, pp 143-54.

Ruzek, S. (1978) *The Women's Health Movement*, New York, NY: Praeger.

Ruzek, S. (1986) 'Feminist Visions of Health: An International Perspective', in J. Mitchell and A. Oakley (eds) *What is Feminism?*, Oxford: Basil Blackwell.

Sale, A.U. (2005) 'Natural Selection?', *Community Care*, 3-9 February, pp 20-3.

Saradjian, J. with Hanks, H. (1996) *Women who Sexually Abuse Children: From Research to Clinical Practice*, Chichester: John Wiley and Sons.

Savage, W. and Leighton, J. (1986) *Savage Enquiry*, London: Virago.

SCCD (Standing Conference for Community Development) (2001) *Strategic Framework for Community Development*, Sheffield: SCCD.

SchNEWS (2005) 'Air Strikes', *SchNEWS*, 2 September.

Schuftan, C. (1996) 'The Community Development Dilemma: What is Really Empowering?', *Community Development Journal*, vol 31, no 3, pp 260-4.

Scott, A. (2001) 'Grounded Politics: Some Thoughts on Feminist Process in the Information Age', *Computers and Society*, vol 44, no 1, pp 5-14.

Scull, A. (1977) *Decarceration: Community Treatment and the Deviant, a Radical View*, Englewood Cliffs, NJ: Prentice Hall.

Seebohm, F. (1968) *Report of the Committee on Local Authority and Allied Personal Social Services*, The Seebohm Report, Cmnd 3703, London: HMSO.

Segal, L. (ed) (1983) *What is to be Done by the Family?*, London: Penguin.

Segal, L. (1987) *Is the Future Female? Troubled Thoughts on Contemporary Feminism*, London: Virago.

SEU (Social Exclusion Unit) (1998) *Bringing Britain Together*, London: The Stationery Office.

SEU (1999) *Learning Lessons*, Report by Policy Action Team 16, London: Cabinet Office.

SEU (2000) *Community Self-Help Report of Policy Action Team 09*, London: The Stationery Office.

SEU (2004) *Tackling Social Exclusion: Taking Stock and Looking to the Future*, London: The Stationery Office.

Sevenhuijsen, S. (1998) *Citizenship and the Ethics of Care*, London: Routledge.

Sewpaul, V. and Hölscher, D. (2004) *Social Work in Times of Neoliberalism: A Postmodern Discourse*, Pretoria: Van Schaik Publishers.

Shakespeare, T. (1999) 'When is a Man Not a Man? When He is Disabled', in J. Wild (ed) *Working with Men for Change*, London: UCL Press.

Shakib, S. (2002) *Afghanistan: Where God Only Comes to Weep: A Woman's Story of Courage, Struggle and Determination*, London: Century.

Shaw, M. and Martin, I. (2000) 'Community Work, Citizenship and Democracy: Remaking the Connections', *Community Development Journal*, vol 35, no 4, pp 401-13.

Shiva, V. (1993) *Monocultures of the Mind*, London: Zed Books.

Shiva, V. (2003) 'Food Rights, Free Trade and Fascism', in M. Gibney (ed) *Globalizing Rights*, Oxford: Oxford University Press.

Sidel, R. (1986) *Women and Children Last: The Plight of Poor Women in Affluent America*, New York, NY: Viking Books.

Sidel, R. and Sidel, V. (1982) *The Health of China*, Boston: Beacon Press.

Siegal, D.L. (1997) 'The Legacy of the Personal: Generating Theory in Feminism's Third Wave', *Hypatia*, vol 12, no 3, pp 46-75.

Sivanandan, A. (1976) 'Race, Class and the State: The Black Experience', *Race and Class*, vol 17, no 4, pp 364-80.

Skeffington, L. (1969) *People and Planning: The Skeffington Report*, London: HMSO.

Skinner, S. (1997) *Building Community Strengths*, London: Community Development Foundation.

Small, J. (1984) 'The Crisis in Adoption', *International Journal of Psychiatry*, vol 30, Spring, pp 120-41.

Smith, M.K. (2005) 'Community Work' (www.infed.org/community/b-comwrk.htm).

Solomon, B. (1976) *Black Empowerment: Social Work in Oppressed Communities*, New York, NY: Columbia University Press.

Sondhi, R. (1982) 'The Asian Resources Centre', in J. Cheetham (ed) *Ethnicity and Social Work*, Oxford: Oxford University Press.

SSEC (Senate Sex Equality Committee) (1989) *Sex Equality Committee Report*, Coventry: University of Warwick Senate Papers.

Stack, C. (1975) *All our Kin: Strategies for Survival in a Black Community*, New York, NY: Harper and Row.

Stanley, L. and Wise, S. (1983; 2nd edn, 1997) *Breaking Out: Feminist Consciousness and Feminist Research*, London: Routledge and Kegan Paul.

Stanley, R. (1998) *High Hopes: The Clinton Presidency and the Politics of Ambition*, London: Routledge.

Staples, R. (1988) *The Black Male's Role in American Society*, San Francisco, CA: Black Scholar Press.

Status of Women (2001) *Women's Economic Independence and Security: A Federal/Provincial/Territorial Strategic Framework from the Ministers Responsible for the Status of Women*, Ottawa: Status of Women.

Steinberg, D.L. (1997) *Bodies in Glass: Genetics, Eugenics, Embryo Ethics*, Manchester: University of Manchester Press.

Stewart, G. and Tutt, N. (1987) *Children in Custody*, Aldershot: Gower.

Strega, S. (2004) *The Case of the Missing Perpetrator: The Absence of Men in Social Workers' Construction of Domestic Violence*, PhD thesis (Southampton, University of Southampton).

Summerskill, B. (2001) 'Fear Grips Old as Care Home Closures Rise', *Guardian Unlimited*, 25 March (http://www.society.guardian.co.uk/longtermcare, accessed 24 May 2005).

SWAF (Scottish Women's Aid Federation) (1980) *Report from Battered Women and the State Conference*, Edinburgh: SWAF.

SWAT (South Wales Association of Tenants) (1982) 'Community Alive Hurts', in A. Curno, A. Lamming, L. Leach, J. Stiles, V. Ward, A. Wright and T. Ziff (eds) *Women in Collective Action*, London: Association of Community Workers.

Thomas, D.N. (1983) *The Making of Community Work*, London: Routledge and Kegan Paul.

Thomas, R. and Green, J. (2006) 'Learning through our Children, Healing for our Children: Best Practice in First Nations Communities' in L. Dominelli (ed) *Revitalising Communities in a Globalising World*, Aldershot: Ashgate.

Tobin, A. (1990) 'Lesbianism and the Labour Party', *Feminist Review*, no 34, Spring, pp 56-66.

Toënnies, F. (1957) *Community and Association*, Michigan: Michigan University Press.

Tolson, A. (1977) *The Limits of Masculinity*, London: Tavistock.

Torkington, C. (1981) 'Women in Action, Preservers of the Status Quo or a Force for Change?', MA dissertation, Coventry: University of Warwick.

Townsend, P. (1979) *Poverty in the United Kingdom*, Harmondsworth: Penguin.

Townsend, P., Davidson, N. and Whitehead, M. (1988) *Inequalities in Health: The Black Report and the Health Divide*, Harmondsworth: Penguin.

Townsend, P. and Gordon D. (eds) (2002) *World Poverty: New Policies to Defeat an Old Enemy*, Bristol: Policy Press.

TRCCC (Tyneside Rape Crisis Centre Collective) (1982) 'Tyneside Rape Crisis Centre', in A. Curno, A. Lamming, L. Leach, J. Stiles, V. Ward, A. Wright and T. Ziff (eds) *Women in Collective Action*, London: Association of Community Workers.

Twelvetrees, A. (2001; 1st edn, 1982) *Community Work* (3rd edn), London: Palgrave.

Twigg, J. and Atkin, K. (1994) *Carers Perceived: Policy and Practice in Informal Care*, Buckingham: Open University Press.

UNDP (United Nations Development Programme) (1996) *The 1996 Report on Human Social Development*, New York, NY: UNDP.

UNDP (1998) *The 1998 Report on Human Social Development*, New York, NY: UNDP.

UNDP (2002) 'Decentralised Governance for Development' (www.undp.org/policy/docs/network/hdr/thematics/Resources_for_HDR_on_Democratic_Governance.htm (accessed 14 February 2006).

Ungerson, C. (1987) *Policy is Personal: Sex, Gender and Informal Care*, London: Tavistock.

Ungerson, C. (1990) *Gender and Caring Work and Welfare in Britain and Scandinavia*, Hemel Hempstead: Harvester/Wheatsheaf.

Van Moorst, H. (1998) 'Australian aboriginal people and access to the law', *Alternative Law Journal*, vol 23, no 6, pp 278-80.

Vancouver Sun, The (1989) 'Child Molester Alleges Three Year Old Child Was Sexually Aggressive', November.

Vincent, C. and Martin, J. (2000) 'School Based Parents' Groups – A Politics of Voice and Representation', *Journal of Education Policy*, vol 15, no 5, pp 459-80.

Wagner, G. (1988) *Residential Care: A Positive Choice. The Wagner Report*, London: NISW/HMSO.

Walker, A. and Hennessy, C.A. (2004) *Growing Older: Quality of Life in Old Age*, Milton Keynes: Open University Press.

Washington Post (2005) 'Senate OKs $82 Billion More for War in Iraq', May 11.

Walby, S. (1990) *Theorising Patriarchy*, Oxford: Basil Blackwell.

Walby, S. (ed) (1997) *New Agendas for Women*, London: Palgrave.

Wandor, M. (1972) *The Body Politic: Women's Liberation in Britain, 1969-1972*, London: Stage One.

Ward, E. (1984) *Father-Daughter Rape*, London: The Women's Press.

WEDO (Women's Environment and Development Organization) (2005) 'The Beijing Platform for Action' (www.wedo.org/campaigns, accessed 24 May 2005).

Weil, M. (ed) (2004) *The Handbook of Community Practice*, London: Sage.

Weinstock, E. (2004) 'Industrial Food Production and Nutrition', in *Dietary Requirements for Older People Using Meals on Wheels* (pamphlet), San Francisco, CA: OWL Publications, p 1.

Weir, A. and Wilson, E. (1984) 'The British Women's Movement', *New Left Review*, no 148, December.

Wendell, S. (1996) *The Rejected Body: Feminist Philosophical Reflections on Disability*, London: Routledge.

WEU (Women and Equality Unit) (2003) *Women and Equality Report*, London: WEU.

Whitehead, A. (2002) *Rethinking Crime and Masculinity*. PhD at Southampton University, Southampton.

Whitlock, M.J. (1987) 'Five More Years of Desolation', *Spare Rib*, vol 180, July, p 15.

Wichterich, C. (2000) *The Globalized Woman Reports from a Future of Inequality*, London: Zed Books.

Williams, C. (2004) 'Community Capacity Building: A Critical Evaluation of the Third Sector Approach', *Review of Policy Research*, vol 21, no 5, pp 729-39.

Williams, F. (1989) *Social Policy: A Critical Introduction – Race, Gender and Class*, Cambridge: Polity Press.

Williams, L. (2004) 'Culture and Community Development: Towards New Conceptualizations and Practice', *Community Development Journal*, vol 39, no 4, pp 345-59.

Wilmot, P. and Young, M. (1957; 3rd edn, 1968) *Family and Class in a London Suburb*, London: Routledge and Kegan Paul.

Wilson, E. (1977a) 'Women in Community', in M. Mayo (ed) *Women in the Community*, London: Routledge and Kegan Paul.

Wilson, E. (1977b) *Women and the Welfare State*, London: Tavistock.

Wilson, E. (1982) 'Women and Community Care', in A. Walker (ed) *Community Care*, Oxford: Basil Blackwell.

Wilson, E. (1983) *What is to be Done about Violence Against Women?*, London: Penguin.

Wilson, E. and Weir, A. (1986) *Hidden Agendas: Theory, Politics and Experience in the Women's Movement*, London: Tavistock.

Wilson, M. (1993) *Crossing the Boundary: Black Women Survive Incest*, London: Virago.

Wilson, T.J. (1996) 'Feminism and Institutionalised Racism: Inclusion and Exclusion at an Australian Women's Refuge', *Feminist Review*, vol 52, Spring, pp 1-26.

Wistow, G., Knapp, M., Hardy, B. and Allen, C. (1994) *Social Care in a Mixed Economy*, Buckingham: Open University Press.

Wolfenberger, W. (1972) *The Principle of Normalisation in the Human Services*, Toronto National Institute on Mental Retardation.

Woodward, V. (2003) 'Participation the Community Work Way', *International Journal of Healthcare Technology and Management*, vol 5, nos 1/2, pp 3-19.

Woolcock, M. (1998) 'Social Capital and Economic Development: Towards a Theoretical Synthesis and Policy Framework', *Theory and Society*, vol 27, pp 151-208.

Worcester, N. and Whatley, M. (1988) 'The Selling of Women's Health Centres: The Response of the Women's Health Movement', in S. Rosser (ed) *Women, Health and Reproduction*, London: Routledge and Kegan Paul.

Younghusband, E. (1978) *Social Work in Britain, 1950-1975*, London: Allen and Unwin.

Yuval-Davis, N. (1997) *Gender and Nation*, London: Sage Publications.

Zucchino, D. (1997) *Myth of the Welfare Queen*, New York, NY: Touchstone Books.

Index

Also available from The Policy Press

Including the excluded
From practice to policy in European community development
Paul Henderson, Community Development Foundation

INCLUDING THE EXCLUDED

From practice to policy in European community development

Paul Henderson

"This useful book draws on a range of experiences across Europe to present some practical strategies for working with communities to promote social inclusion. It brings to life a frequently neglected area of policy and demonstrates the importance of working closely with those who experience poverty and discrimination to tackle complex and seemingly intractable problems." Alison Gilchrist, Director, Practice Development, Community Development Foundation

Paperback £12.99 US$22.50 ISBN-10 1 86134 745 6 ISBN-13 978 1 86134 745 9
234 x 156mm 144 pages June 2005

Making community participation meaningful
A handbook for development and assessment
Danny Burns, Frances Heywood, Marilyn Taylor, Pete Wilde, and Mandy Wilson

"... a useful handbook for anyone working within their local community." LGA update

Paperback £14.95 US$25.50
ISBN-10 1 86134 614 X
ISBN-13 978 1 86134 614 8
A4 REPORT (297 x 210mm)
76 pages July 2004

What works in assessing community participation?
Danny Burns, Frances Heywood, Pete Wilde, and Mandy Wilson

"... very readable and interesting." LGA update

Paperback £13.95 US$23.95
ISBN-10 1 86134 615 8
ISBN-13 978 1 86134 615 5
A4 REPORT (297 x 210mm)
56 pages July 2004

Both these titles published in association with the Joseph Rowntree Foundation

To order copies of this publication or any other Policy Press titles please visit **www.policypress.org.uk** or contact:

In the UK and Europe:
Marston Book Services, PO Box 269,
Abingdon, Oxon, OX14 4YN, UK
Tel: +44 (0)1235 465500
Fax: +44 (0)1235 465556
Email: direct.orders@marston.co.uk

In the USA and Canada:
ISBS, 920 NE 58th Street, Suite 300,
Portland, OR 97213-3786, USA
Tel: +1 800 944 6190 (toll free)
Fax: +1 503 280 8832
Email: info@isbs.com

In Australia and New Zealand:
DA Information Services,
648 Whitehorse Road Mitcham,
Victoria 3132, Australia
Tel: +61 (3) 9210 7777
Fax: +61 (3) 9210 7788
E-mail: service@dadirect.com.au